# Political Poetry across the Centuries

*Edited by*

Hans-Christian Günther

BRILL

LEIDEN | BOSTON

Library of Congress Cataloging-in-Publication Data

Names: Günther, Hans Christian, editor.
Title: Political poetry across the centuries / Edited by Hans-Christian
   Günther.
Description: Leiden ; Boston : Brill, 2016. | Series: Studies on the
   interaction of art, thought and power ; volume 8 | Essays chiefly in
   English; some in German. | Proceedings of an international conference held
   at the Accademia di studi italo-tedeschi in Merano, Italy. | Includes
   bibliographical references and index.
Identifiers: LCCN 2016018476 (print) | LCCN 2016024180 (ebook) | ISBN
   9789004323520 (hardback : alk. paper) | ISBN 9789004323537 (e-book) | ISBN
   9789004323537 (E-book)
Subjects: LCSH: Political poetry—History and criticism—Congresses. |
   European poetry—History and criticism—Congresses. | Politics in
   literature—Congresses.
Classification: LCC PN1081.P64 2016 (print) | LCC PN1081 (ebook) | DDC
   809.1/93581—dc23
LC record available at https://lccn.loc.gov/2016018476

Typeface for the Latin, Greek, and Cyrillic scripts: "Brill". See and download: brill.com/brill-typeface.

ISSN 1877-0029
ISBN 978-90-04-32352-0 (hardback)
ISBN 978-90-04-32353-7 (e-book)

Copyright 2016 by Koninklijke Brill NV, Leiden, The Netherlands.
Koninklijke Brill NV incorporates the imprints Brill, Brill Hes & De Graaf, Brill Nijhoff, Brill Rodopi
and Hotei Publishing.
All rights reserved. No part of this publication may be reproduced, translated, stored in a retrieval system,
or transmitted in any form or by any means, electronic, mechanical, photocopying, recording or otherwise,
without prior written permission from the publisher.
Authorization to photocopy items for internal or personal use is granted by Koninklijke Brill NV provided
that the appropriate fees are paid directly to The Copyright Clearance Center, 222 Rosewood Drive,
Suite 910, Danvers, MA 01923, USA. Fees are subject to change.

This book is printed on acid-free paper and produced in a sustainable manner.

# Contents

List of Contributors    VII
Introduction by the Editor    IX

## Basic Reflections

1   The Poet as Demiurge in Plato    3
     *Dominic J. O'Meara*

2   Dichtung und Politik bei Martin Heidegger    15
     *Bogdan Mincă*

3   Ethik – Politik – Dichtung. Pounds *Patria Mia*    27
     *Ralf Lüfter*

## The Seventeenth Century

4   The Greatest King among Poets, the Greatest Poet among Kings:
   The Poetry of King Teimuraz I    43
     *Donald Rayfield*

5   Knowledge After the Fall: Milton and the Question of Censorship    57
     *Friederike Schmiga*

## The First World War

6   Stefan George als politischer Dichter    77
     *Hans-Christian Günther*

7   Patriotism and Pacifism: The Year 1914 for Futurist Vladimir
   Mayakovskiĭ    102
     *Luigi Magarotto*

## Beyond Europe

8 Dichtung, Propaganda und Polemik im Konflikt zwischen Schah Isma'īl und Sultan Selīm  119
   *Max Scherberger*

9 Maos Gedichte – Versuch einer soziagogischen Analyse  141
   *Harro von Senger*

Index  155

# List of Contributors

*Hans-Christian Günther*
is Associate Professor for Classics in the Albert-Ludwigs-Universität of Freiburg. He has widely published on Greek and Latin literature and philosophy as well as on modern philosophy and politics. He is also the author of many verse translations from various languages.

*Ralf Lüfter*
is Assistant Professor of Moral Philosophy at the Free University of Bozen-Bolzano. His main research areas are ethics, philosophy of economics, theory of science, and phenomenology. He is the director of the Ezra Pound Research Centre located at the Akademie Deutsch-Italienischer Studien Meran.

*Luigi Magarotto*
is Professor Emeritus of Russian and Georgian Literature in the University of Venice. His scholarly publications span both Russian and Georgian literature and history of various epoques.

*Bogdan Mincă*
is Assistant Professor of Philosophy at the University of Bucharest. He has written extensively on Heidegger and Greek philosophy and has translated many works of Heidegger into Rumanian.

*Dominic O'Meara*
is Professor Emeritus of Ancient Philosophy at the University of Fribourg (Switzerland). He has widely published standard works and editions on neoplatonic and Byzantine philosophy.

*Donald Rayfield*
is Professor Emeritus of Russian and Georgian Literature at the University of London. His publications include the standard history of Georgian literature, the standard work on Georgian history and the standard Georgian-English Lexicon.

*Max Scherberger*
is a doctoral student at the Albert-Ludwigs-University of Freiburg. He has already published a monograph on the earliest uyghur ms. *On the ascension of Muhammad* and a wide range of scholarly articles.

*Friederike Schmiga*

is a doctoral student at the Universities of Bari and Leuven. She is mainly interested in medieval philosophy but is a student of English literature as well. She has published a book on English Renaissance Drama.

*Harro von Senger*

is Professor Emeritus of Sinology at the Albert-Ludwigs-University of Freiburg. He is one of the leading experts on modern China with groundbreaking and best-selling books which have even been translated into Chinese.

# Introduction by the Editor

The present volume continues the investigaton of the relationship between intellectuals, artists in particular, and politics, announced in the first volume of this series (*IATP* 1). This volume (as already three others in the series) consists of the proceedings of an international conference held at the Accademia di studi italo-tedeschi in Meran. It limits itself to poetry and is thus narrower and more focussed in scope than the previous ones. However, it centres on authors already treated in previous conferences, namely Plato, Stefan George, Vladimir Mayakowsky, Georgian Poetry, Martin Heidegger, Mao Zedong. The volume returns to a stronger intercultural dimension: once again a nation between Asia and Europe, namely Georgia, is dealt with, along with China and Islamic culture.

My warmest thanks go to the Meran Academy, ITS director Ivo De Gennaro and Riccardo Pozzo, who helped me to finance this conference in rather difficult times.

*H.-C. Günther*
Müllheim, December 2015

*Basic Reflections*

CHAPTER 1

# The Poet as Demiurge in Plato

*Dominic J. O'Meara*

The discussion of poetry in Plato's dialogues is one of the most important ever undertaken by a philosopher and it is also, it seems, one of the most problematic and perhaps disastrous. Plato deals with poetry with what would appear to be no interest in, or concern for, what we moderns value in poetry, subjecting it to severe censorship in the ideal city-state sketched in *Republic* Books II–III and even banishing it, it seems, in Book X. This apparent hostility to poetry is both extraordinary and possibly self-contradictory. Plato himself is, of course, a great writer who has a deep interest in and knowledge of the poetry of his time. And his critique of poetry seems incoherent, both integrating it (albeit heavily censored) and driving it out.

There are many attempts in modern studies to deal with the difficulties and contradictions (real or supposed) surrounding Plato's treatment of poetry.[1] In the following pages, however, I would like to limit myself to one particular approach which I propose to follow in relation to a particular question. I would like to consider Plato's views on poetry as a craft (*technê*) and on the poet as a craftsman, in particular a *dêmiourgos*, i.e. a craftsman who makes a contribution to the public sphere, to the *polis*. Our question will not be "What is poetry and its value in general in Plato?" We will not examine the ontological and aesthetic problems involved in Plato's concept of poetry, but will restrict ourselves to considering these questions: "What does the poet, as a craftsman, contribute to the *polis*? In what way is he, or can he be, a 'demiurge'?" In this regard I would like to emphasize the distinction between the descriptive and the normative, between what Plato considers to be the *actual* political contribution of poets to the city of his time, in particular Athens, and what he thinks their contribution *should* be in a city which, in his view, would be good.[2] I will

---

1  The secondary literature on the subject is very large; for an overview see Levin 2001, ch. 5 and, for more recent work, Destrée/Herrmann (2011). I am indebted in particular to the work of Ferrari 1989 and Burnyeat 1999.

2  This distinction is not always clearly made in the secondary literature, the consequence being that Plato's critique of poetry can come across as applying to poetry *tout court*, and not just to poetry *as actually practised*, as Plato saw it, in his time.

© KONINKLIJKE BRILL NV, LEIDEN, 2016 | DOI 10.1163/9789004323537_002

refer in my discussion mostly to the *Republic*, but will also take Plato's *Laws* into account.

I begin (I) with some remarks about poetry as a craft exercised by craftsmen who are "demiurges" in the sense that they make a contribution to the community, to the *polis*. I will then recall (II) some elements which may serve to characterize craft in general and then (III) relate these elements to poetry in particular, as a way of bringing out Plato's views on (i) the actual contribution of poets as demiurges and (ii) the contribution they should make in a community which is good.

## 1    Poets as Demiurges

We might start with the following passage from Plato's *Symposium*:

> You will agree that there is more than one kind of poetry (ποίησις) in the true sense of the word – that is to say, calling something into existence that was not there before, so that all technical productions (ἐργασίαι) are poetry and all producers (δημιουργοί) are poets (ποιηταί) [...] we don't call them all poets, do we? We give various names to the various arts, and only call the one particular art that deals with music and meter by the name that should be given to them all. And that's the only art that we call poetry, while those who practise it are known as poets.[3]

There are many crafts which produce what was not there before,[4] many producers (*dêmiourgoi*), but the names for producing (*poiêsis*) and producer (*poiêtês*) are applied restrictively in common speech, Socrates says, to just one of these crafts and types of craftsmen, poetry and poets. It also follows from this, of course, that Socrates relates poetry and poets to a wider group, that of the different crafts and craftsmen. Poetry is just one of the various crafts which produce things; poets are craftsmen.

In the wide range of producers which includes the poets, the producers are named by Socrates "demiurges". The term "demiurge" has become almost exclusively associated, in the history of philosophy, with the figure of the divine architect and builder of the world in Plato's myth of the making of the world in the *Timaeus*. However, the term originally had a wider meaning and designated

---

3   *Symposium* 205b8–c9 (trans. M. Joyce, slightly modified).
4   See also Plato's *Statesman* 258e1–2.

# THE POET AS DEMIURGE IN PLATO

skills and trades which contribute to the community, to the *polis*.[5] We can observe this in a quotation from Homer used by Plato in the *Republic*:

> If then the ruler catches anybody else in the city lying, any "of the demiurges (δημιοεργοί), whether a prophet or healer of sickness or a carpenter" (*Od.* XVII, 383–4).[6]

The group of "demiurges" includes prophets, doctors and carpenters, to whom we can add heralds.[7] Elsewhere, Plato includes painters, house builders and ship builders among "demiurges" (*Gorgias* 503e5–6), as well as doctors:

> Every doctor, you see, and every skilled craftsman (δημιουργός) always works for the sake of some end-product as a whole; he handles his materials so that they will give the best results in general, and makes the parts contribute to the good of the whole.[8]

All of these skills are exerted by professionals who are "demiurges" in the sense of making contributions to the community, to the *demos*, to the *polis*. Among these skills is to be found poetry; poets, like other skilled craftsmen, are "demiurges".[9]

## 2 Four Elements of Craft

In order to show how poetry can function as such a craft, I would like to take four elements which may serve to characterize craft in general in Plato and then apply them in particular, in the next section, to poetry.

*Goals or purposes.* The products of a craft are made in relation to a purpose or goal which they are designed to realize. In the context of the critique of poetry in *Republic* X (601de), Plato writes of an instrument, made by

---

5 See Bader 1965: 133–141; a semantic study of the use of the term in Plato is provided by Balansard 2001: 71–82.

6 *Republic* 389d1–3 (trans. G. Grube, slightly modified here and in the following quotations from the *Republic*).

7 Homer, *Od.* XVII, 381–5; XIX, 135. On the public functions of heralds in Plato, see El Murr 2014: 114.

8 Plato, *Laws* 903c5–d1 (trans. T. Saunders, slightly modified here and in the following quotations from the *Laws*).

9 See *Republic* 493d3–4: " If anyone approaches the crowd to exhibit his poetry (ποίησιν) or some other work of his (δημιουργίαν) or service to the city (πόλει διακονίαν)...".

a craftsman, whose purpose is defined by the future user of the instrument: the user *knows* the function which the instrument is to be made to serve and accordingly instructs the craftsman who is to produce it. Thus the flute-player instructs the flute-maker as to the instrument he wants made. The user *knows* the purpose to be achieved by the instrument (ἐπιστήμη), whereas the maker (instructed by the user) merely has a correct belief (πίστις) about this.[10] To the user and maker Plato adds a third figure, that of the painter who paints an image of the instrument: the painter neither knows the instrument, as does the user, nor has a correct opinion about it, as has the maker, but merely imitates the *appearance* of the object, as seen from a particular point-of-view.[11] I return later, in section III, to the implications of these distinctions as regards the critique of poetry.

*Models.* In the same context, in the *Republic*, Plato speaks of a craftsman (*dêmiourgos*) who makes something by referring to a model of the object which he wishes to produce (596b). The examples given here are those of carpenters who wish to produce a table or couch. To produce a couch or a table the craftsman will need to look to a model couch or table. This model shows, I would suggest, what something should be, if it is to function as a couch or table.[12] Going further we could say that there is (i) the goal or purpose which the user envisages (e.g., what the user needs a table *for*); (ii) the model of a table, what something should be, if it is to realize the function of a table; and (iii) the particular table produced by the carpenter. Earlier in the dialogue, Plato had spoken of the philosopher-kings who rule a *polis* which is good by looking, as if they were painters, to a model (*paradeigma*), the Form (principle) of justice and other Forms, in the image of which they paint the canvas of the city (500e2–501c2). And in the *Timaeus* (28c6–29a6), the maker of the world (the demiurge), in order to produce a world which is good, refers to the best of models, Forms, making the world as an image of it.

*Materials.* Having in mind the purpose to be achieved and referring to a paradigm of the object which is to be produced in view of this purpose, the craftsman makes use of various materials (e.g. wood, iron, wool, clay, pigments) in order to realize an object which corresponds, as much as is possible, to the paradigm and is thus fit for the function which it is to serve. Obviously these materials will have to be appropriate to the function to be achieved and will involve various limitations and compromises with respect to the extent to

---

10 See also Plato's *Cratylus* 390b.

11 *Republic* 602ab, with *Laws* 663c; Ferrari 1989: 127 (I return in the next section to the idea of a perspectival view).

12 See also *Cratylus* 389ad.

THE POET AS DEMIURGE IN PLATO

which the object thus produced can actually carry out the function for which it is intended.[13]

*The Product.* As a fourth element we might list the object actually produced by the craftsman. The value of this product will obviously depend on the extent to which it will successfully fulfil the purpose, the function for which it was made.[14]

## 3  Poets as Demiurges now and in a Good City

We can take the elements characterizing craft, as distinguished above, and apply them now to the case of poetry. I would like to do this in particular with regard to the function of the poet as demiurge, i.e. as a skilled producer who contributes to the *polis*. Taking in turn each of the four elements, as applied in the case of poetry, I will describe (i) how Plato sees them as applying to the poetry of his time and of his city, Athens, and (ii) how he holds that they *should* apply to a poetry that would be part of a city which is good.

*The Goal of Poetry.* (i) As Plato sees them in *Republic* Book X, the poets of his time seek to pander to the crowd by imitating what appears to the ignorant multitude to be fine (καλόν).[15] Poets played a fundamental role in the great public events of Athens, in the Panathenaic festival, when they competed in the performance of epic poetry in particular, and in the City Dionysia, when a great part of the population attended the competitions in tragedy and comedy.[16] Central figures in these immensely popular and prestigious events, the poets, in Plato's view, in order to be victorious, played to the lowest irrational desires and passions of the human soul, fostering them so that they take command of our lives, subjecting the soul to the worst regime, that of injustice and the basest pleasures.[17]

(ii) Earlier in the *Republic*, in Book III, Plato describes what poets *ought* to seek to achieve: to produce the "image of good character", of virtue, in the education of the young in a city which is good. Along with other "demiurges" (painters, weavers and builders are mentioned, 401a), they should contribute to an education in the correct moral and political values of such a city (401bd):

---

13  *Gorgias* 503e–504a; see Karfík 2007: 130.

14  *Republic* 601d4–6.

15  602b2–4; also 493bd.

16  See Monoson 2000: 106–7 on the poets at the Dionysia as teachers and educators of the *polis*.

17  *Republic* 605a–607a.

> Is it then the poets only whom we shall command and compel to represent the image of good character in their poems or else not practise among us, or are we to give orders also to the other craftsmen (τοῖς ἄλλοις δημιουργοῖς), and forbid them to represent, whether in pictures or in buildings or in any other works, character that is vicious [...] ? [...] Our [future] guardians ought not to be bred among images of evil as in an evil meadow, culling and grazing much every day from many sources, little by little collecting all unawares a great evil in their own soul. We must seek out such artists (δημιουργοί) as have the talent to pursue the beautiful and the graceful in their work, in order that our young men shall be benefited from all sides like those who live in a healthy place, whence something from these beautiful works will strike their eyes and ears like a breeze that brings health from salubrious places, and lead them unawares from childhood to love of, resemblance to, and harmony with, the beauty of reason.

Unless poets (along with other demiurges) contribute in this way to the education of the young, they are not to be admitted to a city which is good.

Plato's emphasis in the *Republic* on the moralizing function that poetry should have does not mean that the pleasure which poetry can bring is to be dismissed: poetry can be admitted if it is not only pleasant, but useful.[18] In the *Laws* the importance of associating pleasure and pain with moral education is emphasized: the pleasures of poetry and of other educational methods should be linked with the appropriate moral values.[19] And this education concerns not only the young, but continues throughout the life of the citizen of a good state, through constant participation in religious festivals.

In Plato's criticism in the *Republic* of the poets of his time we can detect an underlying issue. The poets claim to represent what is morally good and bad. In this they are just one of a group of various professions who compete with each other in the claim to know the good.[20] Another profession which also makes this claim is rhetoric.[21] Plato rejects the pretention of rhetoric to be the knowl-

---

18    *Republic* x, 607d8–e2; Burnyeat 1999: 319.

19    On this see, for example, *Laws* 11, 653ac, 663a.

20    Plato refers to the quarrel between philosophy and poetry at 607b.

21    See Ferrari 1989: 129. The "wisdom" of the sophists, who flatter the mob by calling what pleases it "good" without knowing what is good, is assimilated to the "wisdom" of the poets (493ad). Rhetors/sophists operate in political assemblies and law-courts, poets in the theatre.

THE POET AS DEMIURGE IN PLATO                                                9

edge of the good, and, consequently, the ruling science in the *polis*.[22] This rule should be exerted by true knowledge of the good, what Plato calls "the science of dialectic" in the *Republic* (511c5). The ruling science is called "political science" in the *Statesman*:[23] it directs and coordinates subordinate expertises, jurisdiction, military science, rhetoric: these subordinate skills cannot claim the ruling function (303d–305e). So, correspondingly, poetry has no claim to be the knowledge of the good and cannot act as a ruling science in the *polis*: if it does, it must be driven out.[24] As imitating many things, but knowing none, its "wisdom" is fraudulent: it cannot count as a true craft with a specific competence. However, it could become such a craft, as subordinate to, and in the service of, a philosophical knowledge of the good, from which it would derive (through the models it receives from this knowledge) what it could claim to "know" (in this limited sense) about the good:[25]

> If a man who in his "wisdom" (σοφίας) can become many persons and imitate many things should arrive in our city and want to give a performance of his poems [...] we would pour myrrh on his head and crown him with wreaths and send him away to another city. We ourselves would employ a more austere and less pleasure-giving poet and story-teller for our own good, one who would imitate the speech of a good man and would express himself in accordance with the models (τύποις) we laid down. (*Republic* 398ab)

*Models.* Poetry can provide moral education by presenting images of the good, in particular by representing the lives and actions of gods, of heroes and of humans. On what models are these representations based? Here I will distinguish again between the poets' current practice, as Plato sees it, and what he thinks their practice ought to be in a good city.

---

22  The pretention of rhetoric to be a ruling science is considered and rejected in the *Gorgias* (see 456ac, 464c–465e).

23  On the relation between dialectic and political science see El Murr 2014: 66–73.

24  Poets such as Homer (called the teacher of Hellas, *Republic* 606e2) are acclaimed as knowing everything (see 598d3–4: πάσσοφος), but they simply imitate everything, knowing nothing (598ce, 599cd; see Burnyeat 1999: 305). They imitate things from the distorting perspective of what pleases the mob (*Laws* 659ac, 663c). The universality of the knowledge which the poet seems to have (as imitating everything) contrasts with the universality of the knowledge which the true philosopher should have, as knowing the principles of things, the Forms (475b–476d; Burnyeat 1999: 308).

25  Compare the correct opinion of the instrument-maker acting under the instructions of the instrument-user who knows (above, p. 6).

(i) Plato denounces the poets (Homer and Hesiod) who portray the gods as causing evil, as deceivers and as open to being corrupted.[26] In contrast to this he proposes (ii) models (τύποι), guidelines (νόμοι) which poets should follow in representing the gods: the gods are good and the causes of good, not of evil; they do not deceive; they cannot be corrupted.[27] These models are provided, not by the poets themselves, but by philosophers who establish a good city (*Republic* II, 379a):

> You and I, Adeimantus, are not poets (ποιηταί) now, but we are founding a city, and it is proper that the founders (οἰκισταί) should know the models (τύποι) which the poets must follow in telling their stories, models from which they will not be allowed to deviate. We are not to compose their stories for them.

The ruling science of a good city will include knowledge of the good, which it can use in order to formulate guidelines which will function as models to be followed by poets in their activity of furthering, through their poetry, the moral education of the citizens. The poets will represent, not only gods, but also humans who exhibit moral values.

We can infer from Plato's introduction of guidelines (or norms) which should inspire the poet if the poet is to contribute to a good city, that he believes that the actual practice of the poets of his time, in Athens, presupposes other moral norms which are false[28] (or perhaps no norms at all). More particularly, the poets take their norms from what appears to be good to the mob and cater to the mob by exploiting these norms.[29]

*Materials.* In the *Republic*, the product of the poet is considered in the first instance to be discourse (*logos*).[30] Plato distinguishes between the content of the discourse and its kind, as indirect (narrative) or direct (impersonating) discourse.[31] Indirect discourse in epic and lyric poetry, when it becomes direct, leads to the poetry of tragedy and comedy (394b6–c5). The discourse can be

---

26    *Republic* II, 377e–392a.

27    For these models (τύποι), see 379a2, 380c7 (νόμων τε καὶ τύπων), 383a2–5, 387c9, 398b3 and d5; Männlein-Robert 2010: 116–117, who translates the term τύπος, as used here, as "Formumriss", "Grundzüge". For the relation between this term and the term παράδειγμα see Hellmann 1992: 318–319.

28    Note 387c9: τὸν δὲ ἐναντίον τύπον.

29    See above p. 7.

30    λογοποιεῖν (378d2–3); μυθολογεῖν (379a2–3); see 398b7.

31    392c6-8–d6 ; see Burnyeat 1999: 266–7.

# THE POET AS DEMIURGE IN PLATO

accompanied by song (taking the form of song) and dance (choral dances). The musical and choreographic components appear to be considered to be ancillary to discourse, as accompanying it.[32] Consequently, we can say that the material used by the poet is in the first place the human voice, which produces sounds structured by the poet by means of meter, rhythm and harmony. To these sounds are added the movements of the body, also structured rhythmically in dance.

The *products* of poetry thus include structured sounds and bodily movements which are joined with discourse, the content of which should conform to the norms set for the poet. The form (the structure of sounds and movements) should correspond to the content of the discourse representing gods and humans. Thus, among the modes of harmony, the *Republic* gives preference to the Dorian and Phrygian modes as corresponding to the virtues of courage and moderation; appropriate rhythms should also be adopted.[33] With this Plato contrasts the actual productions of the poets of his time, in which he finds, not only pandering to false moral norms, but also an indiscriminate exploitation of all sorts of modes, rhythms, mixings, according to the latest fashions and fads, in which the musical dimension can become autonomous, detaching itself from discourse.[34]

## 4  Conclusion

The protagonists of the *Republic*, Socrates, Glaucon and Adeimantus, act as founders and legislators in creating in their discourse (λόγῳ, 369c9) a state which will be good. So too do the protagonists of Plato's *Laws*, the Athenian guest, Cleinias and Megillos, act as founder-legislators in creating a paradigmatic state in their discourse (λόγῳ, 702e1) while walking to Zeus' cave on Mount Ida. In a sense these states-in-discourse are the poetic creations of the protagonists.

> Most honoured guests [addressing the inspired poets of tragedy], we [the founder-legislators of a good state] are poets of tragedy ourselves, and our tragedy is the finest and best we can create. At any rate, our entire

---

32   398d8–9, 399e11–400a2, 400d.

33   399ac. See *Laws* 815a–816c, for two types of dance, for which the legislator makes use of models, τύποι (816c1–2).

34   *Republic* 399e; *Laws* 669e1–2.

state has been constructed so as to be a representation of the finest and noblest life – the very thing we maintain is the truest tragedy. (*Laws* 817b)

The model state which the speakers of the *Laws* create in their discourse is a city whose life is filled with religious festivals, hymns, singing, dancing, poetry, in which the different age-groups take part as members of choruses and as spectators. However, in contrast to the "theatocracy" which Plato criticizes in the Athens of his time, it is a "theatre-state"[35] for which the guidelines (but not the scripts) are written by philosopher-legislators who have knowledge of the good and control the productions of the poets. They are not themselves the poets, but see to it that the poets, whose compositions fill the life of the citizens, provide education in moral values. The qualifications of the poet in the service of this goal are described as follows (*Laws* 829cd):

> But not everyone should be a composer of these things. For a start, the poet must be at least fifty years old, and he must not be one of those people who for all their poetical and musical competence have not a single noble or outstanding achievement to their credit. The poems that ought to be sung (even if in terms of art they leave something to be desired) are those of citizens who, producing (δημιουργοί) fine achievements, are themselves good and are respected in the state.[36]

The poets must have some poetical competence, but this is subordinated to the goal which their productions are to serve: the education of the citizens in moral values.

Poetry is no more banned from the good state of the *Laws* than it is from the good state of the *Republic*.[37] On the contrary, poetry is very much present, as a vital part of the life of the citizens. What is rejected is the poet's claim to omnicompetence, to know everything, while merely imitating things and catering to what pleases the worst desires of the human soul. In a good city, poetry has its place in the city as contributing to the moral and political education of the citizens, working under the supervision of experts in political science and legislation. Within this framework, poetry is everywhere, as part of a permanent festival in which the good life is represented and lived by all.

Plato's critique of poetry relates to the political function of poetry with regard to what would be a good city. Poetry's actual contribution to the community

---

35   I borrow this expression from the title of a book by Clifford Geertz. Plato criticizes Athenian "theatocracy" at *Laws* 701a3.

36   Compare the "austere" poet of the *Republic* 398ab (quoted above, p. 9).

37   Burnyeat 1999: 255, 277.

# THE POET AS DEMIURGE IN PLATO

(the poet as demiurge), to Athens, stands in conflict, as Plato sees it, with the principles of an ideal society. Plato clearly felt that poetry contributed to and reinforced the moral corruption of the city in which he lived. But can there be no room for poetry in our lives, if we live, as we must, in corrupt societies?

We must recall that the poetry of which Plato speaks is not a socially marginal luxury, of negligible political importance, a private pastime cultivated by a few at home, or shared in seminar-rooms or in choice book-stores. On the contrary, it was eminently public, a major part of the life of each Athenian, enjoyed by all at the great Athenian festivals, the Panathenaea and the Dionysia, and on many other occasions, as well as at the heart of the education of children.[38] Plato regards the immense political impact of the poetry of his time as disastrous and advocates, not the destruction of poetry, but its integration in the legislative framework of what would be a good state.

But is there nothing between the very real, corrupting poetry of an evil society and the hypothetical poetry of what might be, one day, somewhere, a good community? Plato's dialogues have been described as "a poetic and philosophical call to the philosophic life".[39] The dialogues stand somewhere in between the poetry of Athens in Plato's time and the poetry of an ideal state: they neither conform to what will guarantee the greatest popular success, nor are they part of what is already a good society. They point to what is required in order to constitute such a society and they anticipate, for us, their readers, aspects of what the poetry of such a society might be.[40]

## Bibliography

Bader, F. (1965), *Les Composés grecs du type de Demiourgos* (Paris).

Balansard, A. (2001), Technè *dans les* Dialogues *de Platon* (Sankt Augustin).

Burnyeat, M. (1999), 'Culture and Society in Plato's *Republic*' in: *The Tanner Lectures on Human Values* 20, 215–324.

Destrée, P./Herrmann, F.-G. (edd.) (2011), *Plato and the Poets* (Leiden).

---

38    Burnyeat 1999: 256.

39    Ferrari 1989: 148.

40    Thus the Athenian guest in the *Laws* (811be) describes his own discourses as like poetry (ποιήσει) and as paradigmatic for a good city. I argue (in a forthcoming book) that Timaeus' speech, in the *Timaeus*, is in certain respects a prose hymn to a god who conforms to the "guidelines" of the *Republic*. And we can imagine that the military feat of ancient Athens in conquering Atlantis, as this was to be recounted after Timaeus' speech by Critias and Hermocrates, would have provided images of virtuous character in humans, in particular courage.

El Murr, D. (2014), *Savoir et gouverner. Essai sur la science politique platonicienne* (Paris).

Ferrari, G. (1989), 'Plato and Poetry', in: G. Kennedy (ed.), *The Cambridge History of Literary Criticism*, vol. I, *Classical Criticism* (Cambridge) 92–148.

Hellmann, M.-C. (1992), *Recherches sur le vocabulaire de l'architecture grecque d'après les inscriptions de Délos* (Athens).

Karfík, F. (2007), 'Que fait et qui est le démiurge dans le *Timée*?' in: A. Macé (ed.), *Etudes platoniciennes* IV. *Les Puissances de l'âme selon Platon* (Paris) 129–50.

Levin, S. (2001), *The Ancient Quarrel between Philosophy and Poetry Revisited* (Oxford).

Männlein-Robert, I. (2010), "Umrisse des Göttlichen. Zur Typologie des idealen Gottes in Platons *Politeia* II", in: D. Koch/I. Männlein-Robert/N. Weidtmann (edd.), *Platon und das Göttliche* (Tübingen) 112–138.

Monoson, S. (2000), *Plato's Democratic Entanglements* (Princeton).

CHAPTER 2

# Dichtung und Politik bei Martin Heidegger

*Bogdan Mincă*

Die Jahre von 1931 bis 1936 stellen eine besondere Etappe auf Heideggers Denkweg dar. In den Jahren 1931/32 wird die so genannte „Kehre" in seinem Denken festgestellt, in den Jahren 1933/34 wurde Heidegger zum Rektor der deutschen Universität gewählt und ab 1936 beginnt er, sein zweites Hauptwerk, die *Beiträge zur Philosophie*, zu schreiben. Wenn die gängige Einteilung in „Heidegger I" und „Heidegger II" irgendeinen Sinn hat, dann kann man behaupten, dass von 1931 bis 1936 der Übergang von „Heidegger I" zu „Heidegger II" sich vollzogen hat.

Welche Schriften hat Heidegger in diesem turbulenten Zeitraum verfasst? Zuerst fällt auf, dass er viel Zeit der griechischen Philosophie gewidmet hat: in den Jahren von 1931 bis 1934 hat er drei Vorlesungen und ein Seminar über das griechische Denken gehalten, nämlich über Aristoteles' Abhandlung *Metaphysik Theta*, über Platons *Höhlengleichnis* und *Theätet*, dann ein Seminar über Platons *Phaidros*, schließlich eine Vorlesung über die Fragmente der Vorsokratiker Anaximander und Parmenides. In seinen Auslegungen zur griechischen Philosophie ging er also rückwärts, in die Richtung des Anfangs des abendländischen Denkens. In den Jahren 1931/32 fällt außerdem die erste Ausarbeitung des Textes *Der Ursprung des Kunstwerkes*, der dann 1935 und 1936 vorgetragen wurde. Als dann Heidegger Rektor der Freiburger Universität wurde, hielt er im Mai 1933 seine berüchtigte Rektoratsrede, *Die Selbstbehauptung der deutschen Universität*. Im Wintersemester 1934/35, nachdem er sein Amt niedergelegt hatte, hielt Heidegger seine erste große Hölderlin-Vorlesung, mit dem Titel: *Hölderlins Hymnen „Germanien" und „Der Rhein"*. Schließlich hielt Heidegger in 1935 die Vorlesung *Einführung in die Metaphysik*, die neben anderem auch eine gewaltige Auslegung des griechischen Denkens und der griechischen Dichtung enthielt.

Inwiefern bilden all diese Texte eine Einheit? Inwiefern sucht Heidegger hier zu einer neuen Klarheit seines Denkweges zu gelangen? Es gibt eine große Vielfalt von Themen, die in diesen Texten behandelt wurden, aber ich möchte behaupten, dass sie alle eine Mitte haben, und dies ist „der Ursprung" oder „der Anfang". Der Text, der wohl am weitesten in die Richtung des Ursprungs geht, ist die Hölderlin-Vorlesung über dessen Hymnen *Germanien* und *Der Rhein*. Gleichzeitig greift diese Vorlesung zumindest auf alles zu, was Heidegger

© KONINKLIJKE BRILL NV, LEIDEN, 2016 | DOI 10.1163/9789004323537_003

von 1931 bis 1936 gedacht und erfahren hat: Seine neue Auslegungen der griechischen Philosophie, die Frage nach dem Wesen der Kunst, der Sprache, der Dichtung und insbesondere der Hölderlinschen Dichtung, dann sein Versuch, die deutsche Universität grundlegend zu reformieren, schließlich seine missglückte Episode mit dem Freiburger Rektorat – alles wurde getragen von der Einsicht, dass Deutschlands Dichter und Denker dazu gerufen sind, dem bei den Griechen ansetzenden Anfang eine neue, besser gesagt eine *andere* Gestalt zu verleihen. Deutschland ist auserwählt, das Land des anderen Anfangs zu sein. Es hat demnach den Auftrag bekommen, eine neue Stiftung des abendländischen Seins zu vollziehen. Hier hängt alles auf engste mit der Problematik des Anfangs und des Ursprungs zusammen, die Heidegger selbst lange Zeit schon bedacht hatte, bevor er sie dann in Hölderlins Hymnen in einer scharfen dichterischen Ausarbeitung wieder fand.

Kommen wir unserem Thema näher. Dichtung und Politik sind zwei Begriffe, die nur im Lichte von Heideggers jahrelanger Beschäftigung mit dem Wesen des Ursprungs verständlich sind. Im Folgenden kann ich nur roh den Zusammenhang von Dichtung und Politik bei Heidegger, im Ausgang von der Hölderlin-Vorlesung, aufweisen. Um es schon im voraus zu sagen, das Thema des Politischen ist bei Heidegger weniger entwickelt als das Thema der Dichtung. Es kommt immer an zweiter oder dritter Stelle. Meiner Meinung nach lässt sich das Politische bei Heidegger leichter von der Problematik des Volkes, und speziell des deutschen Volkes, begreifen. Zum Verständnis des Wesens des Volkes und des innigen Widerspruches, das sein Wesen bestimmt, werde ich im zweiten Teil meines Beitrags einige Gedanken von François Fédier über Heideggers Verständnis des Volkes in der *Rektoratsrede* besprechen. Damit wird die Verwandtschaft von Dichtung und Volk klarer ans Licht treten.

Bevor wir uns dem Wesen der Dichtung bei Heidegger zuwenden, wollen wir einige Zitate aus der Hölderlin-Vorlesung vorbringen, die die Rangordnung von Dichtung, Philosophie und Politik am klarsten darstellen. Hier ist das erste Zitat: „Wir hörten schon, daß das geschichtliche Dasein der Völker, Aufgang, Höhe und Untergang, aus der Dichtung entspringt und aus dieser das eigentliche Wissen im Sinne der Philosophie und aus beiden die Erwirkung des Daseins eines Volkes als eines Volkes durch den Staat – die Politik. Diese ursprüngliche, geschichtliche Zeit der Völker ist daher die Zeit der Dichter, Denker und Staatsschöpfer, d.h. derer, die eigentlich das geschichtliche Dasein eines Volkes gründen und begründen. Sie sind die eigentlich Schaffenden"[41].

---

41    Heidegger 1999: 51.

DICHTUNG UND POLITIK BEI MARTIN HEIDEGGER                    17

Somit wird klar, dass laut Heidegger die Politik als Staatsschöpfung erst dann möglich ist, wenn Dichtung als Stiftung des Seins sich ereignet hat. In der heutigen Zeit aber, die Hölderlins weisende Kraft für das deutsche Volk immer noch nicht erkannt hat, besteht die primäre Aufgabe des Denkers darin, Hölderlins wahre Natur zu enthüllen. Dies ist zumindest Heideggers Aufgabe. Hier das zweite Zitat: „1. Hölderlin ist der Dichter des Dichters und der Dichtung. 2. In einem damit ist Hölderlin der Dichter der Deutschen. 3. Weil Hölderlin dieses Verborgene und Schwere ist, Dichter des Dichters als Dichter der Deutschen, deshalb ist er noch nicht die Macht in der Geschichte unseres Volkes geworden. Weil er das noch nicht ist, muß er es werden. Hierbei mitzuhalten ist »Politik« im höchsten und eigentlichen Sinne..."[42]. In unserer dürftigen Zeit, die blind für den ursprünglichen Ursprung geworden ist, besteht laut Heidegger die genuin politische Handlung des Denkens darin, erst einmal die Macht der Dichtung als solche zum Erblicken zu bringen und ihre freisetzende Kraft zu entfalten. Erst dann kann das Volk soweit zu einem solchen Verständnis der Not kommen, dass aus seiner Mitte jene Staatsschöpfer erwachsen können, die Hölderlins erneuernde, dichterische Stiftung des Seins in einen politischen Entwurf der Gemeinschaft umwandeln können.

Was versteht aber Heidegger genauer unter den Worten „Macht der Dichtung"? Inwiefern soll das Volk, sollen wir „in den Machtbereich der Dichtung einrücken"? Wie denkt er Dichtung überhaupt, so dass sie – einmal sogar „Urdichtung"[43] genannt – *die* anfängliche Macht, ja sogar der Ursprung selbst sei? In der Hölderlin-Vorlesung widmet Heidegger die Einleitung diesem einzigen Thema, nämlich dem Bezug von Dichtung und Sprache.

Heidegger geht phänomenologisch von derjenigen Realität aus, die sich uns zunächst und zumeist dar gibt: unser Verständnis von uns selbst, von der Natur der Dichtung und des Dichters. Alles läuft darauf hinaus, Dichtung nicht mehr als ein bloßes Gedicht zu verstehen, das physisch auf Papier irgendwo liegt und gelegentlich zur Entspannung, zur persönlichen Erbaulichkeit oder zu kulturellen, literarischen Zwecken verwendet wird. „Also müssen wir das Gedicht als nur vorhandenes Lesestück überwinden. Das Gedicht muß sich verwandeln und als Dichtung offenbar werden"[44]. Der Dichter selbst, in diesem Falle Hölderlin, muss nicht mehr als eine Person wahrgenommen werden, die über eine besondere bzw. ausgezeichnete Einbildungskraft verfügt, mithilfe derer er seine Erlebnisse in einem Gedicht sozusagen „verdichtet".

---

42    a.a.O., 214.
43    a.a.O., 218.
44    a.a.O., 19.

Sie, die Dichtung, „wird vorgestellt als *Ausdruck von Erlebnissen*, von welchem Erlebnis-Ausdruck das Gedicht dann der Niederschlag ist"[45]. „Verdichtung", „Ausdruck", „Niederschlag", „Erlebnis": die mechanische, organismische Note dieser Worte ist unüberhörbar: sie hängt mit unserem herrschenden Verständnis von Sein als Kausalität zusammen. Wir werden hier an den Anfang des Vortrags *Der Ursprung des Kunstwerkes* erinnert, wo Heidegger die herrschende Sicht auf das Werk als etwas Körperliches, mit irgendeinem geistigen Wert verhaftetes Ding bespricht. Und doch ist dieses alltägliche Verständnis von der Dichtung nicht etwas Falsches. Genauso wenig wie die allgemeine Sicht auf die Dichtung als das „unschuldigste aller Geschäffte" (Hölderlin). Es liegt im Ursprungshaften der Dichtung und der Sprache, dass sie *auch* dieses wesenslose Verständnis von ihr selbst erlaubt. Heidegger zeigt anhand eines Briefes Hölderlins an seine Mutter, dass Hölderlin Bescheid über diese Zweideutigkeit im Wesen der Dichtung wusste: „Dichtung – sie ist beides: jener Anschein und dieses Sein. Jener alltägliche Anschein gehört zu ihr wie das Tal zum Berg. Hölderlins Dasein hat diesen äußersten Gegensatz des Scheins und des Seins in seiner weitesten Spannung auseinander- und das heißt mit der größten Innigkeit zusammen- und ausgehalten"[46]. Diese Zweideutigkeit im Wesen der Dichtung hängt mit der zwiespältigen Natur des Menschen selbst zusammen, der einerseits das Gehör für das Höchste und Tiefste, d.h. für die Sprache des Ursprungs hat, andererseits zunächst und zumeist in seiner Alltäglichkeit gefangen bleibt. Um in den Machtbereich der Dichtung einzurücken bedarf es folglich eines Kampfes: „Der Kampf um die Dichtung im Gedicht ist der Kampf gegen uns, sofern wir in der Alltäglichkeit des Daseins aus der Dichtung ausgestoßen, blind, lahm und taub an den Strand gesetzt sind und den Wogengang des Meeres weder sehen noch hören noch spüren"[47].

Um es im voraus zu sagen: die ganze Hölderlin-Auslegung Heideggers zentriert in der Problematik des Kampfes, des Streites, der Zweideutigkeit. Dieses Streithafte ist, letztendlich, das Wesen des Ursprungs und des Anfangs selbst. Laut Heidegger hat Hölderlin sein Verständnis von dem Streithaften des Ursprungs aus einer Auseinandersetzung mit Heraklits Gedanke vom Kampf, *polemos*, gewonnen. Der Machtbereich der Dichtung ist somit der Name für jenen uralten Kampf von Sein und Schein, der zuerst von den griechischen Denkern erblickt worden ist. Dieser Kampf ist der Grund der abendländischen

---

45    a.a.O., 26.
46    a.a.O., 35.
47    a.a.O., 22.

DICHTUNG UND POLITIK BEI MARTIN HEIDEGGER 19

Geschichte, genauso wie der Kampf von Sein und Denken, den bekanntlich Parmenides zuerst als eine „Tautologie" gedacht hat: *to gar auto noein estin te kai einai*. Heidegger hat diese wesentlichen Kämpfe Sein-Schein, Sein-Denken eingehend in seiner gleich folgenden Vorlesung *Einführung in die Metaphysik* (GA 40, Sommersemester 1935) dargestellt.

Aber warum wählt hier Heidegger den Namen „Dichtung" für jenen Machtbereich, in den der Mensch, „das geschichtliche Dasein des Menschen", wie Heidegger schreibt, geworfen ist? Dichtung ist die Mitte jener Bezüge, die zwischen Sein, Dasein, Geschichte, und Sprache herrschen. Etymologisch hängt „dichten" mit dem lateinischen *dictare* zusammen, d.h. „etwas wiederholt sagen, vorsagen"[48] zusammen. Aber nicht das lateinische *dictare* hilft uns wahrlich weiter, sondern das griechische *deiknymi*, „zeigen, etwas sichtbar, etwas offenbar machen, und zwar nicht überhaupt, sondern auf dem Wege eines eigenen Weisens"[49] Mithin versteht Heidegger das Dichten als ein Sagen, das *eigentlich, ursprünglich, anfänglich* weisend und offenbar machend ist. Es liegt in der Natur der Sprache überhaupt, das Seiende als ein Seiendes allererst ins Offene, d.h. zum Erscheinen zu bringen. Dichtung ist insofern die eigentliche Art von Sagen, weil dadurch Wahrheit, Unverborgenheit des Seienden allererst entworfen wird. Hier ein Zitat aus dem *Ursprung des Kunstwerkes*, wo Heidegger auf das Wesen der Dichtung zu sprechen kommt: „Das entwerfende Sagen ist Dichtung: die Sage der Welt und der Erde, die Sage vom Spielraum ihres Streites und damit von der Stätte aller Nähe und Ferne der Götter. (...) Die jeweilige Sprache ist das Geschehnis jenes Sagens, in dem geschichtlich einem Volk seine Welt aufgeht und die Erde als das Verschlossene aufbewahrt wird"[50]. Dichtung ist jene Art des Sagens, die am stärksten die *Zwiespältigkeit* aller Dimensionen profiliert und prägt: Welt und Erde, Nähe und Ferne der Götter, Aufgehen und Sichverschließen, Sagbares und Unsagbares.

Kraft ihrer vermittelnden Natur bringt Heidegger die Dichtung in Zusammenhang mit dem *Wink*, den der Dichter von den Göttern bekommt und weiter in das Volk stellt. Den Wink versteht Heidegger als eine Vermittlung von Ferne und Nähe, die beide als solche in ihrem Verhältnis aufgehen lässt: das Ferne wird nur in der Nähe, das Nahe nur in der Ferne als solches offenbar. Eng mit dem Wink verwandt ist der Blitz, den der Dichter – „mit entblößtem Haupte" (Hölderlin) im Gewitter stehend – ins Wort bannt. Erneut wird

---

48  a.a.O., 29.
49  ebd.
50  Heidegger 1977: 61.

der Zusammenhang von Hölderlin und Heraklit sichtbar, sofern Heraklit der Denker des göttlichen Feuers und des Blitzes ist, der Alles, *panta*, auseinander hält und gleichzeitig zusammennimmt.

In der Einleitung zur Hölderlin-Vorlesung geht Heidegger auf die eigentümliche Struktur des Gedichtes „Germanien" ein und zeigt, dass darin ein vielfältiges Sagen am Werke ist: darin spricht zunächst ein Ich, dann ein Wir, dann ein geheimnisvoller Mann (der sich später als der Dichter selbst erweisen wird), schließlich der Adler als Bote der Götter, der selbst das Mädchen Germanien auffordert, die heilige Erde zu nennen. „In ein Gespräch sind wir hineingerissen, das die Sprache zur Sprache bringt ... (...) Ist dieser Wirbel, der uns in das Gespräch reißt, etwas anderes als das Gespräch selbst oder dasselbe? Ist dieser Wirbel die Dichtung, die wir suchen?"[51]. Das Gedicht selbst, in seinem Aufbau, zeigt diesen Wirbel, der von Strophe zu Strophe wächst: „Da der Wirbel nicht vorher, an sich ist, schafft jede Strophe in dieser Wandlung, in dieser Drehung den Wirbel erst und seine verschiedenen Stellen, wenn man überhaupt von »Stellen« in einem Wirbel sprechen kann"[52]. Dichtung ist demnach ein Gespräch, das von Heidegger hier als ein Wirbel, der sich ständig wandelt und dreht, verstanden wird. Seit wann besteht dieses Gespräch? Wann hat es angefangen? Heidegger spricht hier nicht von den Griechen, aber es ist zu vermuten, dass in seiner Sicht die ganze Geschichte des Abendlandes seit den Griechen ein sich immer wandelndes Gespräch ist. Jedes abendländische Volk nimmt an diesem Gespräch teil und fordert ein anderes Volk auf, dieses Gespräch zu übernehmen und sein eigenes Wesen aus diesem Gespräch zu erlangen. Es wäre aufschlussreich, in diesem Zusammenhange den kleinen Text *Wege zur Aussprache*[53] aus 1937 zu berücksichtigen, in dem Heidegger über das geschichtliche Gespräch zwischen Frankreich und Deutschland zu sprechen kommt – gerade in dem Moment, wo diese zwei Länder sich erneut feindlich gegenüberstanden. *Als Gespräch ist demnach die Dichtung wesentlich geschichtlich, und diese Geschichte hat als eigenes Wesen die Wandlung.* Warum das so ist, wird Heidegger in seinem Kommentar zum Gedicht „Der Rhein" andeuten: *das wandelnde Gespräch liegt im Wesen des Streites zwischen dem Ursprung selbst und dem aus ihm Entsprungenen. Diesen Streit nennt Heidegger das Geheimnis überhaupt.*

Hölderlin nennt die Sprache „der Güter Gefährlichstes", und Heidegger versteht diesen Spruch als einen Wink in die zwiespältige Natur der Dichtung

---

51     Heidegger 1999: 45.

52     a.a.O., 47.

53     Heidegger 1983, 15–21.

DICHTUNG UND POLITIK BEI MARTIN HEIDEGGER                    21

und der Sprache, denn sie eröffnet den Raum der größten Gefahr, mit der sich
der Mensch konfrontieren muss. Einmal ist die Gefahr überhaupt, die in dem
Zwiespalt von Sein und Nichtsein besteht. „Kraft der Sprache ist der Mensch
der Zeuge des Seyns. Er steht für dieses ein, hält ihm stand und fällt ihm
anheim. (. . .) Nur wo Sprache, da waltet Welt. Nur wo Welt, d.h. wo Sprache,
da ist höchste Gefahr, *die* Gefahr überhaupt, d.h. die Bedrohung des Seins als
solchen durch das Nichtsein"[54]. Sprache ist somit der Ort, wo diese zwei letzten Mächte, Sein und Nichtsein, ihren Streit austragen können. Der Dichter
vermag den Wink in das Wesen des Seins zu erblicken indem er sich, „mit entblößtem Haupte", im göttlichen Gewitter den Blitzen sich aussetzt. Aber damit
schwebt er in der Gefahr, von diesen selben Blitzen vernichtet zu werden. Der
Entwurf des Seins ist von dem Nichts durchdrungen. Die andere Gefahr ist
der Streit vom Wesen und Unwesen der Sprache selbst, d.h. der Verfall der
Sprache. „Die höchste Beglückung des ersten stiftenden Sagens ist zugleich
der tiefste Schmerz des Verlustes (. . .). Die ursprünglich das *Seyn* begründende
Sprache steht im Verhängnis des notwendigen Verfalls, der Verflachung in das
abgegriffene Gerede, dem sich nichts zu entziehen vermag, eben weil es den
Schein erweckt, als sei in seiner Art des Sagens, wenn es nur ein Sagen sei, das
Seiende getroffen und gefaßt"[55]. Während die Gefahr überhaupt im Verhältnis
von Sein und Nichtsein herrscht, waltet im Verhältnis von Sein und Schein die
Gefahr des Unwesens. *Die Sprache gefährdet sich selbst, weil die Gefährlichkeit
ihr eigenstes Wesen ausmacht.* Dieses zwiespältige, sich selbst gefährdende
Wesen der Sprache hängt wieder mit jenem Geheimnis zusammen, der
im Wesen des Anfangs und des Ursprungs liegt und von Hölderlin in seinem
Gedicht „Der Rhein" dichterisch angedeutet wurde.

Bevor wir uns dieser Sache wenden, wollen wir kurz Heideggers
Bestimmung der Sprache, der Dichtung und ihres Bezuges festhalten. Das
Wesen des Menschen ist die Sprache selbst, die nicht irgendwo an sich ist,
sondern geschieht. Das Geschehen der Sprache macht die Geschichte des
Menschen aus und entwickelt sich als wandelndes Gespräch. „Dichtung ist
das Grundgefüge des geschichtlichen Daseins. Dichtung ist als ursprüngliches
Gespräch der Ursprung der Sprache, mit der als seinem Gefährlichsten der
Mensch in das Sein als solches sich hinauswagt, dort standhält oder fällt und
im Verfall des Geredes sich aufbläht und verödet"[56].

---

54    Heidegger 1999: 62.
55    a.a.O., 63.
56    a.a.O., 76.

Das Gedicht „Der Rhein" gehört in den so genannten Umkreis der Stromdichtungen. In seiner Hölderlin-Vorlesung wählt Heidegger zwei Passagen aus dem Gedicht, die für den Ausleger besonders wegweisend sind[57]. Die erste Passage, die das Vorhaben und den Anspruch der Dichtung ausspricht, lautet: „Halbgötter denk' ich jetzt / Und kennen muß ich die Theuren, / Weil oft ihr Leben so / Die sehnende Brust mir beweget" (x. Strophe, 135–139). Die zweite Passage, die den ganzen Raum der Dichtung ausspricht, lautet: „Ein Räthsel ist Reinentsprungenes. Auch / Der Gesang kaum darf es enthüllen... (IV. Strophe, 46–47). Inwiefern nennt dieses Gedicht „Der Rhein" *auch* das Wesen der Dichtung? Wie man bemerken kann, enthalten beide Passagen *auch* einen Hinweis auf den Dichter: er ist es, der das Wesen des Stromes als ein Halbgott denken muss, weil dessen Leiden auch sein eigenes Leiden ist. Der Dichter leidet mit und ist, in gewissem Sinne, ein Halbgott. Die zweite Passage warnt uns, dass der Gesang des Dichters kaum das Geheimnis des rein entsprungenen Stromes enthüllen darf. Dichtung entspricht am meisten dem Wesen des Geheimnisses, sofern sie einerseits das Geheimnis andeutet, andererseits es verschweigen muss. Wir treffen hier auf eine neue Zweideutigkeit. Das Gedicht „Der Rhein" dichtet somit auch das Wesen der Dichtung: „Indem die Dichtung »Der Rhein« das Seyn der Halbgötter »denkt«, dichterisch stiftet, dichtet sie denkerisch das Wesen der Dichtung. Sofern aber das Seyn der Halbgötter Schicksal ist, muß das Schicksalhafte auch das Seyn der Dichtung und des Dichters bestimmen"[58]. „Halbgott", „Schicksal", „Ursprung" und „Entsprungenes" sind Worte, wodurch Hölderlin – in Heideggers Auslegung – das Geheimnis des Seins als solchen dichtet und denkt. *Das Sein ist es, das die Dichtung auf den Weg zu sich selbst bringt.* In einer Art von *Kehre* offenbart Hölderlins Stiftung des Seins das Sein der Stiftung: „Zum Wesen des Seyns als solchen (...) gehört der stiftende Rückwurf seiner auf sich selbst. Das Seyn läßt Dichtung entspringen, um ursprünglich in ihr sich zu finden und so in ihr sich verschließend als Geheimnis sich zu eröffnen"[59].

Ich kann im Folgenden nur kurz Heideggers auslegende Schritte wiedergeben. Hölderlin denkt das Wesen des Halbgottes, weil der Halbgott *die Mitte* von allem bildet: von ihm lassen sich die Götter, die Menschen, die Erde und das Seiende im Ganzen erst denken. Der Halbgott ist zugleich Untergott und Über-mensch, so dass das Wesen des Gottes und des Menschen erst von ihm her denkbar wird. Die Strophen IV bis IX des Gedichtes „Der Rhein"

---

57  a.a.O., vgl. 240.
58  a.a.O., 237.
59  ebd.

DICHTUNG UND POLITIK BEI MARTIN HEIDEGGER

denken den Halbgott als ein Reinentsprungenes, das nichts inniger will, als seinen Ursprung nicht zu vergessen, ja sogar ihn zu übertreffen. Er hat einen Gegenwille, der losgebunden über die Grenze der ursprünglichen Ungleichheit hinweg schreiten will[60]. Seine Verwegenheit und sein Trotz werden aber gebändigt, so dass das Entsprungene notwendig zum Ursprung zurückkehren muß. Der Ursprung seinerseits ist jener Anfang, der „das Entsprungene überspringt, ihm vor-springend es überdauert und so in der Gründung des Bleibenden gegenwärtig ist"[61]. Der Ursprung umfängt das Entsprungene von seinem Ende her und wird somit zu seinem Ziel.[62] *Zwischen Ursprung und seinem Entsprungenen herrscht demnach der wesentliche Streit überhaupt*, der aber nicht zu einer Vernichtung des einen, des anderen oder der beiden führt, sondern zu einer Einheit. Diese letzte Einheit nennt Hölderlin mit dem Wort „Innigkeit", die Heidegger als „Feind-seligkeit" auslegt: „Die Innigkeit ist jene ursprüngliche Einheit der Feindseligkeit der Mächte des Reinentsprungenen. Sie ist das zu diesem Seyn gehörige Geheimnis"[63]. Hölderlins Verwandtschaft mit Heraklit und dessen Gedanke des *hen diapheron heautō*, des in sich auseinander bringenden und damit sich selbst austragenden Einen, ist unüberhörbar. Diese Innigkeit herrscht im Wesen des Seins, und die Dichtung ist in diese Innigkeit eingefügt[64]. Weil jene Innigkeit das ursprünglichste Geheimnis ist, kann die Dichtung diese Innigkeit nur ahnen, in die sie eingefügt bleibt. Ihr Wort ist demnach nicht nur ihr Wort, sondern auch und *ursprünglicher das Wort von dem, was sie ahnt*. „Dichtung ist das Wort dieses Geahnten, ist dieses selbst als Wort"[65].

Im Folgenden möchte ich ganz kurz das Thema der Politik bei Heidegger aufgreifen, aber nicht allgemein, sondern im Lichte jener wesentlichen Widerwendigkeit, die im Wesen des Seins herrscht, so wie sie von Hölderlin als Innigkeit gedichtet und von Heidegger als Feindseligkeit gedacht wurde. Da mir nicht viel Raum zur Verfügung steht, werde ich nur drei Sätze aus Heideggers Rektoratsrede auswählen und sie kurz auslegen. Eine wesentliche Hilfe bietet mir hier ein Text von François Fédier, der den Titel „En Russie" trägt, 2002 geschrieben wurde und nun seit 2013 im Sammelband *Entendre*

---

60 a.a.O., vgl. 267.
61 a.a.O., 241.
62 a.a.O., vgl. 247.
63 a.a.O., 250.
64 a.a.O., vgl. 258.
65 a.a.O., 257.

24 MINCĂ

*Heidegger* vorliegt. Die Rektoratsrede trägt den Titel: *Die Selbstbehauptung der deutschen Universität.* Gleich am Anfang redet Heidegger von der geistigen Führung der Universität und der Gefolgschaft der Lehrer und Schüler, die alle ihre Wurzel im Wesen der deutschen Universität haben oder haben sollten. Das Paar Führer–Gefolgschaft wird noch einmal am Ende der Rede aufgegriffen, als Heidegger folgende drei Sätze schreibt: „Alle Führung muß der Gefolgschaft die Eigenkraft zugestehen. Jedes Folgen aber trägt in sich den Widerstand. Dieser Wesensgegensatz im Führen und Folgen darf weder verwischt, noch gar ausgelöscht werden"[66]. Was heißt hier Führen? Seine eigene Macht durchsetzen, sei es diktatorisch oder nicht? Oder ein wesentliches Zugestehen, das dem Anderen das eigene Wesen, also die Eigenkraft, zugesteht? Fédier übersetzt „führen" durch *diriger*, und legt dieses als ein *exercer le pouvoir* aus. Normalerweise würde dieses *exercer le pouvoir* als ein *imposer des directives* verstanden. Der Führende setzt *seine* eigenen Entscheidungen, mit Hilfe der Gefolgschaft, in die Tat um. Aber hier hören wir, dass der Führende dazu da ist, um der Gefolgschaft die Eigenkraft zuzugestehen, also dem Anderen sein eigenes Wesen zuzugeben. Und das Wesen der Gefolgschaft wird hier von Heidegger als „Widerstand" verstanden, das von Fédier als *résister au pouvoir* verstanden wird. Mehr erfahren wir hier nicht über die Gefolgschaft. In seinem Text versucht Fédier, diese Gefolgschaft ganz einfach als „Volk" zu verstehen, *le peuple.* Inwiefern wird das Volk in seinem Wesen durch den Widerstand charakterisiert? Laut Fédier widersteht das Volk der Macht, *weil es überhaupt nicht mit Macht zu tun haben will.* Der Widerstand geht nicht primär gegen den Führenden, der die Macht ausübt, denn damit würde das Volk selbst die Machtausübung wollen, was ganz gewiss gegen das Wesen des Volkes geht. In Heideggers Zitat weiter oben wird nicht von Macht, sondern von der *Eigenkraft* der Gefolgschaft geredet. Was soll dann aber ein Volk tun? Es widersteht der Macht des Führenden, *ohne* aber die Machtausübung zu wollen. Ist dies aber nicht ein Zeichen von Passivität? Worin besteht dann seine Eigenkraft? Sie besteht gerade darin, den Führenden als einen Führenden, Machtausübenden *sein zu lassen.* Umgekehrt besteht die Machtausübung des Führenden darin, dem Volk seine eigene Eigenkraft zuzugestehen. Dieses Zugestehen ist aber keine einfache Aktivität, so wie jener Widerstand des Volkes keine einfache Passivität ist. Fédier schreibt: „Le pouvoir ne saurait être exercé – comme il faut – sans résistance; et la résistance véritable ne peut se déployer s'il n'y a pas exercice du pouvoir"[67].

---

66 Heidegger 2000: 116.
67 Fédier 2013: 367.

DICHTUNG UND POLITIK BEI MARTIN HEIDEGGER 25

Zwischen Zugestehen und Widerstand, zwischen dem Führenden und dem Volk, herrscht gerade jener Streit, den Hölderlin in seiner Dichtung „Der Rhein" gedichtet hat. Es handelt sich genauer um jene Widerwendigkeit, die auf der schärfsten Auseinandersetzung basiert, die als solche aber immer in einer ursprünglichen Einheit und Innigkeit zusammengehalten wird: *hen diapheron heautō*. Es handelt sich, in Heideggers Worten, um jene Feind-seligkeit der Mächte des Reinentsprungenen[68], die das letzte Geheimnis des Ursprungs ausmacht.

Warum will aber das Volk nichts mit der Ausübung der Macht zu tun haben? Warum widersteht es aufs Schärfste dem Führenden? Hier wird etwas sichtbar, was in der Hölderlin-Vorlesung nur kurz angedeutet wurde, als Heidegger vom *Unwesen* der Sprache als Gerede zu sprechen kam. Welches wäre dann das Unwesen der Macht? Die Versteifung auf sich selbst und das Vergessen jenes primären Zugestehens, das dem Volk seine Eigenkraft zugesteht. Diese Versteifung würde jenes ursprüngliche Geheimnis zerstören und die anfängliche Widerwendigkeit ignorieren. Fédier nennt diese Versteifung auf sich selbst der Macht „Autokratie", *autocratie*: „la croyance que «je» puisse être, à «moi» seul, la source et la mesure d'un pouvoir"[69]. Das isolierte Ich schwebt immer in der Gefahr, die Macht für sich selbst haben zu wollen und sich letztendlich als der Ursprung der Macht zu betrachten. Nur das Volk hat die Kraft, von jeder Machtausübung abzusehen und gerade *so* dem Unwesen der Macht zu widerstehen. Ursprüngliche Politik, die durch Hölderlins Dichtung jetzt sichtbar wird, besteht demnach darin, den Führenden und das Volk als eine ursprüngliche Gemeinschaft zu gestalten. Ich schließe mit folgendem Zitat Heideggers: „Dichtung – kein Spiel (…), sondern die Erweckung und der Zusammenriß des eigensten Wesens des Einzelnen, wodurch er in den Grund seines Daseins zurückreicht. Kommt jeder Einzelne von dorther, dann ist die wahrhafte Sammlung der Einzelnen in eine ursprüngliche Gemeinschaft schon im voraus geschehen"[70].

### Acknowledgements

The work on this paper was supported by a grant of the Romanian National Authority for Scientific Research and Innovation, CNCS-UEFISCDI, project number PN-II-RU-TE-2014-4-2881.

---

68    Heidegger 1999: vgl. 250.
69    Fédier 2013: 371.
70    Heidegger 1999: 8.

### Literatur

Fédier, François (2013), *Entendre Heidegger et autres exercices d' écoute* (Paris).

Heidegger, Martin (1999), *Hölderlins Hymnen »Germanien« und »Der Rhein«* (GA 39) (Frankfurt/Main).

Heidegger, Martin (1977), 'Der Ursprung des Kunstwerkes', in: *Holzwege* (GA 5) (Frankfurt/Main).

Heidegger, Martin (1983), 'Wege zur Aussprache', in: *Aus der Erfahrung des Denkens (1910–1976)* (GA 13) (Frankfurt/Main).

Heidegger, Martin (2000), *Reden und andere Zeugnisse eines Lebensweges* (GA 16) (Frankfurt/Main).

CHAPTER 3

# Ethik – Politik – Dichtung. Pounds *Patria Mia*[71]

*Ralf Lüfter*

1

Im Ausgang einer frühen Schrift Ezra Pounds soll im Folgenden der Versuch unternommen werden, dem nachzudenken, was politische Dichtung ist und worauf wir uns beziehen, wenn wir im Rahmen dieser Tagung davon sprechen. Wenn in diesem Zusammenhang von einer frühen Schrift die Rede ist, so meint „früh" nicht in erster Linie das Verhältnis zu späteren Schriften, sondern ein in dieser Schrift zur Sprache kommendes anfängliches Eingeholt-Sein in die Nähe eines Anspruchs, dem sich das Werk des Dichters im Ganzen verdankt und das dementsprechend auch für dessen politischen Charakter maßgebend ist.

Der Titel dieser frühen Schrift lautet *Patria mia*. Pound hat sie in den Jahren um 1910 verfasst, noch bevor er während des Ersten Weltkrieges mit den Arbeiten zu den *Cantos* begann, die ihn mehr als ein halbes Jahrhundert beschäftigen sollten. *Patria mia* ist keine besonders umfangreiche Schrift. Sie besteht aus zwei Hauptteilen, die sich ihrerseits noch einmal in zwei bzw. vier Kapitel unterteilen. Die beiden Hauptteile wurden zunächst unabhängig voneinander als eigenständige Beiträge in der britischen Literaturzeitschrift *The New Age* veröffentlicht. Der erste, diagnostische Teil, erschien 1912 unter dem Titel *Patria mia*. Der zweite, prognostische Teil, erschien ein Jahr später unter dem Titel *America: Chances and Remedies*. Pound hat die beiden Texte nach ihrer Erstveröffentlichung noch einmal überarbeitet und zu einem eigenständigen Manuskript zusammengeführt. Dieses sollte von Ralph Fletcher Seymour herausgegeben werden, ging aber in den Wirren eines Verlagskonkurses verloren

---

71  Der vorliegende Text ist eine leicht überarbeitete Version eines Vortrages, der am 2. Mai 2015 im Rahmen der Tagung *Political Poetry across the Centuries* an der Akademie deutsch-italienischer Studien Meran gehalten wurde. Der mündliche Charakter wurde beibehalten. Einiges von dem, was hier angesprochen ist, wurde bereits an anderer Stelle eingeführt und ausführlicher erläutert. Vgl. dazu: Lüfter, R. (2013), *This Land turns evil slowly (Ezra Pound)*, in: M. Signore (Hrsg.), Idee. Semestrale di Filosofia, Scienze Sociali ed Economiche (2013/6), (Lecce) 57–69; Lüfter, R. (2013), *Notizen zu Ezra Pounds Ökonomie*, in: I. De Gennaro, S. Kazmierski, R. Lüfter (Hrsg.), Wirtliche Ökonomie. Philosophische und dichterische Quellen, Teilband 1, Elementa Œconomica Bd. 1, (Nordhausen) 398–417.

---

© KONINKLIJKE BRILL NV, LEIDEN, 2016 | DOI 10.1163/9789004323537_004

und wurde erst Jahrzehnte später wieder gefunden. So kam es, dass *Patria mia*, in der heute vorliegenden Form, erst 1950 in Druck ging[72]. 1960 erschien eine erste, von Eva Hesse besorgte, deutsche Übersetzung des Textes. Zwei Jahre zuvor war eine italienische Übersetzung von Margherita Guidacci erschienen.

*Patria mia* ist eine programmatische Schrift. Nicht nur was die Entwicklung des Werkes von Pound anbelangt, sondern vor allem im Hinblick auf unser gegenwärtiges Zeitalter. Hier gibt einer vor, zu wissen, was in diesem Zeitalter zur Entscheidung steht und was als das Ausständige seine Gegenwart bestimmt. Die Vorgabe, die Pound an dieser Stelle wagt, kommt indes nur dem entgegen, was sich seinerseits längst angekündigt hat und was sich als das Zukünftige derart Bahn bricht, dass es den Menschen dieses Zeitalters von Neuem in die Nähe jenes Anspruchs stellt, von dem er als Mensch immer schon eingeholt ist.

Exemplarisch bringt Pound dieses Neue anhand seines eigenen Vaterlandes zur Sprache. In ihm scheint sich das Schicksal unseres Zeitalters zu erfüllen und dabei in einer Weise offensichtlich zu werden, die eine Diagnose seines gegenwärtigen Zustandes und eine Prognose seiner eigentümlichen Vergangenheit ermöglicht. So hat sich in unserem Zeitalter, wie Pound zu Beginn von *Patria mia* ausführlich erläutert, vor allem im Hinblick auf das Ökonomische eine Ignoranz ins Recht gesetzt, die alles – von der Kunst über die Wissenschaft bis hin zur Politik – überwuchert: Auf dass es nichts anderes mehr geben kann als das Gesetz von Angebot und Nachfrage, wodurch sich ein jedes und ein jeder in die ebenso anspruchslose wie gleichgültige Verfügbarkeit seiner operativen Verwertbarkeit hergestellt sieht. Im Hinblick auf diese hat sich ein jedes und ein jeder als nützlich zu erweisen. Vor allem die Ignoranz gegenüber dem, was ist, hat sich, so Pounds Diagnose, längst zu einem konstitutiven Gesetz (νόμος) für den Bereich des menschlichen Wohnens im Ganzen (οἶκος) erhoben – mithin zu dem konstitutiven Gesetz eines Wissens, das sich gerade dadurch auszeichnet, dass es vor lauter Gleichgültigkeit nichts mehr bleiben lassen kann. Die Anspruchslosigkeit dieser Gleichgültigkeit überwuchert längst und nicht zufällig alle menschlichen Bezüge.

> Man weiß, was man will. Die nächste Frage ist, wie man es bekommt. Und flugs heckt man die Mittel aus. [...] Und alles, was keinen verwertbaren Nutzen zeigt, wird verachtet.
>
> Jedes Bedürfnis dieses neuen „Metropoliten" <des globalisierten Menschen> ist befriedigt, noch ehe es auch nur aufkommt. Er braucht keine Einsichten mehr <er braucht keine Idee mehr>, er hat die Elektrizität.

---

72  Vgl. Hesse 1960: 7–9.

ETHIK – POLITIK – DICHTUNG 29

Nächte wie hier gibt es in keiner anderen Stadt <an keinem anderen Ort>. Ich habe aus hochgelegenen Fenstern auf die Stadt geschaut. So kommt es dann, dass die riesigen Gebäude ihrer Wirklichkeit beraubt eine magische Kraft entfalten. Sie lösen sich auf und werden immateriell, einer sieht nur ihre hell erleuchteten Fenster. Viereck über Viereck entflammt, in Nachtluft gefasst, in Nachtluft geschnitten. Das ist unsere Poesie, so haben wir nach unserem Willen die Sterne vom Himmel geholt.[73]

Was es vom Ökonomischen zu wissen gibt, darum kümmert sich die Ökonomik zur Stunde nicht. In ihrer aktuellen Verfassung geht ihr jeglicher Sinn dafür ab, etwas in dem zu erhalten und als das zu bewahren, was es ist – und es also in eben diesem zu fördern und zu sich kommen zu lassen – was so viel hieße wie: Kunst, Wissenschaft, Politik so zu fördern, dass Kunst Kunst, Wissenschaft Wissenschaft und Politik Politik sein mag und sich in ihr je Eigenes fügen kann. Längst hat die von Pound angezeigte Ignoranz in allen diesen Bereichen Fuß gefasst. Es ist indes kein Zufall, dass gerade die Ökonomik in ihrer gegenwärtigen Form – zusammen mit der modernen Technik, die sich in ihrer Entwicklung auf die Erkenntnisse der mathematischen Naturwissenschaften stützt – das vorherrschende Wissen unseres Zeitalters geworden ist.

Unsere Politik ist heute nur noch ein Zweig des Geschäftslebens.

Und ebenso steht es um die „Kunst (in Amerika)" oder besser gesagt, die Literatur.

Die Kunst <aber> gedeiht auch noch inmitten der dumpfsten und starrsten Ignoranz. Ich glaube, sie gedeiht trotz aller falschen Propheten und kommerziellen Imitatoren; in dem Fall wird die Nation aber nicht gewahr werden, dass es <überhaupt> Kunst gibt und die Mache wird <allerorts> überhand nehmen.

---

73 „They know what they want. The next problem is how to get it. And the devising of means follows swiftly upon this. [...] and that which cannot do something obviously to immediate advantage is despised. [...] This new metropolitan has his desire sated before it is aroused. Electricity has for him made the seeing of visions superfluous. [...] No urban nights are like the nights there. I have looked down across the city from high windows. It is then that the great buildings lose reality and take on their magical powers. They are immaterial; that is to say one sees but the lighted windows. Squares after squares of flame, set and cut into the ether. Here is our poetry, for we have pulled down the stars to our will." Pound 1950: 11–19.

Der ernsthafte Künstler untersteht nicht dem Gesetz von Angebot und Nachfrage. Er gleicht dem Chemiker bei seinen Experimenten, vierzig Resultate sind unbrauchbar, seine Zeit hat keinen Wert; dass die ein-und-vierzigste oder vierhundert-und-vierzigste Verbindung jenes Wunder zeigt, das die Nachwelt bereichern könnte, ist ebenso wahrscheinlich wie unwahrscheinlich. Der Händler aber muss entweder auf Experimente und Entdeckungen verzichten, und sich darauf beschränken, zu produzieren, was gefragt ist, oder aber er muss auch die Ausschussware verkaufen – und jede dieser Lösungen wäre für den Künstler ebenso fatal wie für den Wissenschaftler.[74]

Was hier nach der bloßen Beschreibung eines momentanen Zustandes klingt, bräuchte eine ebenso ausführliche wie eingehende Erörterung, insofern sie Pounds Diagnose unseres Zeitalters vorbereitet und folglich in etwas einführt, das bei Weitem über das hinausgeht, was wir die mehr oder weniger gerechtfertigte Meinung eines Dichters nennen können. Bei einer solchen stehen zu bleiben, würde nun aber weit hinter dem zurückbleiben, was Pound selbst von der Kunst, von der Dichtung – und mithin von seiner eigenen Arbeit – verlangt.

Die Kraft eines Kunstwerks besteht darin, dass der Künstler seine Sache so vollendet, oder auch nur so genau ins Werk setzt, wie er sie seinerseits vermag. Man kann mit ihm einiggehen oder nicht, aber man kann ihn nicht widerlegen.[75]

Eine ausführliche und eingehende Auslegung dieser Passagen, die für ein hinreichendes Verständnis zweifelsohne nötig wäre, vermag das Folgende

---

74　„And our politics are by now no more than a branch of business. [...] And that is ‚art in America', or rather it is literature. [...] The arts can thrive in the midst of densest popular ignorance. They can thrive, I suppose, despite any number of false priests and producers of commercial imitations, but in this latter case the nation will not know that the arts stay alive, and the sham will grow. The serious artist does not play up to the law of supply and demand. He is like the chemist experimenting, forty results are useless, his time is spent without payment, the forty-first or the four hundredth and first combination of elements produces the marvel, for posterity as likely as not. The tradesman must either cease from experiment, from discovery and confine himself to producing that for which there is a demand, or else he must sell his botches, and either of the courses is as fatal to the artist as it would be to the man of science." Pound 1950: 20–24.

75　„The force of a work of art is this, namely, that the artist presents his case, as fully or as minutely as he may choose. You may agree or disagree, but you cannot refute him." Pound 1950: 56.

ETHIK – POLITIK – DICHTUNG

nicht zu leisten, vielleicht kann aber wenigstens die Richtung angezeigt werden, von wo her sich für eine solche noch ausständige Auslegung etwas zu zeigen vermag.

2

Bevor wir nun darauf zu sprechen kommen, sei eine Anmerkung zu dem Thema der Tagung erlaubt, die für den Versuch einer Auseinandersetzung mit Pounds politischer Dichtung wesentlich ist. Schlägt man den Begriff „politische Dichtung" in einem Lexikon nach, so findet man ihn für gewöhnlich in folgender Bedeutung: Sammelbegriff für literarische Werke, die politische Themen oder Vorkommnisse behandeln, um auf Meinungsbildungsprozesse in Staat und Gesellschaft einzuwirken; die politische Dichtung steht im Dienste der Politik, indem sie bestehende politische Zustände bejaht und verherrlicht, oder aber kritisiert und eine Veränderung derselben als Ziel vorgibt.

Mit Blick auf Pounds Arbeit ist der so eingeführte Begriff „politische Dichtung" missverständlich, insofern er gerade das verfehlt, worum es in der Hauptsache geht. Anhand der folgenden Analogie wird das gemeinte Missverständnis unmittelbar klar.

Wenn wir die Ethik als ein praktisches Wissen bezeichnen, dann ist damit nicht gemeint, dass die Ethik ein Wissen von der Praxis ist und also die Praxis der Gegenstand dieses Wissens sei. Vielmehr charakterisiert das Adjektiv „praktisch" das gemeinte Wissen selbst. Praktisch ist nicht etwas – im Verhältnis zum Wissen – anderes, das vom Wissen für dieses in der Weise vorgestellt wird, dass es nach verschiedenen Hinsichten eingesehen und gewusst werden könnte. Anders gesagt: Das Adjektiv „praktisch" bezieht sich nicht auf etwas außerhalb des Wissens, das, um gewusst zu sein, vom Wissen für dieses vergegenständlicht werden müsste. „Praktisch" ist das Wissen als solches, das Wissen als Wissen. Es selbst ist eine Praxis. Es selbst ist von Anfang an und durchgängig konstitutiv für das, was an dieser Stelle „Praxis" genannt werden mag. Daraus folgt: Lediglich dort, wo dieses Wissen von sich weiß, und nur insofern es von sich weiß, ist es zugleich auch ein Wissen von der Praxis. Solange wir aber daran festhalten, dass die Praxis vor allem der Gegenstand dieses Wissens sei und das Wissen selbst ausschließlich dort als praktisch zu gelten habe, wo es sich in einem operativen Zusammenhang anwenden lässt und also nützlich bzw. zweckdienlich wird, bleiben wir von einem hinreichenden Verständnis dessen, was die Wendung „praktisches Wissen" sagt, ausgeschlossen.

In Analogie dazu lässt sich im Hinblick auf den Begriff „politische Dichtung" sagen: Dichtung ist nicht in erster Linie auf Grund der Themen und Vorkommnisse, die sie behandelt, politisch oder auf Grund der Tatsache, dass sie in der einen oder aber anderen Weise auf Meinungsbildungsprozesse in Staat und Gesellschaft einwirkt. Sie ist vielmehr insofern politisch, als es ihr eigen ist, politisch zu sein – insofern ihr Wesen politisch ist. Dichtung als Dichtung ist so gesehen immer schon politisch – nämlich: in der Weise, dass sie jedes Mal das Politische stiftet, dass sie das Politische jedes Mal zur Entscheidung bringt und zum Tragen kommen lässt. Wie wir im Folgenden anhand ausgewählter Textstellen aus den Arbeiten von Pound sehen werden, stiftet die Dichtung und mithin die Kunst das Politische als Ort des Austrags, an dem so etwas wie das Menschliche allererst zu sich kommen und ein Maß für sein Bleiben (ἦθος) finden kann.

> Einige wenige, wirklich behauene Steinblöcke sind eine nahezu hinrei-chende Grundlage für eine neue Zivilisation[76],

schreibt Pound in dem Buch, das der Erinnerung an seinen Freund, dem Bildhauer Henri Gaudier-Brzeska, gewidmet ist. Das „Können", von dem gerade im „Zu-sich-kommen-Können" und „Fügen-Können" die Rede war, meint indes keine außergewöhnliche Leistung eines Menschen, keine besondere Fähigkeit eines Menschen, auf deren Grundlage sich die so genannten Künstler (die Könner) von den Nicht-Künstlern (den Nicht-Könnern) unterscheiden, son-dern das eigentlich menschliche Vermögen „zu können" – nämlich wortwört-lich: „zu kennen" – und das heißt: zu wissen und wissen zu lassen, zu verstehen und verstehen zu lassen. So, dass wir jedes Mal sagen müssen: Wo Mensch, da Wissen. Wo Mensch, da Verstehen. Dass solches „Können" das Seltenste ist, heißt nur, dass auch die Menschen selten sind.

In eins damit besteht laut Pound immer auch die Möglichkeit, nicht zu wis-sen, was es zu wissen gibt, und nicht zu verstehen, was es zu verstehen gibt. In der Ignoranz weist Pound diese Möglichkeit nach und charakterisiert sie als eine dem Menschsein gegenüber fortgesetzt feindliche bzw. un-freundliche Macht.

> Der Feind ist die Ignoranz (unsere eigene).[77]

„Feind" ist hier eine zu ungenaue Übersetzung des englischen Wortes „enemy", das sich vom Lateinischen „inimicus" ableitet und wortwörtlich so viel heißt wie: Nicht-Freund, Un-Freund. Die Ignoranz ist nicht in der Weise gegen das Wissen,

---

76   „A few blocks of stone really carved are very nearly sufficient base for a new civilization."
     Pound 1970: 140.

77   „The enemy is ignorance (our own)." Pound 1975: 344.

ETHIK – POLITIK – DICHTUNG

dass sie das, was es zu Wissen gibt, absichtlich verschweigt oder verleugnet. Die Ignoranz ist insofern gegen das Wissen, als sie sich von dem, was es zu wissen gibt, nicht in Anspruch nehmen lässt und so das eigene Eingeholt-Sein in seine Nähe von vorn herein ausschließt. Heute zeigt sich die Ignoranz vor allem in jenem Wissen, das sich damit begnügt, in einem operativen Zusammenhang zu funktionieren. Das bloße Funktionieren ist diesem Wissen Grund genug, sich im Recht zu wähnen. Sein ausschließendes Wahrheitskriterium ist das Funktionieren, d.h. seine unmittelbare Anwendbarkeit in einem operativen Zusammenhang. Sobald sich ein solches Wissen nun aber am Prüfstein des Verstehens zu messen hat, wird es in seiner Anspruchslosigkeit merklich und erweist sich als ein bloß vermeintliches Wissen. Der Prüfstein des Verstehens wird ihm, wie Pound im *Canto XCIII* sagt, zum „Schlachtblock", an dem es fällt und sich im Hinblick auf das, was es zu wissen gibt, als das erweist, was es ist – nämlich: ignorant. Wissen hängt hier gerade nicht von der unmittelbaren Verfügbarkeit feststellbarer Informationen über einen Sachverhalt ab, sondern von dem, was es zu wissen gibt und was im Verstehen gegründet ein wesentliches Wissen von einem Sachverhalt bildet. Im Hinblick auf den hier grob angedeuteten Unterschied zwischen einem verständigen Wissen und einem unverständigen Wissen, sagt Pound im *Canto XCIII*:

> Ein Schlachtblock für Biographen,
> Was-Sein!
> Haben sie je davon gehört?
> „Ihr da", wie Dante sagt
> „achteraus in dem Beiboot"
> notwendig aber ist incognita
> und in Meeresgrotten
> un lume pien' di spiriti
> und voller Erinnerungen
> Wissen denn zwei beim Wissen dasselbe?[78]

Es gehört zum Wissen selbst, dass die Stiftung des Gemeinsamen als Ort des Austrags, an dem das Menschliche allererst zu sich kommen und ein Maß für sein Bleiben finden kann, jeweils den Einzelnen braucht. Jede echte Gemeinschaft ist die Gemeinschaft Einzelner, nie aber ihre bloße Summe.

---

78 „A butcher's block for biographers, / quiddity! / Have they heard of it? / ‚Oh you,' as Dante says / ,in the dinghy astern there' / There must be incognita / and in sea-caves / un lume pien' di spiriti / and of memories, / Shall two know the same in their knowing?" (Canto XCIII). Pound 1996: 651.

Jede echte Gemeinschaft erwächst aus dem Wissen um die anfängliche Verantwortung für das, was ist – aus dem Wissen um die Verantwortung für das „Was-Sein", dem „Schlachtblock der Biographen". Das Biographische begnügt sich mit vermeintlichem Wissen, mit Informationen, die für sich genommen nichts anderes sind als ein in seine Verfügbarkeit hergestellter, möglichst eindeutig definierter Wissensgehalt, dank dessen ein jeder alles, und alles von jedem auf die gleiche Weise gewusst werden kann. Dem „Was-Sein" aber ist ein jeder in der Weise überlassen, wie er es von sich aus zu verantworten vermag – das heißt: wie weit er sich von dem, was ist, in Anspruch nehmen lässt und von sich her in der Lage ist, das Angesprochen-Sein als solches zur Sprache zu bringen.

„Wissen denn zwei beim Wissen dasselbe?" fragt Pound in dem gerade zitierten Abschnitt des *Canto XCIII*. Wir antworten vorläufig: Sie wissen dasselbe, sofern sie das wissen, was es zu wissen gibt. Jeder aber weiß es für sich, auf die ihm eigene, unvergleichliche Weise – auf jene Weise nämlich, die ihn in das einweist, was er selbst ständig zu sein vermag: ein einmaliger, einzigartiger, unvergleichlicher Mensch. So gehört es zum Wissen eines jeden halbwegs aufmerksamen Lehrers, dass dort, wo ein Schüler das Angezeigte plötzlich versteht und selbstständig mitträgt, es noch einmal, jetzt anders, neu da ist. „Mach es neu", sagt Pound. Dort aber, wo man sich dem gegenüber, was es jedes Mal und immer von Neuem zu wissen gibt, als ignorant erweist und folglich im Hinblick auf das Was-Sein gleichgültig bleibt, können weder Einzelne sein, noch jemals zwei werden, solange zwei nicht bloß die Summe von Gleich und Gleich, sondern eine echte Gemeinschaft sind.

One's not half of two; two are halves of one[79]

sagt Cummings, mit dem Pound wohl nicht nur diese Einsicht gemein hat, sondern den Blick für das, was jede echte Freundschaft trägt.

In der Sorge um das, was ist, und aus dem Wissen von dem, was ist, wird das, was ist, ausgetragen. Der Ort dieses Austrags ist in dem griechischen Wort πόλις gesagt. Die πόλις ist der Ort des anfänglichen Erringens dessen, was es für den Menschen gibt. Gemeint ist jener Austrag, durch den alles innerhalb der πόλις in sein Was-Sein eingesetzt wird und seinen jeweiligen Sinn hat: die Verfassung, die Gesetze, die Institutionen, die Wissenschaft, die Ökonomie, die Kunst etc. Von hier aus bestimmt sich das, was wir „das Politische" nennen können und von dem wir oben gesagt haben, dass es zuallererst in der

---

79  Cummings 1953: 89.

ETHIK – POLITIK – DICHTUNG

Dichtung gestiftet wird und durch sie zur Entscheidung gebracht, für das Gemeinsame tragend bleibt.[80]

### 3

In einem der von T.S. Eliot herausgegebenen *Literarischen Aufsätze* sagt Pound an einer in diesem Zusammenhang bezeichnenden Stelle:

> Erfüllt die Literatur im Staat eine Aufgabe, innerhalb der Gemeinschaft der Menschen, im öffentlichen Bereich, für die res publica, womit eigentlich das Gemeinwohl gemeint ist? Tut sie! Diese Aufgabe besteht indes weder darin, Menschen zur Annahme irgendeiner vorgestellten Meinung oder sechs vorgestellten Meinungen an Stelle irgendeiner anderen vorgestellten Meinung oder einem halbem Dutzend vorgestellter Meinungen zu zwingen, noch darin, ihnen diese [...] schmackhaft zu machen, oder sie ihnen aufzudrängen oder <gar> aufzuoktroyieren. Sie hat <dagegen> mit der Klarheit und der Strenge eines jeden Denkens und Meinens zu tun. Sie hat mit dem Bewahren der Reinheit der seltenen und wenigen geistreichen Augenblicke in der Bildhauerei oder der Mathematik zu tun, ohne Worte kann das Individuum weder denken noch seine Gedanken mitteilen, das Oberhaupt und der Gesetzgeber können weder wirksam handeln noch Gesetze formulieren, ohne Worte, wobei <gerade> die verrufenen und verschmähten *litterati* für die Gediegenheit und Echtheit dieser Worte Sorge tragen. Wo ihre Arbeit verdorben ist – und damit meine ich nicht, wo sie sich anzüglich ausdrücken – <sondern> wo die eigenste Mitte, das eigentliche Wesen ihrer Arbeit, die aufmerksame Hinwendung des Wortes an die Sache verdirbt, [...] verwahrlost <auch> das Gefüge gemeinsam und einzeln ausgetragener Verantwortung und Ordnung im Ganzen. Das ist eine Lektion aus der Geschichte, eine Lektion die noch nicht einmal halbwegs gelernt ist.[81]

---

80  Vgl. Zaccaria 1999: 79–88.

81  „Has literature a function in the state, in the aggregation of humans, in the republic, in the res publica, which ought to mean the public convenience [...]? It has. And this function is not the coercing or emotionally persuading, or bullying or suppressing people into the acceptance of any one set or any six sets of opinions as opposed to any other one sets or half-dozen sets of opinions. It has to do with the clarity and the vigour of »any and every« thought and opinion. It has to do with maintaining the very cleanliness of the rare and limited instances of invention in the plastic arts, or in mathematics, the individual cannot

36 LÜFTER

An anderer Stelle, in einem Text mit dem Titel *ABC of Reading*, heißt es dazu:

> Es ist überaus schwierig, Menschen einen Begriff des unpersönlichen Entsetzens zu vermitteln, den der Verfall der Sprache für jene Menschen mit sich bringt, die verstehen, um was es geht und wohin es führt. Es ist nahezu unmöglich, auch nur einen Bruchteil dieses <unpersönlichen> Entsetzens zur Sprache zu bringen, ohne verbittert zu wirken.
>
> Und dennoch: Der Staatsmann kann nicht regieren, der Wissenschaftler keine Entdeckungen mitteilen, die Menschen können sich nicht über kluge Handlungsweisen einig werden, ohne Sprache – all ihr Tun und Lassen ebenso wie die Umstände, denen sie ausgesetzt sind, werden von den Stärken und Schwächen des Idioms bestimmt.
>
> Ein Volk, das sich an einen schlampigen Stil gewöhnt hat, ist ein Volk, das im Begriff ist, den Halt zu verlieren [...].[82]

Zu der Lektion, die laut Pound noch nicht einmal halbwegs gelernt ist, gehört nicht zuletzt ein Verständnis des Politischen selbst, das ausschließlich aus der Sorge erwächst, die das dichtende Wort braucht, um das menschliche Hören über die Kontingenz des bloß Vorhandenen hinaus in seine „eigenste Mitte" zu weisen. Diese entscheidet und trägt, wie Pound in dem eben zitierten Abschnitt meint, „das Gefüge gemeinsam und einzeln ausgetragener Verantwortung und Ordnung im Ganzen". Pounds Cantos sind auch und vor allem in diesem Sinne „Weisen" – nämlich: „Gesänge" – das heißt: Hinausweisendes Einweisen im dichtenden Wort[83]. Für Pound geht es um den Menschen, um jeden von uns als der,

---

think and communicate his thought, the governor and legislator cannot act effectively or frame his laws, without words, and the solidity and validity of these words is in the care of the damn and despised *litterati*. When their work goes rotten – by that I do not mean when they express indecorous thoughts – but when their very medium, the very essence of their work, the application of word to thing goes rotten [...] the whole machinery of social and of individual thought and order goes to pot. This is a lesson of history, and a lesson not yet half learned." Pound 1968: 21.

82 „It is very difficult to make people understand the impersonal indignation that a decay of writing can cause men who understand what it implies, and the end whereto it leads. It is almost impossible to express any degree of such indignation without being called ,embittered', or something of that sort. Nevertheless ,the statesman cannot govern, the scientist cannot participate his discoveries, men cannot agree on wise action without language', and all their deeds and conditions are affected by the defects or virtues of idiom. And people that grows accustomed to sloppy writing is a people in process of losing grip [...]." Pound 2010: 34.

83 Vgl. De Gennaro 2005.

ETHIK – POLITIK – DICHTUNG

der er ist in seiner Verantwortung für das Gemeinsame, in seiner Verantwortung für die „eigenste Mitte", welche ihre Stiftung durch den Menschen braucht, um für den Menschen der Grund zu sein, auf dem er eine Bleibe haben und sich einrichten kann. So klingen die *Cantos*, an denen Pound, wie gesagt, mehr als ein halbes Jahrhundert arbeiten sollte, nicht zufällig in dem Vers aus:

> Mensch zu sein, nicht Zerstörer.[84]

Mensch-Sein, nicht als bloßes Faktum, das in seiner Faktizität nachträglich festgestellt und als das so Festgestellte nach verschiedenen Hinsichten ausgelegt werden will, sondern Mensch-Sein als das anfängliche Eingeholt-Sein in die Nähe des Anspruchs die „eigenste Mitte" zu stiften – nämlich, des Anspruchs „Mensch *zu* sein". Das Wörtchen „zu" in der Wendung „Mensch zu sein" räumt die Möglichkeit ein, diesem Anspruch zu entsprechen und das anfängliche Eingeholt-Sein in seine Nähe eigens auszustehen oder aber den Anspruch zu verfehlen und im Hinblick auf das Eingeholt-Sein ignorant zu bleiben. Von diesem Anspruch ist jeder von uns als der, der er ist, immer schon eingeholt. Dort nämlich, wo er sich über das bloß Kontingente hinaus vom dichtenden Wort in die „eigenste Mitte" einweisen lässt – das heißt: dort, wo er bereit wird, eigens auf den unpersönlichen Anspruch des dichtenden Wortes zu hören. So bricht in dem Anspruch „Mensch zu sein" eine Möglichkeit auf, in die der Mensch zwar immer schon eingeholt ist, deren Nähe ihm aber zuweilen so fremd ist, dass es allererst wieder ein, wie Pound in *Patria mia* meint, „Erwachen" braucht, um das Eingeholt-Sein angemessen vernehmen zu können und also den Anspruch selbst als „eigenste Mitte" des Mensch-Seins zu erringen.

> Man brachte Huren nach Eleusis
> Leichname sitzen beim Festmahl
> Auf Geheiß von Usura.[85]

Sie haben die käufliche Liebe und damit die kalkulierbare Verfügbarkeit derselben an die Stelle dessen gebracht, was dem Menschen selten genug alles Entstehen und Vergehen als unverfügbares Maß bewahrt. Leichname, nicht Menschen, sitzen am reich gedeckten Tisch – ebenso gleichgültig wie anspruchslos, zeugungsunfähig, im Ganzen unvermögend – dem gegenüber, was es von sich her und von sich aus immer schon gab: Anfänglichen

---

84  „To be men not destroyers." Pound 1996: 823.

85  „They have brought whores for Eleusis / Corpses are set to banquet / At behest of usura" (Canto XLV). Pound 1996: 230.

und unerschöpflichen Reichtum. Auf Geheiß von Usura verbraucht sich das Angesprochen-Sein von diesem ebenso anfänglichen wie unerschöpflichen Reichtum und setzt sich eine Maßlosigkeit ins Recht, die dem Mensch-Sein das rechte Maß für sein Bleiben versagt.

> Bei Usura hat keiner ein Haus aus gutem Stein
> [...]
> bei Usura kein Unterschied mehr
> und keiner hat eine Bleibe für sein Wohnen[86]

So steht für Pound alles menschliche Können, sofern es den Namen verdient, unter dem Anspruch einer – wie es in der Dichtung *The Needle* heißt – „künftigen Gunst", in dessen Nähe „wir" eingeholt unser Tun und Lassen freigesetzt sehen. „Bauen wir", schreibt Pound in dieser Dichtung, „bewegen wir", „bringen wir" in diese „künftige Gunst" hinein das „Bleiben". „Künftig" ist die „Gunst" dort, wo „wir" eingeholt sind in ihre anfängliche Nähe – wo sie uns naht als die eigenste Mitte der zu stiftenden Möglichkeit „Mensch zu sein".

> Narr nicht die Gezeit der Sterne, künftig ist sie.
> Liebste, komm, dies Land nimmt eine üble Wende.
> Die Wellen stürzen unentwegt, sie tragen unverzüglich ab.

> Un-heimliches Vermögen ist unser, bauen wir bei Zeiten Land.
> Bewegen wir und bringen der Gezeit, in ihrer künftigen Gunst,
> Bleiben
> unter unentschiedener Gewalt
> bis dass der Kurs sich wende.[87]

Ist die oben genannte Möglichkeit nicht immer schon und einfach vorhanden? Wie kann es notwendig sein, sie zu stiften und damit dem Menschen allererst eine angemessene Bleibe für sein Wohnen zu gründen? Ist das in der Dichtung genannte Land nicht immer schon und einfach nur vorhanden? Wie kann es eine „üble Wende" nehmen, wie kann es „stürzen" und „abgetragen" werden

---

86    „With Usura hath no man a house of good stone / [...] With Usura is no clear demarcation / And no man can find site for his dwelling" (Canto XLV). Pound 1996: 229.

87    „Mock not the flood of stars, the thing's to be. / O Love, come now, this land turns evil slowly. / The waves bore in, soon will they bear away. // The treasure is ours, make we fast land with it. / Move we and take the tide, with its next favour, / Abide / Under some neutral force / Until this course turneth aside." Pound 1952: 81.

ETHIK – POLITIK – DICHTUNG

und ein „ungeheures Vermögen", ein „zeitiges Bauen" brauchen, auf dass in die „künftige Gunst" hinein „Bleiben" sei?

Das Wort „Land" nennt ursprünglich nichts anderes als eine „freie Gegend", eine „unverstellte und unbebaute Gegend", eine „nicht bewaldete und nicht besiedelte Gegend" – eine Gegend also, die sich für den Anbau eignet". Kurz: eine Brache! Eine Brache für die Aufnahme der Saat, für das Aufbrechen und Umbrechen mit dem Pflug, für das Säen des Korns, für den Austrag des Wachstums, für das Wachsen des Nährenden, für das Tragen der Frucht, für das Ernten, für das Schonen des Grundes. Die Brache für das menschliche Wohnen im Ganzen ist hier als „künftige Gunst" angesprochen – das heißt: als anfängliches Eingeholt-Sein in die Nähe des Anspruchs „Mensch zu sein", dem wir dort folgen, wo wir – und zwar ein jeder als er selbst – vom Dichtenden Wort über das bloß Kontingente hinaus in die „eigenste Mitte" gewiesen sind, das heißt: in die Verantwortung für das Gemeinsame, das Stiftung durch den Menschen braucht, um für den Menschen der Grund zu sein, auf dem er bleiben kann. Zuerst und vor allem ist Dichtung das Stiften der „künftigen Gunst", dank welcher der Bereich für den Austrag des Anspruchs „Mensch zu sein" angezeigt ist und damit der Ort seines Austrags – das Politische – sich zeigt.

4

Dafür braucht es ein „neues Erwachen", ein, wie Pound in *Patria mia* sagt, „Risvegliamento".

Amerika, mein Land, ist nahezu ein Kontinent aber kaum noch eine Nation, denn man kann eine Nation geschichtlich erst dann als solche bezeichnen, wenn sie eine Stadt <einen Ort> hat zu dem alle Wege hinführen und von dem eine Autorität ausgeht.[88]

Ich habe nicht vor, in diesem Text über Amerika herzuziehen, nicht einmal gewisse Schönheitsfehler zu bemerken [...]. Die These, für die ich hier einstehe, ist diese: Amerika <mein Land> hat Aussichten auf eine Renaissance.[89]

---

88    „America, my country, is almost and hardly yet a nation, for no nation can be considered historically as such until it has achieved within itself a city to which all roads lead, and from which there goes out an authority." Pound 1950: 9.

89    „It is not my purpose in this essay to find fault with the country, nor even to enter into criticism of certain [...] The thesis I defend is: that America has a chance for renaissance." Pound 1950: 11.

Wenn ich sage, dass ich an eine absehbare amerikanische Renaissance glaube, so ist „Renaissance" nicht ganz das richtige Wort, aber im gewohnten Sprachgebrauch wird mittlerweile jede Art von Aufbruch so bezeichnet. „Risvegliamento" wäre der bessere Ausdruck, wenn es unbedingt italienisch sein muss.[90]

Hier können wir vorläufig schließen und sagen: Wir erwachen wieder, in dem wir schon sind und für das wir schon sind – nämlich: in und für das anfängliche und als solches bleibende Eingeholt-Sein in die Nähe des Anspruchs Mensch zu werden, um auf diese Weise allererst Mensch zu sein.

### Literatur

Cummings, E.E. (1953), *i six nonlectures* (London).

De Gennaro, I. (2005), *Polis und Sprache*, in: M. Flatscher, G. Pöltner (Hrsg.), *Heidegger und die Antike* (Frankfurt am Main / New York).

Hesse, E. (1960), *Vorwort*, in: E. Hesse (Hrsg.), *Ezra Pound Patria Mia* (Zürich).

Moody, A.D. (2007), *Ezra Pound Poet. A Portrait of the Man & his Work, Vol. I, The Young Genius 1885–1920* (Oxford).

Moody, A.D. (2014), *Ezra Pound Poet. A Portrait of the Man & his Work, Vol. II, The Epic Years 1921–1939* (Oxford).

Pound, E. (2010), *ABC of Reading* (New York).

Pound, E. (1970), *A Memoire of Gaudier-Brzeska* (New York).

Pound, E. (1996), *The Cantos* (New York).

Pound, E. (1968), *Literary Essays* (New York).

Pound, E. (1950), *Patria Mia and the Treatise on Harmony* (London).

Pound, E. (1952), *Personae. Collected Shorter Poems* (London).

Pound, E. (1975), *Selected Prose. 1909–1965* (New York).

Zaccaria, G. (1999), *L'inizio greco del pensiero. Heidegger e l'essenza futura della filosofia* (Milano).

---

90 „When I say that I believe in the immanence of an American Renaissance, ‚Renaissance' is not le mot juste, but it has come by usage to mean almost any sort of awakening. ‚Risvegliamento' would be the better term if one must stick to Italian." Pound 1950: 53.

*The Seventeenth Century*

∵

CHAPTER 4

# The Greatest King among Poets, the Greatest Poet among Kings: The Poetry of King Teimuraz I

*Donald Rayfield*

King Teimuraz I (1589–1663), King of Kakheti (with interruptions) from 1605 to 1648 and of Kartli from 1625 to 1633, not only had one of the most turbulent reigns in history, but a family background worthy of Euripides: 'Vernimm, ich bin aus Tantalus Geschlecht,' he could well have cried out. His father, Davit King of Kakheti, forced his own sickly father Aleksandre to renounce the throne for a monastery in 1602, only to drop dead (after being cursed by Aleksandre); in 1605 Aleksandre was murdered, together with the heir to the throne Giorgi, by Teimuraz's uncle Konstantine, who had spent his childhood as a hostage in Iran and was instructed by Shah Abbas I to kill his father for his dealings with Russian envoys and for his reluctance to make war on the Turks. Teimuraz's mother took the lead in an uprising which ended with Konstantine's death and her adolescent son Teimuraz becoming king. (A similar parricide and fratricide, by King Giorgi II 'the Evil' had occurred two generations earlier in the Kakhetian house.) Teimuraz's mother – the inspiration for his poetic career – had a similarly bloody background: she came from the Mukhranbatoni Bagratids of Kartli: it was her grandfather Bagrat who established the line as a protest against his too unwarlike brother Giorgi IX of Kartli and who, after enduring a long siege, killed 'Evil' Giorgi, the great-grandfather of Ketevan's husband Davit.

Teimuraz had early experience of warfare, Iran and Shah Abbas I, the mortal enemy of his family: in 1605 he had been brought to Shah Abbas's camp by his grandfather to fight in the Iranians' Armenian campaign. In 1610, Teimuraz, together with the young king Luarsab II of Kartli, was summoned by Shah Abbas for a summer's hunting. Shah Abbas seemed pleased by Luarsab's valour in fighting the Ottomans in the west and angry at Teimuraz's refusal to do so in the east. (Perversely, however, the Shah would imprison and execute Luarsab, but let Teimuraz live and rule.)

Very soon, Teimuraz felt more grief. His much loved young wife Ana died of diphtheria, and in 1612, against church rules, for the couple had the same grandfather, the Shah ordered Teimuraz to marry King Luarsab's elder sister. Although Abbas had a Georgian mother and several Georgian wives, and had

© KONINKLIJKE BRILL NV, LEIDEN, 2016 | DOI 10.1163/9789004323537_005

FIGURE 4.1  *King Teimuraz I and Queen Khorashan, drawn by Cristofore de Castelli.*

entrusted much of the government of Iran to ethnic Georgians, he was morbidly suspicious of their loyalty, especially given the closeness of the Russian forces across the Caspian and the Caucasus and the shared Orthodox religion.

In 1613 Teimuraz was forced to send as hostages to Iran his two young sons and his mother. Over the next four years Shah Abbas's armies devastated Kartli and Kakhetia, effectively abolishing the kingdoms and deporting 30,000 of the surviving population to the depths of Iran. Teimuraz only infuriated him further by appealing to Moscow for help: Moscow's demands that Teimuraz be restored were the final straw. Abbas had Teimuraz's sons castrated (both died of the operation), had King Luarsab strangled and, finally, demanded that Queen Ketevan convert to Islam or be tortured to death. On 22 September 1624 Ketevan was subjected to unspeakable torture, supervised (as was the castration of Aleksandre and Levan) by the governor of Shiraz, Imam-Quli Khan, by birth a Georgian, Undiladze. Imam-Quli-Khan had close connections to his victims: Queen Ketevan was the mother-in-law to Imam-Quli-Khan's brother. Arguably, he did no more than his duty and even evaded it when possible: despite his very high rank, he had failed to take part in the Shah's invasions of Georgia, and for four years hidden from Ketevan her grandchildren's fate.

Détail du supplice de la Reine Ketevan à Chiraz le 22 septembre 1624.

FIGURE 4.2 *The Martyrdom of Queen Ketevan*, Convento da Graça, Lisbon.

Détail de la remise des os de la Reine Martyr à Gori à son fils Taimouraz I en 1628 par le Père Ambrosio dos Anjos.

FIGURE 4.3 *The Return of Ketevan's Remains*, Convento da Graça, Lisbon.

> Then they bound her hand and foot, tautened her wrists
> Tore off her breasts with tongs, put red-hot pans on her,
> Thrust spades into her forehead, they did all they were asked,
> They split open the back of her head, alas, to say so is my punishment.
> *Martyrdom* (66)

> The monks secretly gathered bits, whatever had escaped the spades,
> They identified them, but did not let the Persian officials find them,
> They put them in a coffin, embalmed them with musk and perfume,
> The body cured diseases of anyone touching the lid. (75)

Some of Ketevan's remains were retrieved by Augustinian missionaries and in 1628 brought, with a full account of what the missionaries had witnessed, to Teimuraz, then clinging onto power in Gori, desperately sending a diplomatic mission to Spain and Italy, treacherously turning on his greatest ally, Giorgi Saakadze. In 1629 Shah Abbas died; Teimuraz once again miscalculated: he supported the succession of one of Abbas's sons, instead of his grandson Sefi Shah. As a result, an Iranian nominee ruled in Tbilisi, while Teimuraz ruled

THE GREATEST KING AMONG POETS, THE GREATEST POET AMONG KINGS     47

only Kakhetia and inner Kartli. He turned to poetry, and created one of the world's most original and unimaginable poems, the Passion of his mother.[91]

In some ways it resembles a mediaeval Georgian passion, for instance that of Shushanik, in which a pious observer relates the obstinate resistance of an aristocratic woman to an ultimatum of convert or die and reports her defiant last prayers, a mixture of phrases from New Testament and Nicaean creed. But Teimuraz's approach is different. We have 270 four-line stanzas in Rustavelian form, i.e. all four lines with virtuoso three- or four-syllable homophonic or homonymic rhymes, a form associated with Persian-style romance and epic; we have an extraordinary range of feeling, from a wish to share the torture, to an appreciation of the virtues of the chief executioner as opposed to the malice of the Shah's orders. While the Shah is described as a 'merciless king, A torturer of Christians, a spiller of simple people's blood, Sitting in Herod's place . . .', his agent the governor of Shiraz is, in Teimuraz's eyes, innocent:

> When Imam-Quli-Khan heard these horrible things
> He was most amazed and said: 'How can this befit me?
> I know that she won't accept Islam if she is not given time,
> How can I propose Teimuraz's mother something unbefitting? (31)[92]

> Wise tongues cannot praise enough the ruler of Shiraz,
> His underlings praise him as humble, sweet and merciful,
> He is deserving of God, for heavenly powers defend him:
> Three months he told her nothing, though he saw her often. (32)

> Imam-Quli-Khan is shown proposing to Ketevan a compromise by which she outwardly converts, but inwardly remains a Christian. She refuses on the ground that 'who would show me respect, or let me return to my patrimony or even let me come near them?' (36)

Teimuraz's tolerance and understanding of the governor's quandary sits uneasily with the empathy and guilt shown by the poet as he describes the unbearable torture Ketevan was subjected to in terms of the crucifixion:

---

91    To this date the best introduction to Teimuraz's poem is Z. Avalishvili 'Teimuraz and his poem *The Martyrdom of Queen Ketevan* in Georgica (London) 1937, 1, 4–5. It is discussed extensively in the monography by M. Gugushvili *Teimuraz p'irveli* Tbilisi, 1981.

92    Numbers in brackets refer to stanzas according to versions printed in A. Baramidze (et al. eds) *Teimuraz p'irveli: txzulebata sruli k'rebuli* Tbilisi, 1934.

Poor me, remembering that day, I forget all preceding days.
They thrust red-hot irons through her chest right to her back.
I am the robber who regrets I wasn't nearby, I rue the fact
That I wasn't crucified on her right-hand side, for this I shed tears. (67)

The poems' conclusion is typical in his abrupt swing from humility to pride: on the one hand Teimuraz declares himself 'unable to cleanse himself of sin', awaiting the 'worm that does not sleep and the fire that has been kindled' (82); on the other, he is 'amazed that [*in writing the poem*] I have done deeds that are outstanding, dared to set my hand to what is the preserve of the wise.' (84)

What Teimuraz relates is derived from the reports of the Augustinian missionaries, whose account is the basis for contemporary history Pietro della Valle's account to the Vatican, for the Armenian historian Arakel of Tabriz and, eventually for Andreas Gryphius's drama *Katharina von Georgien* of 1663. Teimuraz's poem, however, is almost as interesting for what it omits as for what it includes. Firstly, there is an absence of guilt: if Teimuraz had answered Shah Abbas's summons to help attack Shemakha, his mother and sons might not have been held hostage, but this he does not mention, any more than the fact that his mother herself offered Abbas the use of her own thousand-strong guard. Secondly, Shah Abbas's motives are reduced to those of a cruel fanatic: that in itself tallies with Abbas's genocidal actions in Kakheti and the murder and blinding of his own sons and strangling of King Luarsab, but it fails to appreciate (as Teimuraz would himself in 1627) Abbas's complexity. Abbas did not hate Christians: Augustinian missionaries were allowed enormous freedom and treated with great respect; a herd of pigs was kept at the Shah's court to supply exiled Georgians and European missionaries with roast pork for Christmas.[93] True, the Georgian Orthodox church came under suspicion as a potential fifth column for Orthodox Russia. Arakel of Tabriz offers a reason for Abbas's demand that Ketevan accept Islam: converted Armenians in Iran, asked why their mothers would not follow them into Islam, replied, 'If Teimuraz's mother is a Christian, why then should be become Muslim?'[94] Ketevan was therefore required to set an example. The Augustinian Father Ambrosio, the missionary Cristofore de Castelli[95] and the dramatist Andreas Gryphius interpret Abbas's actions as that of a spurned lover, assuming that

---

93 Roberto Gulbenkian *L'Ambassade en Perse de Luis Pereira de Lacerda et des Pères Portugais...* Lisbon, 1972, p. 56.

94 Arak'el Davrizhets' (trans. K'arlo K'uts'ia) *tsnobebi sakartvelos shesaxeb* Tbilisi, 1974, p. 42.

95 'quam ipse ut vidit cepit concupiscentie igne, ac libidinus uri, ebriisque amoris tentando eius castitatem' *see* Don Cristofore de Castelli (*transcribed & translated by* Bezhan

# THE GREATEST KING AMONG POETS, THE GREATEST POET AMONG KINGS 49

Abbas was so smitten by Ketevan's beauty, intellect and character that he over-looked her age (she was in her late fifties when martyred).

In a letter to the Pope, written after he had received the remains of Ketevan, Teimuraz did allege a more complex motivation: 'This infidel king of Persia, unable to overcome her firmness and her love of carnal purity, first imprisoned her for her faith...'[96]

Teimuraz was well aware that he was not only commemorating his mother's martyrdom, but entering into a life-long emulation of, if not contest with, Rustaveli. Not only his use of the virtuous Rustavelian rhyming scheme, but the allusions to Rustaveli's heroes demonstrate this: As Ketevan watches her priest Giorgi quail at the prospect of torture, her resolve only strengthens: she says, 'Now here is the time when whoever wishes should accompany me (62,2) echoing Rustaveli's Tariel telling his followers 'Now is the time when whoever wants should accompany me! (585,4).

The 1630s Teimuraz devoted to ruthlessness worthy of Abbas, but far less successful: he incited his son-in-law Zurab Duke of Aragvi to murder Simon Khan, then beheaded Zurab and sent his head to Shah Sefi, assuming he had killed two birds with one stone, enabling himself to claim all Kartli for himself and to remarry his daughter Darejan to Crown Prince Aleksandre of Imeretia, and thus be the grandfather of a king of a reunited Georgia. Simon Khan's uncle however, the kingmaker of Persia, was named King Rostom of Kartli, while Kakhetia was invaded by the Shah's nominee Selim Khan. Teimuraz, after trying to rob the Theatine missionaries in Gori, had to flee to Imeretia in 1633. After periodic raids via the mountains of Kakhetia, and giving Shah Sefi his daughter Tinatin in marriage (she was soon strangled by Sefi), Teimuraz was recognized again as King of Kakhetia, but still persisted in seek-ing support from Moscow and in trying to have King Rostom of Kartli assas-sinated. Finally, in 1644 a new Shah, Abbas II, ordered Teimuraz's death (in the end, Teimuraz's last son was killed in battle); only his womenfolk's intercession and King Rostom's chivalry allowed Teimuraz to escape to live with his new son-in-law, King Aleksandre III of Imeretia.

Part of Teimuraz's reprieve was secured by his paying blood-money for his earlier murders: here, in his penitent grants of estates to the church, he shows a monk's humility quite at odds with his Machiavellian politics: in 1631, he writes 'I the utterly worst of kings, crowned not because of good deeds, but by the mercy of God...' 'I, utterly inadequate in knowledge, utterly defective in

---

Giorgadze) *tsnobebi da albomi sakartvelos shesaxeb* Tbilisi, 1977, p. 41 (*Georgian*), p. 270 (*Latin*).

96    M. Tamarashvili *Ist'oria k'atolik'obisa kartvelta shoris* Tbilisi, 1902, p. 108.

behaviour, lacking in goodness, in hope and in great fear, utterly stunned by my guilt, not as a king made by the choice of your Son, but as the worst, hoping in you, your humble slave, the unwanted Teimuraz'.[97]

All the more perplexing is the fact that this is the time when Teimuraz turns to poetry rooted in earthly passion and in Persian sources. By 1633, while in Gori, he had composed his version of *Leila and Majnun*, originally an Arab collation of an infatuated poet's biography and of that poet's love poetry, but after some 40 verse versions in Persian an established classic. Teimuraz talks of what he has read and heard, and uses the word translation to categorize his importation from Persian into Georgian, as if all he wanted was the challenge of rendering 'sweet Persian sounds' into 'hard' Georgian.

Until recently, it was assumed that Teimuraz had merely translated *Leila and Majnun* from the Persian of Nizami of Ganja, the first of many poets, famous and obscure, to tell this Romeo-and-Juliet type story of tragic love. When comparison showed no trace of translation, a search was made for other sources: in 1960 and 1961 a M. Mamatsashvili[98] worked through versions by Nizami, Jami, Mekteb of Shiraz, Khosro Deznevi, Navoi, Hussein Baiqara of Herat, Ruh al Amin and Fizuli, many of whom were near contemporaries whose work Teimuraz might have encountered when in Shiraz. Finally, in the Bodleian, Mamatsashvili came across the sole extant manuscript of a version of *Leila and Majnun* by Saad ed-Din Rahai Hafi and in 1967 suggested Hatefi (a nephew of the more famous Jami) as the prototype of Teimuraz's version, or that both stem from an unknown earlier poem. Of all these versions, Teimuraz mentions only Saad ed Din (as *shikh sadi*): 'I take as my point of departure Shikh-Seid's story of Leila and Majnun'. In fact, every incident in Teimuraz's version can be found in one or more Persian version, as he himself admits at the poem's end (270): 'I haven't invented anything I haven't heard'; but not a single line of Teimuraz can be shown to be a translation (in the modern sense). The term *targmani* had wider meaning: interpretation, variation, adaptation, even pastiche. Generally, Teimuraz follows Nizami, but when he differs he is closer to the 15th century Herat school (Baiqara, Hatefi, Jami). In Teimuraz the Sufic elements are conspicuously missing and replaced by a Christian invocation and epilogue. Above all, his 1,000 odd lines condense what Persian poets express in three times the length, and instead off the easy-going *beit*, rhymed couplet, of Persian, Teimuraz imposes on himself the demands of the homonymic rhyming four line quatrains of the Rustavelian metre.

---

97 I. Javaxishvili *Kartul eris ist'oria* vol v. Tbilisi, 1953, p. 9.

98 M. Mamatsashvili 'Teimuraz p'irvelis leilmajnunianis sp'arsuli ts'qaros sak'itxistvis', in *xelovnebis inst'it'ut'is moambe II* Tbilisi, 1960, pp. 111–34 and *III*, 1961, pp. 87–94.

THE GREATEST KING AMONG POETS, THE GREATEST POET AMONG KINGS 51

Nizami of Ganja wrote the first, best-known and the finest version, and there are good reasons for Teimuraz choosing it. It was commissioned by Aghsartan Shah of Shirvan, himself Georgian on his mother's side (and a cousin of King Giorgi III), and for a long period a refugee from Turkic *begs* at the court of Queen Tamar and Davit Soslan. In Shirvan many poets flourished, including Khakani who claimed to speak Georgian as well as Persian and Turkish, and they were well-known to Georgian imitators and translators.

After a prolonged pious invocation, Nizami explains that he writes *Leila and Majnun* not of his own will, but under Aghsartan's orders. Teimuraz alleges the same reluctance, fearing that writing on worldly love, instead of divine matters, is a sin: 'I fear that the world's bad concerns will distract me, that taking refuge with things will bring my soul to fire, that the lure of idle words will add trouble to trouble, and nobody will be able to give me the key for Peter to let me into paradise.' But he has still asked God to give him 'the wit so as by grace to set to translating Persian writings into Georgian'. He concludes, now proudly, that 'A poet should, I think, create and make ornate words ... It is better for someone who is eloquent and has sharp wits to speak: neither rose nor violet, I fancy, is better than the stories of foreign, sweet wise men'.

Like *Leila and Majnun*, the poem of *Ioseb and Zuleika* (*iosebzilikhaniani*) was written in Gori and retells the Biblical story of Potiphar's wife falling in love with Joseph, in a way reminiscent of Jami's Persian poem, but in a far more condensed and less mystical way. This poem, because of its Biblical origins, was praised by the Theatine missionaries, who told the Pope (in the first report to the West on a work of Georgian literature) in December 1628 that 'Teimuraz was the best of poets, for he has composed the history of Joseph'.[99] As in *Leila and Majnun* Teimuraz substitutes a Christian prologue for a Sufic one: in fact he vacillates between abusing Islam: 'I am amazed: if that's what they believe, they are mentally defective.' (132) and evoking an Islamic paradise for Leila and Majnun after death: 'This is their paradise, as Mohammed ordained it: maidens and boy constantly lie at their side, Their covered limbs, he said, reach three metres, Whoever says and believes this story, shame on their beard!' (261), and admits his eclectic sources: 'The story of infatuated lovers is gathered in this writing of mine, I shall create about them a bouquet of verse, we won't see anyone made wretched, I shall put into Georgian all the story told by Persians.' Again, pride at his composition is mixed with fear of damnation for frivolity: 'It will do me no good in eternity, alas, I sorrow for my soul.'

The puzzle about Teimuraz's poem is that it has some resemblance to an anonymous Georgian version, thought to have been written about fifty years

---

99    M. Tamarashvili *op. cit.* p. 102.

previously and to be derived from a lost imitation of Jami. In fact some lines of the anonymous version are similar to Teimuraz's: 'The King summoned his ministers and all his healers (*anon* 25,1) / 'The king summoned the doctors, complaining of the princely problem (*Teimuraz* 62,1); 'Now I advise, o tutor, the building of such a house (*anon.* 420,1) / 'What I advise, o king, we should build a tower to be erected' (*Teimuraz* 250,1), but the similarities do not amount to plagiarism. More significant are the echoes of Rustaveli, ever more frequent in Teimuraz's work and ambitions: the idyllic garden party in Rustaveli[100] (*stanzas* 1113–4) resembles Teimuraz's in *Iosebzilikhaniani* (122–5). Nevertheless, Teimuraz's succinct narration reduces the story of Zuleikha's forbidden and hopeless love for her Hebrew slave to the narrative elements we find in *Qu'ran* 12 and eradicates the symbolism of divine love in the Persian versions.

Teimuraz's last period was spent as the guest of his son-in-law Aleksandre, in a palace in the mountain stronghold duchy of Racha. His efforts at diplomacy all came to nought: he had Aleksandre adopt his grandson Giorgi, in the hope of eventually uniting Georgia; he tried to reconcile the quarrelling rulers of Mingrelia and Guria with Imeretia to unite at least western Georgia. He negotiated with Russian envoys, sending an embassy to Moscow in 1649, asking for 20,000 armed men (the age-old vain Georgian request) and a dynastic intermarriage. Eventually, in 1653 Teimuraz sent his grandson Erekle to Russia (where Erekle, known as Nikolai, probably fathered Peter the Great), and in 1658 went himself to plead his cause. On his return he found his wife and his son-in-law had died. His last refuge collapsed, his daughter Darejan and the whole of western Georgia sinking into depravity, Teimuraz was deported to die as a monk and a prisoner of Shah Abbas II; but the exiled king had one more spurt of poetic creativity. Some of it was religious: a poem on *The Seven Church Councils* and an alphabetic poem of praise. Others were in a form new to Georgian, the *gabaaseba* or dispute.

Of his two disputes, the 100-quatrains of *The Comparison between Spring and Autumn* are the finest: it is the first example of nature poetry, often resembling eighteenth-century English seasonal studies, in Georgian, evoking landscapes, verdure, harvests, as spring and autumn alternate in boasting of their superiority. As to who wins the dispute, Teimuraz is silent. It is an unusually joyful poem: 'This is the best to be expected from us', even though Teimuraz never escapes his thoughts on four last things: 'Let us laugh for a day, for we must mourn for many a year / At the end comes death, earth and stones on our heart.' (103) Teimuraz now seems reconciled to the 'sin' of writing about earthly, not heavenly things: there is no audience for Christian poetry:

---

100 Rustaveli tanza references are to the *saiubileo* edition of his *vepxist'qaosani*, Tbilisi, 1988.

THE GREATEST KING AMONG POETS, THE GREATEST POET AMONG KINGS 53

> Nobody wants the Gospels, nor the Acts of the Apostles,
> Don't be amazed that they've forgotten what the Creator has done...
> If I said anything profound, I've wasted my time, I'll get no listeners...
> Many godly books have rotted, buried in the ground...(5–6)

The *Dispute between Wine and Lips* is a short lyric, comparing the beauty of red wine in white crystal with red lips over white teeth. It is unique in Teimuraz's work for its unsullied sensuality, and was gathered by him in his *Majama*, a collection of eight lyrical verses, many of which reflect a profound gloom. *Majama* is a Persian term for anthology, and Teimuraz was the first to use it in Georgian for a cycle of lyrics. At the end of the anthology he categorizes it as a lighter form, 'something to put quickly in your breast pocket, or to tuck under your belt'. Political and personal despair infuses them: 'You who give the soul no rest, breath like a beast's / The door to the bridal chamber is shut in our face, we are told, 'Do not come in.' The purpose of the anthology is 'I want to write the poor, outlandish verses, collected here, in order not to be forgotten.' The following poems complain that the sun gives him no joy, has killed his roses, deprived him of light. Elsewhere, unrequited love, typified by the frustrated nightingale trying to unite with the rose, is the source of misery. Only the eighth poem, in praise of his daughter Darejan and his son-in-law Aleksandre is full of joy and admiration: knowing that Darejan was already infamous for her depravity and ruthlessness, the reader may find it hard to take without a grain of salt the praise of her virtues.

> I've forgotten others' praise, let me now praise her:
> Her eyelids are as full as the moon, you'll see the sun in her eyelashes
> A pool full of ink is the beauty of her brow,
> Cursed be the lover who hasn't tormented himself for her. *Majama, VIII, 3*]

Of Teimuraz's three other lyrics the most typical and moving is his *Reproach to the World*: imbued with the spirit of *Ecclesiastes*, Teimuraz manages this time to use Rustavelian rhyme without resorting to syntactical and lexical obscurity, to express his disillusion:

> The Lord knows that the world does not last long for anyone,
> At first it is pleasant and sweet, it treats us lovingly,
> Then it stops, and at the end betrays, turns nasty,
> I refute anyone who trusts it or who comes to terms with it. (11)

Before he took holy orders, Teimuraz wrote two extended poems that have something of the *gabaaseba* (dispute) and something of this frustration and

FIGURE 4.4  *Darejan the Deceitful, Teimuraz's daughter, drawn by Cristofore de Castelli.*

disillusionment about them. Both appear to be variations on Persian topics. The best known is *Vardbulbuliani* (*The Poem of the Rose and the Nightingale*), a theme which Teimuraz broached twenty years earlier in Joseph and Zuleika. Now he attributes the theme to Mulla Aja of Isfahan, as far as we know a poet whom he has invented. The lush, even romantic, nature descriptions, however, are typical of Teimuraz's evocation of spring. Fundamentally, this is an episode of courtly love, deliberately reminiscent of Rustaveli, but with a tragic end: the rose tells the nightingale: 'Rustaveli praised me, you know, thorns, roots and all, / Go away, be infatuated, why do you burn here next to me?' (73) The nightingale resigns itself to silence and solitude, and Teimuraz asks God to forgive him his 'idle, fruitless words'.

Of the same type, (also attributed to the fictitious Mulla Aja) but with more mystical implications is *Shamiparvaniani* (*The Candle and the Moth*), where the unhappy lover must, as in Persian tradition, be willing to burn to death in his love for the unattainable. Here Teimuraz finally merges the erotic and the divine, as Davit Guramishvili would do a century later in his Ukrainian poem *Zubovka*. In this, perhaps final work Teimuraz sums up all he has written as a means of distracting himself from an 'endless Nile of tears' and the reversal of the wheel of fate. But the moral is bitter:

> If you are burned by an undying fire, you have a heart that is wounded,
> See the burning moth, dead, give up the ghost...
> This is how you burn any kind of madness and infatuation. (23–4)

History judges Teimuraz the king harshly: although he was barely an adult when he let his mother and sons suffer the wrath of Shah Abbas, his subsequent behaviour is easy to condemn – turning on his ally Giorgi Saakadze, who might have saved Georgia from Iran, entrapping and murdering his son-in-law, repaying King Rostom's tolerance with murderous plots – offering pledges to Russia that would later be a pretext for incorporating all Georgia into the Russian empire. As a poet, he provoked very different reactions. He was extrvagantly admired by Archil, a descendant like Ketevan of the Mukhranbatoni founder, and briefly King of Kakhetia and of Imeretia, before giving up hope and emigrating to Russia. Archil may have met Teimuraz during the latter's last days in Imeretia; certainly he admired his poetry enough to write one of the longest poems in the Georgian language, *The Dispute of Rustaveli and Teimuraz* which is both biography and comparison and leaves undecided which is the greater poet:

No Georgian language poet can be compared to these two,
To Rustaveli the eloquent versifier, to the King (Teimuraz) the aloë tree.
(*gabaaaseba* 37)

Others have deplored Teimuraz for his inadequate reactions and his conceit. The 19c. radical Purtseladze wrote in 1911: 'Teimuraz added poetry to banqueting, luxury and hunting...He imagined, like Nero with his music, poetry and acting, that no poet had ever equalled him...ugly mindless verse...the victim of a thousand tragic events, not once was he struck by a worthwhile heartfelt idea.'[101] Other critics have wondered how a man who fought so hard with Shah Abbas could be so infatuated with the Persian language and Persian poetic tropes.

It is true that Teimuraz's pursuit of rhyme – *O qui dira les torts de la rime?* – often makes the second half of a Teimuraz line seem contrived, even bathetic after a strong first half. But not always. We should remember that Kings who write poetry do not benefit from constructive criticism. Among King-Poets of Teimuraz's stature only Mao Tze-Dong comes to mind, even though it was a tradition for Bagratid kings to write verse (David the Builder's *Songs of Repentance*, the impressive œuvre of Archil of Imeretia and Kakhetia, the gentle lyrics of the unwarlike Teimuraz II).

## Bibliography

Arak'el Davrizhets' (trans. K'arlo K'uts'ia) *tsnobebi sakartvelos shesaxeb* Tbilisi, 1974.

Avalishvili, Z. 'Teimuraz and his poem *The Martyrdom of Queen Ketevan*' in Georgica (London) 1937.

Baramidze, A. (et al. eds) *Teimuraz p'irveli: txzulebata sruli k'rebuli* Tbilisi, 1934.

de Castelli, Don Cristofore (*transcribed & translated by* Bezhan Giorgadze) *tsnobebi da albomi sakartvelos shesaxeb* Tbilisi, 1977.

Gugushvili, M. *Teimuraz p'irveli* Tbilisi, 1981.

Gulbenkian, Roberto *L'Ambassade en Perse de Luis Pereira de Lacerda et des Pères Portugais...* Lisbon, 1972.

Javaxishvili, I. *Kartul eris ist'oria* vol v. Tbilisi, 1953.

Mamatsashvili, M. 'Teimuraz p'irvelis leilmajnunianis sp'arsuli ts'qaros sak'itxistvis', in *xelovnebis inst'it'ut'is moambe II, III* Tbilisi, 1960–1.

Purtseladze, Anton *Giorgi Saak'adze da misi dro* Tbilisi, 1911.

Tamarashvili, M. *Ist'oria k'atolik'obisa kartvelta shoris* Tbilisi, 1902.

---

101    Anton Purtseladze *Giorgi Saak'adze da misi dro* Tbilisi, 1911, pp. 374–5.

CHAPTER 5

# Knowledge After the Fall: Milton and the Question of Censorship

*Friederike Schmiga*

In November 1644, John Milton published a short treatise entitled *Areopagitica, A Speech for the Liberty of Unlicensed Printing to the Parliament of England*.[102] In June of the previous year, the Long Parliament had issued a Licensing Order "which stipulated that all printed matter be first approved and licensed by a government agent, [and] then officially entered in the *Register* of the Stationer's Company".[103] Milton himself came to be affected by this Order when in August 1644 the Stationer's Company mounted a complaint to Parliament that Milton and his publisher had failed to obtain licensing for his divorce tracts. Three months later, Milton published the *Areopagitica*. Casting himself as an adviser of the "Lords and Commons of England"[104], he addresses the concerns of his critics and of the political supporters of the Licensing Order, and undertakes

---

102 Although it is called a "speech", Milton never held nor intended to hold it as a speech before Parliament. Rather, as various scholars have argued, the title and the choice of genre serve to establish a connection with two important precedents from antiquity, in particular the Greek orator Isocrates and the Apostle Paul. On the former see e.g. Wittreich (1972), on the latter Burt (1998). The conscious parallel to Isocrates and the motto from Euripides' *The Suppliants* are used by Dowling (2006) to suggest an "against the grain" interpretation of the *Areopagitica*.

103 Dobranski (1999:13). Research on the problem of censorship in relation to the *Areopagitica* includes the following valuable studies: Tanner (1977) provides a comparative survey of censorship in English literary history from Milton to D.H. Lawrence and Joseph Conrad; Patterson (1984) develops a whole "hermeneutics of censorship" in the early modern period; Meyer (2011) reads early modern tracts as documents of fundamentalist tendencies during the Reformation. Among those who focus on Milton's *Areopagitica* in particular are Limouze (1980), Blum (1987), Norbrook (1994) and Tournu (1999). Limouze (1980) foregrounds Milton's insistence on private morality and authorial self-regulation as necessary complements to a free press. A remarkable recent contribution shows the relevance of Milton's argument to the Arab world (Issa 2015).

104 The works of Milton are quoted according to the edition by Merritt Y. Hughes (1975) *John Milton. Complete Poems and Major Prose*. All references to the *Areopagitica* are to page numbers; those to *Paradise Lost* are to book and line.

© KONINKLIJKE BRILL NV, LEIDEN, 2016 | DOI 10.1163/9789004323537_006

to demonstrate the ineffectiveness and at worst the damage wrought by the political practice of licensing.

The force of Milton's pamphlet stems – to a considerable degree – from the fact that he speaks on behalf of his own profession, as an active intellectual engaged in the political, theological and cultural debates of his day, as a representative of England's literary and scholarly elite, and – last but not least – as a poet who considered his literary vocation to be closely connected to a broader educational project. In the *Areopagitica* especially, Milton takes position with regard to an issue that had important ramifications for the emerging figure of the intellectual and allowed him, among other things, to define the public and scientific responsibility of those who – by publishing their work – contribute to the intellectual project of their times.[105] Of the four considerations concerning the practice of licensing which Milton develops in this work, the second clarifies "what is to be thought in general of reading, whatever sort the books be" (720), and it develops a broader perspective on the political and eschatological relevance of publications. This reflection allows Milton to conclude that books, and indeed all kinds of books, ought to be produced, published and circulated freely, without the restraints imposed by licensing, that is by politically or religiously motivated censorship. At the heart of this perspective lies the conviction that even "bad" books, in effect, can be put to good use for the following reason:

> Good and evil we know in the field of this world grow up together almost inseparably [...]. It was from out the rind of one apple tasted, that the knowledge of good and evil, as two twins cleaving together, leaped forth into the world. And perhaps this is that doom which Adam fell into of knowing good and evil, that is to say, of knowing good by evil. (728)

According to Milton, it follows from this state of affairs that human beings inevitably must also know evil in order to know good. It is effectively impossible to have any knowledge or wisdom at all without knowing good and evil together through a contrastive dynamics. Thus, he continues his train of argument:

> Assuredly we bring not innocence into the world, we bring impurity much rather, that which purifies us is trial, and trial is by what is contrary. [...] Since therefore the knowledge and survey of vice is in this world so necessary to the constituting of human virtue, and the scanning of error

---

105    See Norbrook (1994) for a discussion of the *Areopagitica*'s impact on the emerging early modern public sphere.

KNOWLEDGE AFTER THE FALL 59

> to the confirmation of truth, how can we more safely, and with less danger, scout into the regions of sin and falsity than by reading all manner of tractates and hearing all manner of reasons? And this is the benefit which may be had of books promiscuously read. (728–729)

In these lines, Milton posits a connection between the post-lapsarian human condition on the one hand and the role of books and the free press on the other. Indeed, the notion that all kinds of books, that is all kinds of ideas, invariably contribute to an effort, both individual and shared, of knowledge acquisition and thus invariably have a political relevance, is really founded upon a specific conception of human knowledge. Similarly, Milton's confutation of the political and cultural practice of censorship rests – to a considerable extent – upon his views concerning the conditions under which humankind is forced to acquire knowledge after humankind's "first disobedience" and attendant fall from the original state.

The connection between censorship and the fallen condition of human knowledge leads us from the 1644 pamphlet to one of Milton's mature masterworks, in which he develops a sophisticated and complex interpretation of humanity's origins. Indeed, it is an essential part of Milton's educational project in his great epic poem *Paradise Lost*, which he wrote about 15–20 years after *Areopagitica*, to provide, in the form of a Christian epic narrating the circumstances of the fall of Adam and Eve, the biblical and theological justification for the present state of humankind and human knowledge.[106] The poet defines the scope of his task as follows:

---

106 The question of what role Milton attributed to learning and knowledge and whether he changed his mind on this matter towards the final years of his life has attracted much scholarly attention and generated a wealth of research. Particularly in his early and middle works (e.g. *Of Education, Areopagitica*), Milton showed himself to be a fervent supporter of learning and one of the most erudite writers in the English language. From his earliest years, he received an excellent education and dedicated also much of his adult life to the study of literature and theology (for more details on Milton's life, context and works, see Barbara K. Lewalski (2000b), *The Life of John Milton. A Critical Biography*). Many scholars have sought to explain how a poet of Milton's calibre could have written the condemnation of human (in particular pagan) learning voiced by the Christ figure in *Paradise Regained*. In the context of this paper, only a few selected studies can be drawn to the reader's attention. Sensabaugh (1946) paints the picture of an aging and disillusioned Milton; the reply by Samuel (1949) suggests an interpretation of Christ's statements that fits Milton's previously voiced views on the purpose and contents of education. Classic monographic studies are Schultz (1955) on *Milton and Forbidden Knowledge*, Svendsen (1956) on *Milton and Science*, and Jacobus (1976) on *Sudden Apprehension. Aspects of Knowledge in Paradise Lost*.

Of Man's first disobedience and the fruit
Of that forbidden tree, whose mortal taste
brought death into the world and all our woe
[…] Sing *Heav'nly Muse*, that on the secret top
of Oreb or of Sinai didst *inspire*
That shepherd who *first taught* the chosen seed,
In the beginning, how the heav'ns and earth
Rose out of chaos. […]
And chiefly thou, O Spirit, […]
*Instruct* me, for thou know'st […]
[…] What in me is dark
Illumine, what is low raise and support,
That to the heighth of this great argument
I may assert Eternal Providence
And justify the ways of God to men.     (1, 1–26, emphasis added)

In the famous opening lines of *Paradise Lost*, Milton presents himself as a prophetic teacher in the tradition of Moses, whom he calls "That shepherd, who first taught the chosen seed, / In the beginning, how the heav'ns and earth / Rose out of chaos" (1, 8–10). By invoking the same heavenly Muse that inspired the great biblical teacher, Milton casts himself as a second Moses entrusted with the task of teaching God's new chosen people, the English (an idea which Milton only hints at in *Paradise Lost*). The role of the prophetic poet allows Milton to use his poetic voice to fulfil a specific educational function: thanks to his privileged access to a particular kind of knowledge (mostly revealed or divinely inspired), Milton sets out, in the poem's most frequently quoted words, "to justify the ways of God to men" (1, 26), that is to explain the justice of the fall not as an isolated event but as a part of an overarching divine scheme.

Importantly, these teachings of the prophetic poet do not only aim at providing theological education for his readers, but they have important and far-reaching ramifications for many social and political issues of seventeenth-century England.[107] In this paper, I would like to focus on one of these ramifications, namely the necessity to abolish licensing and thereby

---

107    For a general analysis of how Milton used the poem to communicate political ideas and convictions, see the informative and illuminating essay by Barbara Lewalski (2000a). Against those who are inclined to regard *Paradise Lost* as a retreat from the political scene, Lewalski contends: "I mean to argue here that Milton's poem is a more daring political gesture than we often realize, even as it is also a poem for the ages by a prophet poet who placed himself with (or above) Homer, Virgil, Ariosto, Tasso, and the rest. It undertakes a strenuous project of educating readers in the virtues, values, and attitudes that make a

KNOWLEDGE AFTER THE FALL                                          61

political censorship, by exploring the theological foundation (as developed in *Paradise Lost*) of Milton's conception of human knowledge in the transition from the pre- to the post-lapsarian state. Thus, the aim is to reconstruct the logic of the *Areopagitica*'s second argument against licensing (i.e. the argument from the general utility of books) by drawing on *Paradise Lost* to understand the way in which the "first disobedience" changed humankind's relation to their knowledge. In particular, there are two aspects that I would like to discuss in more detail: first, the general assumption underlying Milton's argument in the passage from the *Areopagitica* quoted previously, namely the notion that knowledge is natural and therefore to some degree even necessary for humankind; second, the idea that the possibility of evil is the precondition for human freedom and at the same time the reason why human virtue is subject to continuous testing, or trial. In conclusion, it will emerge that censorship tends to hinder rather than promote the intellectual advancement of society and of England in particular, precisely because it seeks to suppress evil.

1      **Knowledge is Constitutive of Human Nature and Necessary for Human Beings in Order to Fulfil their Part in the Economy of Creation**

In Book 7 of *Paradise Lost*, Milton presents a reworking and interpretation of the first chapters of *Genesis*, which narrate God's creation of the earth and its inhabitants:

> There wanted yet the master work, the end
> Of all yet done: a creature who not prone
> And brute as other creatures but endued
> With sanctity of reason might erect
> His stature and, upright with front serene,
> *Govern the rest, self-knowing*, and from thence
> Magnanimous to correspond with Heaven,
> *But grateful to acknowledge whence his goodness*
> *Descends*, thither with heart and voice and eyes
> Directed in devotion to adore
> And worship God supreme who made him chief
> Of all His works.      (7, 505–516, emphasis added)

---

people worthy of liberty, and we need to recognize just how emphatic its political lessons were and are." (2000a: 140–141)

According to Milton's interpretation of the biblical story, man was explicitly created to know and to act on the basis of his knowledge, especially knowledge of himself, the other creatures and of heavenly things, as far as they are revealed to him through his "correspondence with heaven". Man is referred to as the "master work", the "end of all yet done", a creature endowed with reason and capable of acquiring knowledge, which is why he is placed in a position to "govern the rest, self-knowing". It is worth noting how Milton connects man's privilege of dominion with the privilege of knowledge: Adam receives the right to rule the earth directly from God, but Milton has God insist that Adam understand the reason why he holds this prerogative, namely his being created as an image of God, a rational being. However, man's outstanding position, signalled by his rationality and its attendant privileges – dominion over the earth and the possibility to communicate with heavenly beings – obliges him at the same time to be constantly aware of and to acknowledge his dependence on God as the ultimate source of all goodness. The gift of reason implies both the pleasure and the duty to know himself as well as to worship his creator.

In Milton's version, Adam, the first human being and future progenitor of the human race, receives the knowledge he needs in order to do his part in the divinely instituted economy of creation right at the beginning. When he awakens for the first time, Adam immediately voices his natural desire to know, in particular his own nature, his whereabouts and the cause of his existence. He addresses the natural world around him:

> Tell if ye saw how came I thus, how here.
> Not of myself: *by some great Maker, then,*
> In goodness and in pow'r preeminent.
> Tell me *how may I know Him, how adore*
> From whom I have that thus I move and live
> And feel that I am happier than I know.     (8, 277–82, emphasis added)

Although Adam possesses reason, he does not yet possess knowledge.[108] Interestingly, the phrasing of his plea for knowledge shows that he is indeed a rational *as well as* a humble creature, given that he uses the few facts he knows

---

108   See also Lewalski (1969) who argues that growth and intellectual growth in particular are part of the human experience according to Milton's interpretation of the pre-lapsarian state. This is corroborated, for instance, by Raphael's admonition: "God made thee perfect, not immutable" (5, 524). Perfection as conceptualised in *Paradise Lost* means precisely growth: "primal man's nature is shown to be complex and constantly developing, not simple and stable" (Lewalski 1969: 99).

KNOWLEDGE AFTER THE FALL 63

to conclude that all must be the work of "some great Maker". In this sense, Adam desires knowledge not in a spirit of curiosity – as he would be if he were driven by a self-referential desire to know solely for the sake of knowing or if he wished to obtain further proof of his Maker's omnipotence – but as a precondition for praising the creator and expressing his gratefulness. His wonder is intimately linked with admiration and reflects an informed awareness of his happy state. Since Adam is unable to acquire by himself such knowledge as he seeks, having no human teachers to rely on, God acts as a kind of archetypal teacher, giving Adam an initial education. First and foremost, he informs Adam of the freedom to do whatever pleases him *except* eating the fruits from "the tree whose operation brings / Knowledge of good and ill (which I have set / The pledge of thy obedience and thy faith)" (8, 323–325). Once this point has been made unmistakably clear, God engages in a friendly conversation with Adam, which – contrary to what it may seem at first – amounts to a first "trial" of human virtue.

The divine instruction which Adam receives consists, in other words, not only in an act of authorial exhortation but also in a demonstration of the creature's rational capacity. In particular, human reason is shown to involve two complementary aspects: on the one hand, an intuitive or receptive faculty which allows Adam to name and discern the nature of the earth's animals over whom he is supposed to exert dominion;[109] on the other hand, a discursive ability which enables him to use his knowledge – whether acquired through "sudden apprehension" (8, 354) worked by God or through verbal instruction – in an appropriate manner.[110] Applying rational deliberation to the newly acquired insights about God, himself and the other living creatures on earth, Adam is able to justify his desire for a suitable companion and to answer the mock objections brought forward by God.[111] At the end of the debate, the divine interlocutor admits:

---

109    To seal Adam's lordship over the earth, God wishes all the animals "to receive / From thee their names and pay thee fealty / With low subjection" (8, 343–345). Adam recalls that with natural ease "I named them as they passed and understood / Their nature: with such knowledge God endued / My sudden apprehension" (8, 352–354). For further analysis of the link between reason and language in this and other passages, see Leonard (1999).

110    Remarkably, Milton treats the naming episode with relative brevity in the space of 17 lines (8, 338–354) while the testing of Adam's reasoning faculty extends over almost 100 lines (8, 355–451).

111    God first objects that Adam is not solitary on earth but enjoys the company of various animals, to which the latter replies that he too needs one of his kind in order to be fully happy (see 8, 369–398). The second objection is more delicate to answer since God proposes his own model of "solitary" happiness. As in the previous case, Adam manages to pin down

> Thus far *to try thee*, Adam, I was pleased
> *And find thee knowing* not of beasts alone
> Which thou hast rightly named but of thyself,
> Expressing well the spirit within thee free,
> My image, not imparted to the brute [...]
> *Good reason* was thou freely shouldst dislike:
> And be so minded still! I, ere thou spak'st
> Knew it not good for Man to be alone
> And no such company as then thou saw'st
> Intended thee – *for trial only brought*,
> To see how thou could'st judge of fit and meet.      (8, 437–448, emphasis added)

By dramatising God's first testing of Adam's rational capacity, Milton provides an exemplary demonstration of how human beings ought to use reason and knowledge. If used well, they provide the means to rationalise desire and to justify the choice of a given alternative in a situation where more than one solution appears acceptable. As Adam's plea for a suitable companion shows, faced with a given desire, one must decide, *with good reason*, whether to pursue it or to restrain from enacting it. Thus, if there are certain kinds or areas of knowledge that are natural and necessary for Adam and hence for his future descendants, then this is due to the fact that human beings need rational criteria in order to be able to judge and govern their desires.[112] At the same time, the first dialogue between God and Adam serves to establish the boundaries of human knowledge through the prohibition to eat from the Tree of Knowledge of Good and Evil. In this way, Milton places the problem of knowledge within a delicate balance between legitimacy and illegitimacy from the very beginning of Adam's (and by implication: humankind's) existence. Even though knowledge is natural and necessary to man, as is his desire to know things concerning himself as well as heavenly things, there is one kind of forbidden knowledge which cannot be acquired without risking the original state of happiness.

---

the flawed assumption thanks to his ability to discern the difference in nature between God and himself: "Thou in Thyself art perfect and in Thee / Is no deficiency found. Not so is Man / But in degree the cause of his desire / By conversation with his like to help / Or solace his defects." (8, 415–419)

112    On the naturalness of desire in the unfallen state and its intricate relation to the phenomenon of temptation, see Campbell (2014). For an analysis of Milton's staging of the process of human self-knowledge, see Fields (1968: esp. 395–396). According to Fields, "the story of Adam is the story of Everyman in self-realization" (395).

KNOWLEDGE AFTER THE FALL 65

2    **Trial of Virtue is Essential to Human Freedom because it Means the Actual Possibility of Evil without which the Choice to do Good would be Meaningless**

To a significant extent, Milton's justification of God's ways to men in *Paradise Lost* rests upon the correct understanding of the meaning and implications of this divinely instituted interdiction. As Satan, the chief among the fallen angels, plots his revenge on God, which he seeks to enact by corrupting the latter's most recent work of creation, Milton introduces into the story of the fall a novel and vital complication. In order to warn Adam and Eve of Satan's machinations, Milton's God sends one of his archangels, Raphael, on an educational mission to teach the couple, by the "terrible example" (6, 910) of the rebel angels' fall, that happiness – whether human or angelic – depends on obedience and, what is more important, that obedience is not to be taken for granted but is constantly put to trial and must be renewed over and over again. Interestingly, Milton does not present Raphael's narration as an unsolicited lesson but motivates it with an inquiry on the human part. Encouraged by the friendly demeanour of the archangel, Adam raises the question (quite as if it had already been on his mind for some time): "But say, / What meant that caution joined, 'if ye be found / Obedient'? Can we want obedience then / To him [...]?" (5, 512–515).[113] Raphael elucidates the divine "caution" in a twofold way: first, by explaining the underlying rationale (5, 519–543); and second, by illustrating the actual possibility of disobedience (hence of evil) with the help of his narrative relating the fall of the rebel angels (the remainder of Book 5 up to the end of Book 6). Humans and angels, as rational creatures, are created truly free and unless they freely choose to worship and serve God, they do not act according to the dignity of their respective natures, Raphael explains:

> Attend! That thou art happy owe to God.
> That thou continuest such owe to thyself,
> That is, to thy obedience: therein stand!
> This was that caution giv'n thee. Be advised!
> God made thee *perfect, not immutable,*
> And good made he thee. But to persevere

---

113    Adam repeatedly addresses Raphael with epithets that define his role as a heavenly teacher, for instance "[d]ivine instructor" (5, 546), "[d]ivine Interpreter" (7, 72) and "divine / Historian" (8, 6–7); for a more detailed analysis of the role of Raphael, see Reeves (1997). Interestingly, Raphael briefly alludes to Adam's future role as the first teacher of mankind: "that posterity / Informed by thee might know" (7, 638–639).

> He left in thy pow'r, ordained thy will
> By nature free, not overruled by fate
> Inextricable or strict necessity.
> Our voluntary service He requires,
> Not our necessitated: such with Him
> Finds no acceptance, nor *can* find. For how
> Can hearts, not free, be *tried* whether they serve
> Willing or no, who will but what they must
> By destiny and can no other choose?     (5, 520–534, emphasis added)

For rational creatures to *remain* in the state of happiness, they must freely choose to serve God, and the only way of guaranteeing that their service is indeed paid voluntarily is to have them face a real choice between obedience and disobedience, between good and evil, and to have them face that choice not once or twice but continuously. In other words, the notion of human freedom necessitates, according to Milton's *Paradise Lost*, the actual possibility of evil.

Thus, the Tree of Knowledge of Good and Evil, which embodies and symbolises God's single prohibition, represents a constant trial to Adam and Eve's virtue – not, however, a temptation meant to seduce them, which is how Satan interprets its presence in the Garden of Eden.[114] In the logic of *Paradise Lost*, the tree functions as a guarantee of human freedom and it provides the human couple with a continuous occasion to show their obedience and their capacity to withstand the possibility of doing evil. It follows from this observation that, according to Milton's interpretation of the prohibition, trial is not exclusive to the post-lapsarian state; rather, it is an indispensable element already present in the paradisal stage, as God's initial testing of Adam's capacity to reason on the basis of self-knowledge testifies. Yet trial before the fall differs significantly from trial after the fall and the impact of "Man's first disobedience" on the nature of this essential element of human freedom remains to be clarified.

To illuminate this point, it is necessary to consider the constellation of factors determining the human creature. As a matter of fact, man's position in the hierarchy of being is defined by two (rather than just one) aspects: his rationality and his deeds. Through reason, man is capable of establishing a relation to truth and to being; through his actions, he is placed in a certain relation to

---

114    The distinction is very subtle and it must be admitted that one cannot exclude the possibility that the tree *was* meant as a temptation, as Campbell's subtle discussion of the notion of temptation in *Paradise Lost* makes clear (2014). On the necessity of trial before the fall, see also Reichert (1981).

KNOWLEDGE AFTER THE FALL 67

goodness. Importantly, these two aspects are mutually related in a two-directional manner: in the ideal (i.e. original) state, man's reason governs his decisions (and thus his actions) just as man's actions define the parameters of his reasoning. In other words, one's knowledge of reality is a decisive factor when judging desires and making decisions, and one's active participation in goodness shapes one's perception and evaluation of reality. The underlying reason for this reciprocal impact is that man's actions circumscribe the space of actual experience while his rationality opens up the realm of possibility (hence the necessity to choose, namely between possible ways of action). Thomas Blackburn has shown that Adam and Eve have knowledge of evil *before the fall* but only in the form of "conceptual" knowledge rather than through their own experience: "the Fall does not consist of an access of knowledge, as we usually conceive of it, but of a shift in the mode of man's knowledge of good and evil".[115] In the light of this insight, it becomes clear that the prohibition is not about forbidden knowledge in an objective sense but about a foundational experience involving a failure on the part of human reason (namely a misjudgement) and subsequently an illegitimate action which has a disinhibiting effect and impairs man's capacity to distinguish good from evil precisely because the realm of actual experience by now includes both.[116] Before the fall, Adam and Eve knew of evil as a theoretical or abstract concept but as a pure object of knowledge it affected neither their cognitive capacity nor the rationality of their choices. Doing and experiencing good informed human reason in such a way as to dispose the human creature to acquire true knowledge and to choose well. After the fall, by contrast, evil as well as good form part of the human experience and affect reason both as a source of knowledge (evil manifesting itself, for instance, in the form of error) and as a ruler of desire (in this case, manifesting itself in the shape of unreasonable decisions or sinful actions).

In the light of this analysis, the following distinction emerges. In the prelapsarian state, trial, as represented by the Tree of Knowledge, means the

---

115  Blackburn 1971: 126. And further: "In the state of innocence, Adam and Eve live a total *experience* of good; their knowledge of evil, on the other hand, is conceptual. They know the word *evil*, what it meant when the state so named has been actualized elsewhere [i.e. for the rebel angels], and what act could cause it to be actualized in their own existence. But so long as they remain faithful to God's command, evil remains only a potentiality in their lives: good alone is known as actual and innocence is preserved. When Adam and Eve fall, however, this actual-potential polarity is destroyed. By their disobedience evil is actualized as a part of their direct personal experience." (Blackburn 1971: 126, emphasis in the original)

116  See Patrides (1962) on the standard interpretation of the Tree of Knowledge in the Christian Tradition, of which Milton forms part.

choice between, on the one hand, doing good and therefore having experience only of good (while evil, as testified to by Adam's reaction upon learning of the rebel angels, is almost unimaginable, a kind of abstract concept)[117] and, on the other hand, doing and experiencing evil through the very act of disobedience (thereby losing the possibility to know/do *pure* good). As a consequence, the actuality of both good and evil inevitably shapes the circumstances under which man is forced to acquire knowledge and to take decisions after the fall. Essentially, this view of human knowledge informs also the prose tract on licensing from 1644, although Milton explores and dramatises the theological foundation only many years later in his epic poem.[118] In the *Areopagitica*, he focuses rather on the implications of the first act of evil for humankind's individual and shared effort of recovering truth. Since it is no longer possible for fallen humankind to circumvent or evade evil (both falsity and sin), the challenge consists *not* in suppressing evil but in dealing with it in the *least damaging* manner:

> Good and evil we know in the field of this world grow up together almost inseparably; and the knowledge of good is so involved and interwoven with the knowledge of evil, and in so many cunning resemblances hardly to be discerned, that those confused seeds which were imposed upon Psyche as an incessant labour to cull out, and sort asunder, were not more intermixed. It was from out the rind of one apple tasted, that the knowledge of good and evil, as two twins cleaving together, leaped forth into the world. And perhaps this is that doom which Adam fell into of knowing good and evil, that is to say, of knowing good *by evil*. As therefore the state of man now is; what wisdom can there be to choose, what continence to forbear without the knowledge of evil? He that can apprehend and consider vice with all her baits and seeming pleasures, *and yet abstain, and yet distinguish, and yet prefer that which is truly better,* he is the true warfaring Christian. (728, emphasis added)

As a consequence, trial in the post-lapsarian state stands for a choice between knowing evil *and* revelling in doing it, or, on the contrary, knowing evil and

---

117    When Adam asks Raphael to narrate the circumstances of the rebel angels' fall, he muses that "[t]he full relation [...] must needs be strange" (5, 556); afterwards, he expresses his gratefulness for having been forewarned of Satan's desire for revenge because these are things "which human knowledge could not reach" (7, 75).

118    Milton planned and wrote his first great epic poem *Paradise Lost* in the period from 1650 to 1665, the first edition appeared in 1667 (see Lewalski 2000a: 141).

KNOWLEDGE AFTER THE FALL

"yet abstain, and yet distinguish, and yet prefer that which is truly better". The difference, in other words, is between those who seek to reduce the impact of evil on their lives by exploring the fullness of fallen life merely *on a theoretical level*, that is by considering as many ideas and courses of action as possible *before* making a careful choice, and those who indiscriminately embrace every possible intellectual and moral experience, and thus welcome good *and* evil into the realm of their individual lived experience. With respect to the argument brought forward in Milton's Areopagitican speech, Blackburn observes: "The unfallen Adam and Eve, in fact, are held up in *Areopagitica* as a model of morality for fallen man."[119] Paradoxical as it may seem, ever since humankind experienced evil for the first time, whereby evil was made a determining factor of the human condition, the descendants of Adam and Eve must come to terms with evil not by attempting to avoid it entirely, but by returning to the "model of morality" characteristic of the original state and thus by exposing themselves to evil *through rational consideration only*, not, however, through actual experience, namely by committing errors or sinful deeds time and again. The difficulty of post-lapsarian trial thus lies in the fact that humankind must attempt to identify and reject a part of reality, precisely because for them (qua descendants of fallen Adam and Eve) reality is made up equally of good and evil. To withstand trial successfully in this constellation means to resist a significant portion of reality and – on the basis of a rational consideration of the various theoretical and practical alternatives and subsequently of a careful choice – to turn those aspects of the world that are tainted by evil into a mere possibility again, into a potential yet declined option.

### Conclusion

Against the biblical and theological background that informs Milton's conception of human knowledge and its transformation caused by the fall, the urgency of his argument against licensing and censorship in the *Areopagitica* is thrown into sharp relief. From the beginning of man's existence, created as a

---

119    Blackburn 1971: 133. Many scholars have pointed out that although Milton's *Areopagitica* argues for the necessity of a free press, it does not argue for amorality (see e.g. Limouze 1980). Indeed, Milton rejects only one specific form of licensing, namely pre-publication licensing enacted by the state. At the same time, he encourages a form of moral self-regulation on the part of the author (see Limouze 1980: 112–114), and the need for post-publication debate in order to distinguish truth from falsity (see e.g. Dowling 2006: 282–283).

rational creature in the image of God, knowledge has been a constitutive part of human nature. His knowledge determines his position in the hierarchy of beings, his relation to other creatures on the one hand and to God on the other. Remarkably, Milton does not conceive of knowledge as a static phenomenon but as a dynamic process through which man increasingly comes to know himself, his state (whether pre- or post-lapsarian), his fellow creatures and partly heavenly things, provided that they were revealed to him. Knowledge is natural to man, and so is his desire for it. Yet ever since Adam and Eve's first disobedience transformed the nature of trial and replaced the pre-lapsarian freedom to know and choose good because it was contiguous with their experience of reality with the post-lapsarian freedom to know and choose good through a contrastive differentiation between good and evil, man cannot access knowledge of good without at least conceptual knowledge of evil. For this reason, Milton's second argument developed in the *Areopagitica* and concerned with the utility of all kinds of books, whether true or false, concludes as follows:

> Assuredly we bring not innocence into the world, we bring impurity much rather, that which purifies us is trial, and trial is by what is contrary. That virtue therefore which is but a youngling in the *contemplation* of evil, and knows not the utmost that vice promises to her followers, and rejects it, is but a blank virtue, not a pure [...]. Since therefore *the knowledge and survey* of vice is in this world so necessary to the constituting of human virtue, and the *scanning* of error to the confirmation of truth, how can we *more safely*, and *with less danger*, scout into the regions of sin and falsity than by reading all manner of tractates and hearing all manner of reasons? And this is the benefit which may be had of books promiscuously read. (728–729, emphasis added)

According to this view, the practice of licensing and censorship as reintroduced and implemented by the Long Parliament of England inevitably has negative consequences for humankind's shared effort to identify and bring together the dispersed pieces of truth which in a fallen world are intimately mixed with falsehood and evil. Since good may be derived not only from good books (or ideas) but, by way of contrast and differentiation, also from bad books (or ideas), any attempt to remove falsehood (or at least certain manifestations of it) from the reach of the broader public will actually limit, rather than increase human liberty. This train of thought can be placed within Stephen Burt's analysis according to which the *Areopagitica* elaborates – along with a demonstration of the futility of actual censorship practices – a constructive justification for the freedom of the press and of expression by building upon an implied parallelism

KNOWLEDGE AFTER THE FALL

as established, for instance, by the title's reference to the *Areopagus*: "Paul's speech at Athens becomes Milton's demonstration of the necessity of argument, of the deep connection between true faith and inquiry" (Burt 1998: 26). From this "deep connection", Milton is shown to draw his conclusions regarding the role of the state:

> [C]ivil authority is to admit as one of its purposes (as, in fact, the highest purpose of all human institutions) the discovery and propagation of true religion; but, because we are fallen and must try truth by contraries, because we have no way to be sure beyond argument, and, perhaps, because we cannot know exactly what our beliefs are without arguing about them, government can best serve true religion through a policy of toleration and near-total press freedom. (Burt 1998: 28)

If the possibility or reality of evil, which includes the existence and availability of seditious, false or otherwise harmful books, is censored – though for the public good – such an attempt is doomed to fail and to reduce the freedom of those who are meant to be protected. To push Milton's reasoning to its utmost consequence, one could say that the only time in human history when censorship was useful was precisely in the pre-lapsarian state, if one is inclined to see God's prohibition as an act of benevolent censorship aiming at protecting his creatures from the knowledge of good *and* evil, or rather from the knowledge of good *by evil*. However, since man's first disobedience and concomitant experience of evil, the grounds for censorship have collapsed because after man's violation of God's censored tree, human knowledge cannot be damaged, but at best (when purely theoretical) benefit from the acquaintance with evil. Milton's polemical intervention against the Licensing Order of 1643 is a powerful and stimulating document of his belief in the theological and political relevance of an open intellectual and poetical space – a space which follows its own logic of discovery according to which the differentiation of good from evil is the end, not the beginning, of public debate.

### Bibliography

Blackburn, T.H. (1971), 'Uncloister'd Virtue. Adam and Eve in Milton's Paradise', in: *Milton Studies* 3, 119–137.

Blum, A. (1987), 'The Author's Authority. *Areopagitica* and the Labour of Licensing', in: *Re-membering Milton. Essays on the Text and Traditions*, ed. M. Nyquist and M.W. Ferguson (New York) 74–96.

Burt, S. (1998), 'To The Unknown God. St. Paul and Athens in Milton's *Areopagitica*', in: *Milton Quarterly* 32:1, 23–31.

Campbell, W.G. (2014), 'Temptation', in: *The Cambridge Companion to Paradise Lost*, ed. L. Schwartz (Cambridge) 164–178.

Dobranski, S.B. (1999), 'Milton's Social Life', in: *The Cambridge Companion to Milton*, ed. D. Danielson (Cambridge) 1–24.

Dowling, P.M. (2006), 'Civil Liberty and Philosophic Liberty in John Milton's *Areopagitica*', in: *Interpretation* 33:3, 281–294.

Fields, A.W. (1968), 'Milton and Self-Knowledge', in: *PMLA* 83:2, 392–399.

Hughes, M.Y. (1975), *John Milton. Complete Poems and Major Prose* (Indianapolis).

Issa, I. (2015), 'Milton's *Areopagitica* in the Arab World Today', in: *English Studies* 96:1, 82–101.

Jacobus, L.A. (1976), *Sudden Apprehension. Aspects of Knowledge in Paradise Lost* (The Hague).

Leonard, J. (1999), 'Language and Knowledge in *Paradise Lost*', in: *The Cambridge Companion to Milton*, ed. D. Danielson (Cambridge) 130–143.

Lewalski, B. (1969), 'Innocence and Experience in Milton's Eden', in: *New Essays on Paradise Lost*, ed. T. Kranidas (Berkeley) 86–117.

Lewalski, B. (2000a), '*Paradise Lost* and Milton's Politics', in: *Milton Studies* 38, 141–168.

Lewalski, B. (2000b), *The Life of John Milton. A Critical Biography* (Oxford).

Limouze, H.S. (1980), 'The Surest Suppressing. Writer and Censor in Milton's *Areopagitica*', in: *Centennial Review* 24:1, 103–117.

Meyer, J. (2011), 'Sense and Censorship: Licensing or Silencing? Early English Fundamentalism and the Reading Public: From Roger Ashcam to John Milton', in: *Anglistik* 22:2, 35–48.

Norbrook, D. (1994), '*Areopagitica*, Censorship and the Early Modern Public Sphere', in: *The Administration of Aesthetics*, ed. R. Burt (Minneapolis) 3–33.

Patrides, C.A. (1962), 'The Tree of Knowledge in the Christian Tradition', in: *Studia Neophilologica* 34, 239–242.

Patterson, A. (1984), *Censorship and Interpretation: The Conditions of Writing and Reading in Early Modern England* (Madison).

Reeves, C.E. (1997), 'Lest Wilfully Transgressing. Raphael's Narration and Knowledge in *Paradise Lost*', in: *Milton Studies* 34, 83–98.

Reichert, J. (1981), 'Against His Better Knowledge. A Case for Adam', in: *ELH* 48:1, 83–109.

Samuel, I. (1949), 'Milton on Learning and Wisdom', in: *PMLA* 64:4, 708–723.

Schultz, H. (1955), *Milton and Forbidden Knowledge* (New York).

Sensabaugh, G.F. (1946), 'Milton on Learning', in: *Studies in Philology* 43:2, 258–272.

Svendsen, K. (1956), *Milton and Science* (Cambridge, Mass.).

Tanner, T. (1977), 'Licence and Licencing: To the Presse or to the Spunge', in: *Journal of the History of Ideas* 38:1, 3–18.

Tournu, C. (1999), 'Un bon livre, le Livre, les livres. L'*Areopagitica* de John Milton: de la liberté de la presse à la presse de la liberté', in: *XVII–XVIII. Bulletin de la société d'études anglo-américaines des XVIIᵉ et XVIIIᵉ siècles* 48, 41–54.

Wittreich, J. (1972), 'Milton's *Areopagitica*. Its Isocratean and Ironic Contexts', in: *Milton Studies* 4, 101–112.

## The First World War

CHAPTER 6

# Stefan George als politischer Dichter

*Hans-Christian Günther*

Stefan George als politischer Dichter – das klingt genauso merkwürdig wie selbstverständlich; merkwürdig, da man mit Stefan George esoterischen Ästhetizismus jenseits allen Alltagsgetriebes verbindet, selbstverständlich, da Stefan George mit seinem Kreis eine für einen Dichter geradezu einmalige gesellschaftlich- politische Wirkung entfaltete. Gewiss, Stefan Georges Leben fiel in eine Zeit eines der gewaltigsten Umbrüche des politischen und geistigen Lebens Europas, des ersten Weltkrieges. Bereits dieses Kriegsereignis selbst hat nicht nur eine Welle nationaler Begeisterung auch unter Künstlern und Intellektuellen ausgelöst, die zunächst jeden erfasste, der nicht einer dezidiert pazifistischen oder extrem antibürgerlichen Gesinnung anhing, es hat auch durchaus nationale-politische Dichtung hervorgebracht, wenn auch von geringem Wert, die heute vergessen ist, freilich vielleicht auch deshalb, weil sich ihre Verfasser später in edelkonservativen Humanisten verwandelten bzw. zu solchen stilisieren ließen. Sie hat freilich auch eine unmittelbare künstlerische Verarbeitung des Grauens des Krieges in jener Kriegsgeneration hervorgebracht, die auch, was einige der größten Künstler der Zeit, zahlreiche Opfer kostete (unter deutschen Dichtern etwa August Stramm, Ernst Stadler und, wenn auch nicht auf dem Feld, Ernst Trakl, unter den großen Malern Franz Marc und August Macke). Dieser Krieg ließ auch, zumal im Lande der Verlierer Deutschland und Österreich, kaum einen Künstler von dem Zusammenbruch der Behaglichkeit und inneren und äußeren Sicherheit unberührt. Insofern war im Grunde genommen jede künstlerische Reaktion auf dieses Ereignis eine Verarbeitung dieser Situation und somit eine politische.

Stefan George war inmitten dieser geschichtlich-intellektuellen Landschaft ein Fixpunkt mit einer mächtigen Ausstrahlung, die weit über seinen damals längst etablierten Kreis von Jüngern ausstrahlte, ein Kreis, der im übrigen nur zum geringsten Teil aus wirklichen Künstlern bestand. Er strahlte aus auf viele Dichter, die nicht unmittelbar dazugehörten, auch Gelehrte; letztlich wirkte er auch *e contrario* auf diejenigen, die ihn belächelten oder gar frontal ablehnten und verspotteten. Insbesondere wirkte er auch auf so manchen derer, die später – zumindest nach der offiziellen Version zum inneren Widerstand gegen den Nationalsozialismus gerechnet und nach dem Krieg zu den bürgerlichen Helden der faulen geistigen Erneuerung bzw. christlich-humanistischen

Wiederverspießerung, wie ich es einmal nennen möchte, nach dem zweiten Weltkrieg wurden,[120] wie Rudolf Borchardt oder der Verfasser der von Alfred Heuß favorisierten neuen Nationalhymne der Bundesrepublik als Land von Glaube Hoffnung, Liebe, Rudolf Alexander Schröder.

Letzterer, im übrigen vielgepriesener Verfasser einer gerade noch lesbaren Vergilnachdichtung und einer in kaum einem Gedicht das Lächerliche vermeidenden Horazübersetzung, hat übrigens 1935 einen Vortrag zu Horaz als politischem Dichter gehalten, in dem er – eigentlich seltsamerweise, denkt man an das Datum, oder auch nicht – davon sprach, dass politische Dichtung heute etwas so Heikles an sich habe, dass man selbst den Alten, d.h. antiken Dichtern nur ungern eine politische Überzeugung zugestehe, obwohl politische Dichtung damals eine Selbstverständlichkeit gewesen sei.[121] Der Vortrag ist im übrigen noch heute in einem weit verbreiteten modernen Sammelband abgedruckt, den einer der schlimmsten Naziphilologen, Hans Oppermann, zusammengestellt hat, der vom Universitätsdienst enthoben im Nachkriegsdeutschland dennoch eine beachtliche Karriere nicht nur als Gymnasiallehrer, sondern auch Herausgeber und Verfasser von Aufsätzen gemacht hat, die er genausogut auch schon im 'Nationalsozialistischen Gymnasium' hätte veröffentlichen können.[122] Dennoch, Schröders Bemerkung ist durchaus korrekt, und seine Rede enthält durchaus viel Treffendes und durchaus Wichtiges.

Nun hat freilich Stefan George längst vor dem Krieg, nämlich in seinem Gedichtband 'Der Siebente Ring' von 1907, eine scheinbare Wende vollzogen, eine Wende vom zeitfernen esoterischen Ästheten, der jede explizite Erwähnung des Alltäglichen, seiner konkreten historischen Umgebung peinlich zu meiden schien, ja abgesehen von der Sammlung Algabal selbst jede Vermeidung des Historisch-Konkreten überhaupt. Diese Wende des 'Siebenten Rings', wo George sich in Gedichten konkret zu Historie, ja selbst zur Gegenwart äußerst, wo er wie nirgends sonst einen ganzen Teil des Buches zu Ansprachen an die Gefährten seines Umfeldes verwendet, hat George in der Einleitung des Buches selbst markiert, wo er sagt:

---

120 Bernd von Heisseler hat noch 1936 ein Georgepamphlet verfasst, indem er den Schluss des ‚Dichters in der Zeit der Wirren' auf Hitler gedeutet hat; er hat das nach dem Krieg 1958 fast unverändert wiedergedruckt, nur den Bezug auf Hitler emphatisch geleugnet, ohne zu sagen, dass er einst das Gegenteil behauptet hatte (das Buch ist übrigens durchaus lesenswert). Das sind die (chritlich-humanistischen) Wendehälse, die nach dem Krieg Deutschland erneuert haben. Heidegger, der genug Taktgefühl und Respekt vor den Opfern hatte, um zu schweigen, beschimpfen die braunschnüffelnden Pinscher bis heute.

121 Schröder (1972).

122 Vgl. http://archiv.ub.uni-heidelberg.de/propylaeumdok/390/1/Malitz_Roemertum_im_Dritten_Reich_1998.pdf.

STEFAN GEORGE ALS POLITISCHER DICHTER 79

> Ihr meiner zeit genossen kanntet schon
> Bemasset schon und schaltet mich – ihr fehltet.
> Als ihr in lärm und wüster gier des lebens
>
> Mit plumpem tritt und rohem finger ranntet:
>
> Da galt ich für den salbentrunknen prinzen
> Der sanft geschaukelt seine takte zählte
> In schlanker anmut oder kühler würde ·
> In blasser erdenferner festlichkeit.

Anderwo spricht er durchaus davon, dass 'was früher klang im Tempeltone, die Menschen nun mehr in ihre Sprache dünke'. Doch am Ende des eben zitierten Einleitungsgedichtes sagt er über diese 'Wende':

> Ihr sehet wechsel · doch ich tat das gleiche.

Ich habe bereits in einem erst vor kurzem hier in Meran vorgetragenen Beitrag, Georges Haltung zum Politischen, seine Antwort auf dem ersten Weltkrieg im speziellen sowie die Frage, warum er dieses Ereignis nicht brauchte, um sich in seiner Dichtung 'politisch' zu äußern und was das Politische für ihn bedeutete, behandelt.[123] Ich will dies hier nicht wiederholen, sondern vielmehr fortführen, indem ich nun diejenigen Gedichte Georges insgesamt summarisch in den Blick nehme, die man insofern als politische bezeichnen könnte, als er sich in ihnen direkt zu historischen Ereignissen oder Personen seiner Gegenwart oder Vergangenheit äußerst. Dabei muss ich freilich einen Rahmen abstecken und so in einigen Sätzen bereits Gesagtes wiederholen.

Ich habe bereits gesagt und zur Genüge begründet, dass Georges einmalige politische Hellsichtigkeit und treffende Analyse seines geschichtlichen Umfeldes eines Ereignisses wie des Ersten Weltkrieges, den er längst vorausgesehen hatte nicht bedurfte, um politisch aufzuwachen;[124] ich habe auch gesagt, dass seine Wendung im 'Siebenten Ring' eng mit der Etablierung eines festen Kreises von Jüngern um George und dem Maximinkult verbunden ist. Diese letzten Punkt möchte ich hier folgendermaßen präzisieren: Georges

---

123 Günther (im Druck).

124 So sagt er im ‚Jahrhundertspruch‘ am Ende des ‚Siebenten Rings‘ auch explizit: Ein Vierter: Schlacht: Ich sah von fern getümmel einer schlacht/So wie sie bald in unsren ebnen kracht./Ich sah die kleine schar ums banner stehn.../Und alle andren haben nichts gesehn.

Wendung hin zum Geschichtlich-Konkreten im 'Siebenten Ring' ist unlösbar mit der Institutionalisierung des Georgekreises (man sprach von einem 'Staat', s. unten) als Kultverein um die Maximinreligion verbunden. Insofern diese Religion sich als eine Religion der Vergöttlichung einer konkreten Person als Inbegriff und lebendiges Unterpfand der Vergöttlichung des Leibes, der Aufhebung jeder Differenz zwischen ästhetischer Transzendenz und konkreter Wirklichkeit definiert, ist diese Wendung zum Historisch-Konkreten innerlich absolut kohärent.

Die explizit zeitgeschichtlichen Gedichte des 'Siebenten Ringes' bilden den mit 'Zeitgedichte' überschriebenen Anfangszyklus des Buches, aus dessen 'Das Zeitgedicht' betitelten Einleitungsgedicht ich schon zitiert habe. In dem streng um die Mitte der Maximingedichte herum gebauten Buch steht diesem Anfangsteil am Ende spiegelbildlich ein Teil spruchhafter epigrammatischer Gedichte gegenüber, die sich zumeist an Personen des Kreises wenden oder deutsche Städte und in einem Zyklus kleinerer Gedichte den Rhein, den deutschen Fluss par excellence besingen. Dieser Schlusszyklus scheint so durchaus den von George selbst in einem der Schlussgedichte verkündeten Anspruch zu erfüllen, von dem ich die Schlusszeilen bereits zitiert habe und dessen vollständiger Text lautet:

> Ganz ging hervor aus vaterländischer brache
> Dies werk und ging dem ende zu ganz ohne
> Fernluft . was früher klang im tempeltone
> Deucht nun die menschen mehr in ihrer sprache.

Sieht man sich nun aber die Themen der Gedichte des Anfangszyklus an, ergibt sich zunächst ein ganz anderes Bild. Nur ein Teil ist Orten oder Persönlichkeiten des deutschen Kulturraumes gewidmet: Goethe, Nietzsche, Böcklin. Programmatisch am Anfang steht als einziger Dichter neben Goethe Dante. Den Anfang der zweiten Hälfte macht Leo XIII, der bereits erwähnte Algabal, es folgt ein Titel wie 'Franken', wo sogar ein auf Französisch verfasster Vers abschließt. Die neben Speyer einzig genannte deutsche Stadt Trier wird unter ihrem berühmtesten römischen Monument, der Porta Nigra, genannt und aus der Perspektive eines römischen Sklaven gesehen. Die österreichische Prinzessin Sissi taucht in einem Gedicht 'Die Schwestern' neben ihrer Verwandten Sophie von Alencon auf. Unter den Gefährten aus dem Kreis erschein neben dem Jugendfreund Carl August Klein ein im russisch-türkischen Krieg Gefallener unter dem Titel eines Ortes in Griechenland, Pente Pigadia. Diese Aufzählung zeigt an, dass der Anfangsteil einerseits zunächst demonstrativ den geographischen Raum über Deutschland hinaus vor allem in das Gebiet der *romanitas* hinein weitet, das geschichtliche Zeitfeld reicht von der Antike über das Mittelalter zur Gegenwart. Und gerade das Gedicht 'Die Gräber zu Speier' weist am weitesten aus dem geographischen und geistigen Raum des zeitgenössischen Deutschland hinaus: es endet mit dem Staufer Friedrich II, der zentralen Gestalt des Deutschtums als politische Größe für George, als seiner Erfüllung und Bestimmung (die Zusammenarbeit mit Ernst Kantorowicz, die in dessen berühmtem Buch von 1927 mündete, liegt viel später). Damit reicht es selbst über die römisch-griechische Antike bis in den Orient hinein (George spricht von 'Weisheit der Kabbala').[125] Diese orientalischen Wurzeln klingen auch in Algabal an, der einzigen konkreten historischen Gestalt, die vor dem , Siebenten Ring' in Georges Werk auftaucht.

Bevor ich näher auf einige weitere Einzelheiten eingehe, muss ich noch zwei hier relevante Tatsachen zu Georges Leben und Werk erwähnen. Der 'Siebente Ring' fällt nicht nur in die Zeit, als sich der Kreis um George fest etabliert hatte, er fällt auch in die Zeit von Georges Zusammenarbeit mit einem der großen Gelehrten des Kreises, mit Gundolf, dessen 'Caesar in der deutschen Literatur' bereits 1904 erschienen war und dessen Habilitation mit 'Shakespeare und der deutsche Geist' 1911 erfolgte. Somit fällt in diese Zeit auch die gemeinsame Shakespeareübersetzung mit Georges Übertragung der Sonette; auch die Danteübersetzung und die beiden Bände mit fremden Dichtern gehören hierher.

Auch hier deutet sich etwas Analoges wie in den eben aufgeführten Gedichttiteln an: das Deutsche reicht über den politisch-geographischen Raum Deutschlands hinaus: es geht um die fremden Wurzeln des Deutschtums und ihre Aneignung im deutschen Geist. Fast könnte man sagen: es geht um die Formung des Deutschtums als des Amalgams, in dem Europa zu seiner Bestimmung findet.

Zum zweiten ist hier erwähnenswert die Begegnung mit dem Hölderlinentdecker und -herausgeber Hellingrath, die freilich erst nach die Veröffentlichung des 'Siebenten Ringes' 1907 fällt und erst 1909 stattfand, Hellingrath der mit Georges 'Stern des Bundes' im Gepäck in den ersten Weltkrieg zog und 1916 bei Verdun fiel. Mit seiner Wiederentdeckung Hölderlins war er zugleich der Initiator jenes 'hölderlinschen Deutschlands',

---

125    Vor allen aber strahlte von der Staufischen/ Ahnmutter aus dem süden her zu gast/ Gerufen an dem arm des schönen Enzio/ Der Grösste Friedrich · wahren volkes sehnen ·/ Zum Karlen- und Ottonen-plan im blick/ Des Morgenlandes ungeheuren traum ·/ Weisheit der Kabbala und Römerwürde/ Feste von Agrigent und Selinunt.

für das eben jene zugleich von Georges 'Stern des Bundes' geprägte Generation in den ersten Weltkrieg zog.

Auch Martin Heidegger gehörte zu dieser Generation, er, der später – in dezidiertem Gegensatz zur Vereinnahmung Hölderlins, wie im übrigen auch Nietzsches, für einen chauvinistischen Deutschnationalismus und eine totalitär verkürzte Interpretation des Politischen – die denkerisch bedeutsamste Hölderlindeutung entwickelt hat, in der er das 'Vaterländische' in Hölderlins Vision des Deutschen anhand von Hölderlins Stromdichtung als den (Rück)gang zur Quelle gedeutet hat.[126] Auch der 'Siebente Ring' enthält im Schlussteil einen Zyklus von sechs kurzen Gedichten mit dem Titel 'Der Rhein', der Inbegriff des deutschen Flusses, dem auch Hölderlin sein größtes Stromgedicht gewidmet hat.

Für den in Bingen geborenen Stefan George ist der Rhein auch ganz persönlich der Fluss der Herkunft. So geht den Rheingedichten ein Gedicht von epigrammatischer Kürze mit dem Titel 'Einem Dichter' voran, das in einem Landschaftsbild von vier Zeilen alles konzentriert, was George in 'Das Zeitgedicht' von sich gesagt hatte:

> Schönste farben hellste strahlen
> Gebt ihr da ihr grünt und quellt
> Voll der ahnung aller qualen
> Mitten in der blumenwelt.

Und schon im vorletzten Teil des 'Siebenten Ringes' steht ein Gedicht 'Rhein', ein Gedicht, das wie das auf es folgende zumeist aus Fragen besteht, so wie wir es in einem jener letzten kurzen Gedichte des Dichters am Ende seines letzten Werkes, dem 'Neuen Reich'[127] finden:

> Blüht am hange nicht die rebe?
> Wars ein schein nicht der verklärte?
> Warst es du nicht mein gefährte
> Den ich suche seit ich lebe?
>
> Jagt vom flusse feuchter schwaden
> Duft des haines licht der lande?
> Dichter brodem wirst du laden ·
> Folg ich dir nur spur im sande?

---

126 Günther 2006; zu Heidegger und Hölderlin vgl. auch Helting 1999.
127 'Welch ein kühn-leicher schritt...'.

# STEFAN GEORGE ALS POLITISCHER DICHTER

»Dich zu ehren dir zu dienen
Seid geopfert frühere prächte ·
Seid vergessen tag und nächte!«
Summt beharrlich lied der bienen.

Weite runde wo sich mische
Ferne hoffnung glück der stunde!
Nur noch droben in der nische
Zeigt der Heilige alte wunde …

Es steht nach einem 'Südliche Landschaft' überschrieben Zyklus. In seiner Evokation der sonnendurchgluteten Rebenlandschaft des Rheins malt George die Flusslandschaft selbst als südliche. Sie wird so zum Symbol der Herkunft des Dichters aus dem Süden. Der vorhergehende Zyklus wie viele andere Gedichte des 'Siebenten Ringes' nimmt die südlichen Landschaften voll Sonne und Meer des Jugendwerks, das Algabal in seinem Titel trägt, auf. Im Rheinzyklus des Schlussteils wird der Rhein zum Fluss der Herkunft und Verheißung des Neuen, das Neue, das entsteht aus dem sich Entledigen des Wertlosen, der Reinigung der Vergangenheit. Im vierten Gedicht, bevor er im fünften die Rebenlandschaft des Rheins nun explizit als eine gesegnete beschreibt, heißt es:

Nun fragt nur bei dem furchtbaren gereut
Ob sich das land vor solchem dung nicht scheut!
Den eklen schutt von rötel kalk und teer
Spei ich hinaus ins reinigende Meer.

Auch in seinem großen politischen Gedicht 'Der Dichter in der Zeit der Wirren' sollte George später von dem 'jungen Geschlecht' sprechen, "das von sich spie, was mürb und feig und lau". Und im Schlussgedicht des Rheinzyklus spricht der Dichter dann – am Ende – von seiner Herkunft, der Herkunft des Deutschen aus dem Römischen. Die Wiederfindung jener Herkunft ist Unterpfand und Verheißung des Neuen:

Sprecht von des festes von des reiches nähe –
Sprecht erst vom neuen wein im alten schlauch:
Wenn ganz durch eure seelen dumpf und zähe
Mein feurig blut sich regt. mein römischer hauch!

Diese Herkunft als Zukunft ist das, was George in 'Das Zeitgedicht 2' am Ende des Einleitungszyklus so nennt:

Eins das von je war (keiner kennt es) währet
Und blum und jugend lacht und sang erklingt.

Dies ist gewiss dem sehr nahe, was Heidegger in den Hölderlinvorlesungen 'den Gang zur Quelle' nennt, es ist präzise das, was Heidegger im griechischen *arché* als dem 'verfügenden Ausgang' bzw. der 'ausgänglichen Verfügung' gedacht hat. Diese erstaunliche seherische Vorwegnahme noch vor der Entdeckung Hölderlins entspringt einer gemeinsamen Sensibilität für ein geistiges Klima des herannahenden geschichtlichen Moments – im Heideggerischen Sinne.[128] Es ist nur allzu verständlich, wenn neben Trakl George Heideggers moderner Bezugspunkt in seiner Reflexion auf das Verhältnis von Dichten und Denken ist.[129]

Der oben in seiner Thematik kurz umrissene Programmzyklus 'Das Zeitgedicht' besteht aus einer Reihe von einzeln entstandenen Gelegenheitsgedichten, die bis ins Jahr 1899 zurückreichen. Am Anfang steht in exponierter Stellung das Gedicht zu Dante, mit dem sich der Seherdichter seit seiner Arbeit an der Danteübersetzung immer mehr identifizierte und in dessen Kostüm er auch beim Dichterkarneval 1904 in München aufgetreten war. Dantes Lebensweg vom Leiden an der geist- und führerlosen politischen Gegenwart zum Dichter der Erlösung in Geist und Liebe[130] steht Georges Beschreibung seines eigenen Lebensweges in 'Das Zeitgedicht' in spiegelbildlicher Analogie gegenüber. Das deutet auch bereits der Titel 'Dante und das Zeitgedicht' an.

Das folgende Gedicht gehört eng mit dem Dantegedicht zusammen. Es geht um den zweiten Dichter – den einzig anderen des Zyklus –, in dem George sich spiegelt; und es ist ein deutscher Dichter. Die Wahl freilich mag zunächst, denkt man an Georges vorzügliche dichterische Affinitäten, überraschen: es ist Goethe. George verwendet ein älteres Gedicht zur 150-jahrfeier von Goethes Geburtstags. Der Titel Goethe-Tag passt dabei vorzüglich in das Programm des Zyklus, der sich zum guten Teil aus älteren Gelegenheitsgedichten zum Tod von Persönlichkeiten wie Nietzsche, Böcklin, Leo XIII, Kaiserin Sissi und ihrer Schwester oder eines im Krieg gefallenen Mitglieds des Kreises zusammensetzt. Der Titel Goethe-Tag deutet an, worum es George geht: es geht um eine

---

128 S. Günther (2015).

129 Von Hermann 1999.

130 Das Dantegedicht steht implizit den Berufungsgedichten aus dem 'Teppich des Lebens' sehr nahe, besonders dem ersten 'Ich suchte bleichen eifers nach dem Horte'. Die Begegnung mit dem Engel erinnert mich stark an die Berufung Jesaias oder auch die Verkündigung.

STEFAN GEORGE ALS POLITISCHER DICHTER

Vergegenwärtigung des Vergangenen, um das Heraufbeschwören einer in die Gegenwart hereinragenden Vergangenheit.

Goethe spielte und spielt auch später – zumindest an der Oberfläche – eine geringe, eine erstaunlich geringe Rolle in Georges Dichten. Freilich sollte man bedenken, dass der einzige wirklich große Literaturwissenschaftler des Kreises, dessen Verbindung zu George in eben die Zeit des 'Siebenten Ringes' gehört, Gundolf sein Lebenswerk mit einer Goethemonographie gekrönt hat, dass auch später bei Kommerell Goethe eine herausragende Bedeutung haben wird. Am Verständnis des Goethegedichtes mit seiner prominenten Stellung am Anfang des Zyklus, der Identifikation Georges mit deutscher Dichtung in Goethes Person, hängt wiederum viel, um zu klären, was Georges explizite Zuwendung zum konkret Geschichtlichen, zum Deutschen und mithin zu dem, was er in seinem Abschlussgedicht mit 'vaterländisch' meint, bedeutet.

In 'Goethe-Tag' spricht Stefan George von Goethe zunächst als Emblem deutscher bürgerlicher Kultur. Sein Gedicht richtet sich zunächst gegen die Vereinnahmung Goethes durch den geistlosen, spießigen Kulturbetrieb, der Goethe zum Emblem des feisten, pseudohumanistischen Edeldeutschtums des geistamputierten wilhelminischen Deutschland gemacht hat. Dem gegenüber stellt George implizit den Goethe mit seiner Zuwendung zum Anderen, dem Südlichen, so wie er es im 'Neuen Reich' in seinem zweitem großen Goethegedicht mit dem Titel 'Goethes letzte Nacht in Italien' ganz am Anfang des Buches explizit macht. In 'Goethe-Tag' steht Goethe explizit als derjenige da, der weit über seine Zeit hinausreicht, der Grenzüberschreiter, der den wertlosen Ballast beschränkten deutschen Spießertums unbemerkt von anderen längst hinter sich gelassen hat. Ganz analog zu Georges Selbstdarstellung in 'Das Zeitgedicht' wird Goethe als derjenige dargestellt, der sein geheimes Leid unter der Gelassenheit, dem Lächeln seines Entrücktseins in den Bereich des Ewig-Schönens der Dichtung birgt, dem Bereich, von wo aus der Dichter heiter auf alle menschlichen Leidenschaften herabsieht, wie Goethe es im 'Wilhelm Meister' ausdrückt. Ohne jeden expliziten Anklang gestaltet George hier tatsächlich ein, wenn nicht das Grundanliegen von Goethes Auffassung der Aufgabe des Dichters, wie er es etwa im 'Wilhelm Meister', in der 'Novelle', dem 'Märchen', in manchem Wort zu Eckermann oder in jenen unsterblichen Versen kurz ausgedrückt hat, wo er vielleicht am schönsten gesagt hat, was er unter seinem Ideal des Menschen als dem an der Antike geläuterten schönen Menschen verstand:

> Zwischen oben zwischen unten schweb ich hin in munterer Schau,
> Ich ergötze mich am Bunten, ich erquicke mich am Blau.
> Und wenn mich am Tag die Ferne heller Berge sehnlich zieht,

Nachts das Übermaß der Sterne prächtig mir zu Häupten glüht:
Alle Tage alle Nächte rühm ich so des Menschen Los:
Denkt er ewig sich ins Rechte, ist er ewig schön und groß.

Das ist der Goethe, der sagen konnte: wie es auch sei, das Leben, es ist gut.[131]

Diese innere Affinität sollte uns davor warnen, Georges Verhältnis zu Goethe am Äußerlichen zu messen. Es mag angesichts der Vereinnahmung Goethes durch das Bildungsspießertum, der Begeisterung für den neuentdeckten Hölderlin eine ‚Jugend ohne Goethe' und mit Hölderlin gegeben haben,[132] gerade auch um George, wahrscheinlich der bedeutendste Einfluss auf die deutsche Jugend seiner Zeit. Nur sollte man George nicht mit dieser Jugend, überhaupt nicht mit Personen seines Kreises identifizieren. Ebenso sollte man alle Aussagen von Mitgliedern des Kreises über George und Aussagen von George ihnen gegenüber mit Vorsicht genießen. Es ist naiv, anzunehmen, dass George die jungen Leute, die ihn umschwärmten und die er durchaus auch zur Befriedigung seiner Eitelkeit oder seiner sexuellen Bedürfnisse benötigte, wirklich ernst genommen hat, noch haben die meisten viel von ihm verstanden. Dasselbe gilt für das bürgerliche Umfeld Georges oder den spießigen Zeremonienmeister des Kreises Wolters, der in Georges Abkürzung ss für einen ‚Sehr Süßen' eher ‚Staatsstütze' hineinlas.[133] Der Kreis besaß mit Gundolf, Kantorowicz und dem zu Unrecht weitgehend vergessenen Josef

---

131 Trotz der unweigerlichen modenen Verwandlung hat niemand das griechische Menschenbild tiefer durchschaut und erneuert als Goethe. Der griechische Mensch sieht die Welt, im Sinne des Kosmos, als ein Georgnetsein, in dem vernünftige Ordnung, Natur, Schönes und Göttliches eine Einheit bilden (das ist nichts Selbstverständliches – ganz im Gegenteil). Das ist so trotz der 'pessimistischen' Sicht des menschlichen Lebens als voll Mühe und Leid. Dieses Leid wird hingenommen mit der Gelassenheit dessen, der weiß, dass er nicht der Maßstab der Welt ist, dem die Welt nichts schuldet, der nur ein unendlich kleiner Teil von ihr ist. Die aus der menschglichen Perspektive unvollkommene und weder voll begreifbare noch gerechte, gute, sondern stets ambivalente Welt ist doch von einem höheren Standpunkt aus 'schön und gut', und der Mensch ist der, in dessen Geist sich diese Schönheit und Gutheit alleine spiegeln kann, wenn er seinen Geist in die Sphäre des Göttlichen, des ihn Überschreiteten weitet. Und dies kann er nur als der Unvollkommene und Zerbrechliche zugleich, denn nur er kann zugleich auch das Unvollkommene und Schlechte überhaupt erfahren und so im Überschreiten seiner selbst doch in heiterer Gelassenheit in das Vollkommene aufheben.

132 Schmitt 1991: 152. Auch von Heidegger hat man behauptet, er habe Goethe kaum zur Kenntnis genommen. Ich halte das in dieser unqualifizierten Form für falsch, kann aber hier nicht näher darauf eingehen.

133 Karlauf 2007.

Liegle[134] immerhin drei wirklich bedeutende akademische Gelehrte, mit Kommerell zumindest noch einen respektablen Intellektuellen. Wirrköpfe wie Klages und Schuler blieben bezeichnenderweise nicht; und von Staatsbeamten oder letztlich mittelmäßigen bürgerlichen Akademikern, die allenfalls zu verfehlter Hobbydichtung fähig waren, zu erwarten, dass sie George geistig auch nur entfernt gewachsen waren oder er sie wirklich ernst genommen haben sollte, ist abwegig. Georges Botschaft ist eine dichterische, die nur dichterisch gesagt und nur dichterisch verstanden werden kann, und einen Dichter besaß der Kreis nur einen, Karl Wolfskehl, der George seit früher Zeit begleitete, der bei aller Devotion gegenüber dem 'Meister' (wie er George stets nannte) seine eigene geistige Physiognomie besaß,[135] der George bis zu seinem Ende im Exil treu blieb und den auch George nie als seinen wirklichen Geistesverwandten aufgab, trotz aller Versuche anderer, die beiden zu entfremden.

Doch um nun zu Goethe zurückzukommen: Goethe steht wie selbstverständlich im Hintergrund von Georges Dichtung und geistiger Welt als die Deutschland als geistige Größe prägende Gestalt. Durch Goethe wurde deutscher Geist zur prägenden geistigen Kraft Europas, das Deutschland Goethes war die Erfüllung des europäischen Geistes schlechthin, aber gerade so war Goethes Deutschland keine nationale, keine geographisch begrenzte und vor allem keine konkret politische Größe. Goethes Deutschland war das Amalgam europäischen Geistes, in dem sich die Wiedergeburt der Herkunft des europäischen Geistes aus der Antike ereignen konnte. In diesem Rückgang zum Anfang weist nicht nur das Deutsche über sich selbst hinaus, das Europäische in seiner Anfänglichkeit öffnet sich zugleich über Europa hinaus, um es mit Heidegger zu sagen, ‚zu den anderen Anfängen'. Am bedeutsamsten war für Goethe seine Begegnung mit der islamischen Kultur, während er ansonsten das Fremde – bis hin zu China – ganz in seiner dezidiert selektive Rezeptionsweise in das Eigene einschmolz,[136] hat er sich noch gegen Ende seines Lebens im West-Östlichen Divan auf ein ganz anderes eingelassen und sich in diesem Fremden selbst aufgegeben und verwandelt.[137]

---

134 S. Kerkhecker 2007 und 2009.

135 Vgl. Scheffold 2013.

136 Sein Gedicht „Dämmerung senkte sich von oben" trifft den Geist der Naturerfahrung chinesischer Lyrik der Tangzeit so unvergleichlich, dass ein chinesischer Germanist meinte, es müsse die Übersetzung eines verlorenen Gedichtes von Li Bai sein.

137 'Wie nimmt ein leidenschaftlich Stammeln/ Geschrieben sich so seltsam aus!', sagt Goethe selbst. Heute reden die Proleten von Goethe, die sich darum raufen 'ob der Islam zu Deutschland gehöre' und wie oder wie nicht. Es ist ein Armutszeugnis für unsere 'Intellektuellen', von denen bisher, soweit ich sehe, kein Germanist noch Mittelalterforscher, die es alle wissen (müssten), das Rückgrat hatte, auzustehen und klar

Georges Rolle in seiner Zeit entspricht der Goethes so präzise, dass ein expliziter Bezug nicht nur unnötig, sondern unmöglich wäre. Goethe steht unweigerlich im Hintergrund von Georges Mission der Erneuerung und Bewahrung Deutschlands als der große Verschwiegene, der nur zweimal, jedoch da umso emphatischer aus dem Schatten heraustritt, in zwei Gedichten, in denen George Goethe davor zu retten versucht, zum Emblem deutschen Bildungsspießertums zu verkommen, etwas, was ihm leider bis heute nicht gelungen ist, in den beiden großen eben erwähnten Goethegedichten. Im zweite, weit bedeutenderen des ‚Neuen Reichs', auf das ich hier nicht im einzelnen eingehen, steht Goethe neben, ja vor Hölderlin, der jetzt mit dem Hyperionzyklus auch in Georges Dichtung hereinrückt. Goethe erscheint hier als der Dichtervater des von ihm allein gehegten 'Traums', wie es im 'Goethe-Tag' heißt, von der Erfüllung des Deutschtums im Griechischen:

> Abschied reisst durch die brust – von dem heiligen boden
> Wo ich erstmals wesen wandeln im licht
> Sah und durch reste der säulen der Seligen reigen . .
> Ich den ihr preisend ›herz eures volkes‹ genannt
> ›Echtesten erben‹: hier hab ich vor armut gezittert ·
> Hier ward erst mensch der hier wiederbegonnen als kind.
> Durch die nebel schon hör ich euch schmälende stimmen:
> ›Hellas' lotus liess ihn die heimat vergessen‹ . . .
> O dass mein wort ihr verstündet – kein weiseres frommt euch –
> ›Nicht nur in tropfen · nein traget auch fürder in strömen
> Von eurem blute das edelste jenseit der berge ·
> Anteil und sinn euch solang ihr noch unerlöst‹.

> Euch betraf nicht beglückterer stämme geschick
> Denen ein Seher erstand am beginn ihrer zeiten
> Der noch ein sohn war und nicht ein enkel der Gäa
> Der nicht der irdischen schichten geheimnis nur spürte
> Der auch als gast in ambrosischen hallen geweilt
> Der dort ein scheit des feuers stahl für sein volk
> Das nun sein lebenlang ganz nicht mehr tastet in irre
> Der in die schluchten der grausigen Hüterinnen
> Die an den wurzeln im Untersten sitzen · sich wagte
> Die widerstrebenden schreienden niederrang

---

zu sagen, dass nicht Kulturproleten und halb/ungebildete Politiker das letzte Wort darüber haben, was europäische oder deutsche Kultur ist. Aber anscheinend haben sie es.

STEFAN GEORGE ALS POLITISCHER DICHTER

Ihnen die formel entreissend mit der er beschwört...
Solch einer ward euch nicht und ich bin es nicht.

Früh einst – so denkt es mir – trug ein bewimpeltes schiff
Uns in das nachbarlich rheinische rebengeländ..
Hellblauer himmel des herbstes besonnte die gaue
Weisse häuser und eichen-kronige gipfel..
Und sie luden die lezten trauben am hügel
Schmückten mit kränzen die bütten · die festlichen winzer ·
Nackte und golden gepuzte mit flatternden bändern..
Lachend mit tosendem sange beim dufte des mostes
Also stürmte die strasse am tiefgrünen strom
Purpurnes weinlaub im haare der bacchische zug.
Dort an dem römischen Walle · der grenze des Reichs ·
Sah ich in ahnung mein heimliches muttergefild.

Unter euch lebt ich im lande der träume und töne
In euren domen verweilt ich · ehrfürchtiger beter ·
Bis mich aus spitzen und schnörkeln aus nebel und trübe
Angstschrei der seele hinüber zur sonne rief.
Heimwärts bring ich euch einen lebendigen strahl ·
Dränge zutiefst in den busen die dunkleren flammen ·
Euch ein verhängnis solang ihr verworren noch west.
Nehmt diesen strahl in euch auf – o nennt ihn nicht kälte! –
Und ich streu euch inzwischen im buntesten wechsel
Steine und kräuter und erze: nun alles · nun nichts..
Bis sich verklebung der augen euch löst und ihr merket:
Zauber des Dings – und des Leibes · der göttlichen norm.

Lange zwar sträuben sich gegen die Freudige Botschaft
Grad eure klügsten · sie streichen die wallenden bärte ·[138]
Zeigen mit fingern in stockige bücher und rufen:

---

138   Vgl. in 'Der Krieg': Nie wird dem Seher dank.. er trifft auf hohn/Und steine · ruft er unheil –
wut und steine/ Wenn es hereinbrach. Angehäufte frevel/Von allen zwang und glück
genannt · verhehlter/ Abfall von Mensch zu Larve heischen busse../ Was ist IHM mord
von hunderttausenden/ Vorm mord am Leben selbst? Er kann nicht schwärmen/ Von hei-
mischer tugend und von welscher tücke./ Hier hat das weib das klagt · der satte bürger ·/
Der graue bart ehr schuld als stich und schuss/ Des widerparts an unsrer söhn und enkel/
Verglasten augen und zerfeztem leib.

> ›Feind unsres vaterlands · opfrer an falschem altar‹...
> Ach wenn die fülle der zeiten gekommen: dann werden
> Wieder ein tausendjahr eurer Gebieter und Weisen
> Nüchternste sinne und trotzigste nacken gefüge
> Ärmlicher schar von verzückten landflüchtigen folgen
> Sich bekehren zur wildesten wundergeschichte
> Leibhaft das fleisch und das blut eines Mittlers geniessen
> Knieen im staube ein weiteres tausendjahr
> Vor einem knaben den ihr zum gott erhebt.

Hier ist der Rhein ganz explizit der Fluss der Herkunft aus dem Süden, und wenn es heißt, den Deutschen fehle der Seher am Anfang der Zeiten, so deutet George eben hier in diesem Goethegedicht die Notwendigkeit des Deutschen zum Rückgang, zum 'Gang zur Quelle' an. Er – bei George – geht über den Rhein, über das Römische. Hat George gesehen, dass das, was er hier über das Deutsche sagt, dass ihm der eigene Anfang fehlt, es nur über den Rückgang zum Ursprung im Fremden zu sich findet, genauso bereits für das Römische gilt. Das Römische, das erst zum Träger großer Kultur wird in der Hinwendung zum Fremden, zum Griechischen.[139] Dort findet es seine Erfüllung in der Aneignung und Verwandlung dieses Fremden, und so wird das Römische zum Paradigma Europas. Mag sein, dass George sich dessen nicht in seinen vollen Implikationen, nicht in seiner Bedeutung zum Verständnis der römischen Kultur in ihrer Größe bewusst war – Goethe hat das nicht verstanden, Schiller in seinem Werk zur naiven und sentimentalischen Naturbetrachtung schon eher –, George hat es in seiner Dichtung ahnend ausgesprochen.

Im Hyperionzyklus lebt dieser Traum weiter, er wird gelebt im Scheitern und weist so im Scheitern auf die Erlösung in einer lichten Zukunft, die das letzte Gedicht (III) vorwegnimmt:

> Ich kam zur heimat: solch gewog von blüten
> Empfing mich nie.. ein pochen war im feld
> In meinem hain von schlafenden gewalten ·
> Ich sah euch fluss und berg und gau im bann
> Und brüder euch als künftige sonnen-erben:
> In eurem scheuen auge ruht ein traum
> Einst wird in euch zu blut der sehnsucht sinnen...
> Mein leidend leben neigt dem schlummer zu
> Doch gütig lohnt der Himmlischen verheissung

---

139 Die eigentümliche Entwicklung der römischen Literatur hat besonders Leo 1967 gesehen.

STEFAN GEORGE ALS POLITISCHER DICHTER 91

Dem frommen .. der im Reich nie wandeln darf:
Ich werde heldengrab · ich werde scholle
Der heilige sprossen zur vollendung nahn:
MIT DIESEN KOMMT DAS ZWEITE ALTER · LIEBE
GEBAR DIE WELT · LIEBE GEBIERT SIE NEU.
Ich sprach den spruch · der zirkel ist gezogen ..
Eh mich das dunkel überholt entrückt
Mich hohe schau: bald geht mit leichten sohlen
Durch teure flur greifbar im glanz der Gott.

Goethe gelang es, den Traum des Deutschtums zu leben, in positiv mit seinem
Leben zu füllen in seiner Gegen-wart – wie kein anderer je; Hölderlin ist der
Dichter der Zu-kunft: er lebt im Scheitern den Traum der Zu-kunft. Er wird
im Scheitern zum Verweis auf den Dichter der Zukunft, der Dichter, der das
Deutschtum erlöst, der kommende Dichterseher, der einst der Gegenwart den
Seher am Anfang der Zeiten neu zu-kommen lässt, derjenige, der auch George
nicht ist, den er in 'Goethes letzte Nacht in Italien' ankündigt.

Ich kann das hier nicht näher ausführen; es gehört auch nicht unmittelbar
zum Thema dieses Vortrags. Ich muss mich darauf beschränken, Georges Bezug
auf Goethe hier nun summarisch ohne präzise Textbelege zusammenzufassen.

Georges Erneuerung des Deutschtums ist Goethes Neugründung des
Deutschtums analog, in dieser Analogie jedoch auch notwendigerweise ver-
schieden. Die Ablösung der kulturellen Dominanz Frankreichs durch das
Deutschland der Weimarer Klassik bedeutete einen Bruch mit der Kontinuität
der europäischen Kultur mit ihren antiken Wurzeln in der *romanitas*.[140] Gerade
Goethe steht für die Wiederentdeckung des antiken Griechenlands in seiner
Andersartigkeit von der *romanitas*. Goethe war zu groß für eine pauschale
Verkennung der Größe römischer Kulturleistung, gerade seine Hochschätzung
Ovids in seiner gewiss nicht ovidfreundlichen Zeit beweist das. Jedoch rückte
mit dem Antikenbild der Weimarer Klassik das Römische an die Stelle des
Zweitrangigen, bloß Abgeleiteten.[141] Dies ging einher mit einer Abwertung der

---

140 Günther (in Vorbereitung).

141 Freilich muss man bedenken, dass Goethe das Griechische nur in seiner von einer
römischen Patina überlagerten Form in Italien kennengelernt hat, und das ist für sein
Griechenlandbild höchst bedeutsam. Sieht man Goethes Haus in Weimar, so ist es
unmittelbar beeindruckend, wie konsequent die gesamte Einrichtung antikisierend-
klassizistisch ist; so wie Goethe auf der italienischen Reise sich ausschließlich für das
antike Italien begeisterte und seine großartige mittelalterliche oder barocke Kultur links
liegenließ, das Antike jedoch in jedem noch so zweitrangigen Objekt bewunderte. Doch

französischen Klassik zugunsten Shakespeares, und diesen letzteren Aspekt nun hat gerade George und sein Kreis mit seiner Shakespeareverehrung fortgesetzt.

Bei George fällt nun freilich gerade seine starke Betonung des Römischen auf, das viel stärker thematisiert wird als das Griechische, das bei George lange kaum über einige pauschale Erwähnungen hinausgeht. Gestalt gewinnt es erst eben in jenem Gedicht 'Goethes letzte Nacht in Italien', wo Goethe der Vater des griechischen Traums des Deutschtums wird. Erst hier und im Hyperion gestaltet er, was er später als die noch zu erfüllende schicksalhafte Zukunft des Abendlandes in den Vers fasst:

Apollo lehnt geheim an Baldur.

Der Bezug zur *romanitas* läuft bei George natürlich über das Mittelalter, seiner Emphase auf dem römischen Element der imperialen Idee des heiligen römischen Reiches, die in der Erfüllung des Deutschtums in seinen lateinischen Wurzeln, die im Mythos des Staufers Friedrich II gipfelt. Das Mittelalter, das bei Goethe weitgehend ausgeblendet wird, ist natürlich zunächst ein Erbe der Romantik. Dass es bei George im wesentlichen der Erneuerung einer über Deutschland im engeren Sinne hinausgehenden Reichsidee dient, ordnet sich andererseits ihn verschiedene Ausprägungen derartiger politischer Alternativkonzepte zu Bismarcks Kleindeutschland ein, das George so glühend verachtete.[142] Nun spielt für Goethe Deutschland als politische Größe keinerlei Rolle, ganz zu schweigen von irgendeiner imperialen Idee; das lag außerhalb der geschichtlichen Situation seiner Zeit. Ganz anders bei George.

Spezifisch für George ist freilich zunächst, betrachtet man seine Vision der an das Mittelalter anknüpfenden Reichsidee, dass sie über das Mittelalter hinaus in die *romanitas* weist, und da liegt der wesentliche Unterschied zu Goethe: für George hat gerade das Deutsche eine ins Römische weisende Kontinuität

---

sein Bild des Griechischen war klassizistisch, so wie es das römische war; das veranschaulicht nichts besser als seine Weimarer Wohnung. Man lese nur die Reiseberichte über Griechenland Hauptmanns oder Hofmannsthals, im Grunde genommen kann man bereits die Dichtung Byrons heranziehen. Wer Griechenland kennt, der wird unmittelbar erfühlen, dass das Griechenlanderlebnis dessen, der Griechenland, die griechische Landschaft, das griechische Licht, die Trümmer der antike in dieser Landschaft erlebt, das Griechische ganz anders erscheinen wird als demjenigen, der Italien, seine Landschaft und die Antike, auch die echt griechische im Süden in diesem Ambiente erlebt.

142  S. Günther (2015).

STEFAN GEORGE ALS POLITISCHER DICHTER

mit der Antike, während für Goethe die Wiederentdeckung der authentischen Antike im Griechischen im Grunde genommen einen Bruch mit dem von einer Kontinuität geprägten Antikebezug der romanischen Kultur war. Dort, wo das antike Rom bei George in einer spezifischen Gestalt erscheint, erscheint es freilich nicht in der klassischen römischen Kulturepoche, es erscheint in seiner spätantiken Form, zudem in seinem Synkretismus mit dem Orient. Die zentrale schon im Frühwerk dominante Gestalt ist Algabal, eine Chiffre für den Verfall wie für den Zug zum Fremden, Geheimnisvollen zugleich. Das entspricht präzise dem, wofür Friedrich II in dem oben zitierten Gedicht 'Die Gräber von Speier' steht (das Gedicht steht im Kontext von Georges Empörung über die Öffnung der Gräber durch das Kaiserreich Wilhelms II).

Dass das Mittelalter in die römische Antike hineinweist und zugleich in deren dekadente und synkretistische Ausprägung in der Spätantike[143] hängt an Georges Interpretation der mittelalterlichen Reichsidee, wie er sie vor allem in den 'Gräbern von Speier' deutlich macht, und in ihrer Bedeutung für die Gegenwart wie es besonders scharf in 'Die Schwestern' deutlich wird.

In 'Die Gräber von Speier' legt George den Akzent gerade nicht auf den Stifter des Domes, Konrad II, den die deutschnationale Geschichtsschreibung, und nicht nur sie, als den erfolgreichen Gründer einer weltlich ausgerichteten Staatsmacht ansieht, auch nicht auf seinen erfolgreichen Nachfolger Heinrich III, sondern auf das Scheitern Heinrichs IV, und er charakterisiert die Salierherrscher von Anfang am als , im missglück fest, in busse groß'. Die vorletzte Strophe ist den Habsburgern gewidmet, wobei er vom Ende 'jahrtausendalter herrschaft' und 'tiefster schmach noch heut nicht heiler wunde' spricht:

> Urvater Rudolf steigt herauf mit sippe ·
> Er sah in seinem haus des Reiches pracht
> Bis zu dem edlen Max dem lezten ritter ·
> Sah tiefste schmach noch heut nicht heiler wunde
> Durch mönchezank empörung fremdengeissel ·
> Sah der jahrtausendalten herrschaft ende
> Und nun die grausigen blitze um die reste
> Des stamms dem unsre treue klage gilt.

---

143  Man kann hier Kavafis vergleichen, bei dem die klassische Antike kaum eine Rolle spielt; seine ‚historischen' Gedichte leben vor allem in der Spätantike und zum Teil im byzantinischen Mittelalter; vgl. Günther/ Kerkhecker 9ff.

In den 'Schwestern' spricht George von der Schönheit im frühen Tod der Erben des untergehenden Reiches einer Endzeit, die 'herrlicher als Andre/ Bescholtne kronen das erlauchte haar' trugen.

In dieser Geschichte des Versagens ist Friedrich II 'ein fremder gast', eine Episode, deren geistige Strahlkraft geheimnisvoll in die Gegenwart hineinleuchtet.

Die Geschichte des heiligen römischen Reiches ist für George die Geschichte eines politischen Versagens, seine positive Hinterlassenschaft das Aushalten dieses Versagens in Würde und Schönheit, seine Botschaft an die Gegenwart die Überwindung dieses Versagens im Verzicht auf einen konkret politische Anspruch und Wiedergewinnung einer ursprünglichen geistigen Dimension des Deutschen im Blick auf den jenseits jeder geographisch konkreten Dimension liegenden geheimnisvollen verborgenen Ursprung, der eben genau das Aushalten jenes Geheimnisvollen, den Verzicht auf die Profanisierung durch plumpe äußerliche Aneignung fordert.

Hiermit ist der Horizont abgesteckt, vor dem man Georges im engsten Sinne politische Gedichte in 'Das Neue Reich', 'Der Krieg', 'Der Dichter in der Zeit der Wirren' und 'Auf einen jungen Führer in dem ersten Weltkrieg' würdigen kann. Hier kommentiert George dichterisch unmittelbar das Zeitgeschehen, und diese Gedichte beziehen sich alle auf das epochale Ereignis des ersten Weltkrieges und die ihn umgebende politische Situation Deutschlands. Ich habe sie mit ihrem Fokus auf den ersten Weltkrieg bereits anderswo behandelt und möchte das hier nicht wiederholen.[144] Aus dem Horizont des hier Gesagten will ich mich vielmehr der Frage zuwenden, wie George in diesen Gedichten die, soweit ich sehe, größte im engsten Sinne 'politische' Dichtung seit der augusteischen Zeit in Europa gelingen konnte.

Ich habe diesen Beitrag mit den Erstaunen begonnen, wie der lange Zeit scheinbar dezidiert weltentrückte Ästhet Stefan George plötzlich sich zum explizit politischen Dichter wandeln konnte. Ich habe die Frage mit Stefan Georges Selbstdeutung seiner Wendung zum Zeitgeschehen in 'Das Zeitgedicht' beantwortet. Kein menschliches Handeln spielt sich in einem luftleeren Raum ab; auch die explizite Verweigerung ist ein politischer Akt. Das war George bewusst, er sagt es in den Worten:

> Gesang verklärter wolken ward zum schrei!
> Ihr sahet wechsel. doch ich tat das gleiche ...

---

144  S. Günther (2015).

Aber er sagt mehr. Seine Wendung zum Zeitgeschehen bedurfte des Anstoßes von außen nicht. Ebenso wie er ohne Anlass sich dem Außen zuwendet, bleibt er auch in den abgründigsten Umwälzungen derselbe, der mit dem 'Stern des Bundes' sein politisch wirkungsmächtigstes und doch ganz dem Weltgeschehen entrücktes Werk verfasst. Das Politische ist eine organische integrale Dimension seines Dichtens, aber nicht so, dass seine Dichtung des Politischen im äußerlichen banalen Sinne als Anregung bedürfte: sein Dichten umgreift das Politische als eine integrale Dimension des Menschlichen. Doch seine Dichtung geht noch nicht einmal in jenem Menschlichen auf, jenes Menschliche ist einbegriffen in die kosmische Dimension des Dichtens, welches das Menschliche in seiner Geschichtlichkeit im ursprünglichen Sinne deutet.

George gelingt eine dichterische Beschreibung des Grauens des technischen Krieges in wenigen Versen, die eindrücklicher ist als die authentischste Beschreibung eines Beteiligten, eine treffendere Analyse der politisch-gesellschaftlichen Situation, die zu diesem Krieg führte und die aus ihm hervorging, als der tiefschürfendsten Monographie eines Historikers;[145] dies gelingt ihm, da er die geschichtliche Bestimmung des Deutschtums in ihrer weltgeschichtlichen, ihrer kosmischen Dimension gestaltet aus der Perspektive des Dichters, dem einzig diese Dimension sich erschließt. Nur im Weltbezug des Dichters waltet der ursprünglich schöpferische Weltbezug des Menschen, der den Dichter der rein innerweltlich, bloß zeitlich gedachten Gegenwart immer schon voraus sein lässt. Der schöpferische Geist des Dichters lebt in der Gegenwart der Zu-kunft, der Gegenwart als der je neuen Zu-kunft der Herkunft. Das ist Georges Dichtersehertum; als Dichterseher in diesem Sinne verleiht er dem konkret geschichtlichen Augenblick durch den Eingang in seine Dichtung Dauer, lässt ihn im zeitlichen Wechsel das Eine sehen, 'das von je war, das kein andrer sieht, das währet' und ihm Gestalt verleihen im Sinne dessen, was Goethe so gedichtet hat:

> Lass den Anfang mit dem Ende
> Sich in eins zusammenziehn,
> Schneller als die Gegenstände
> Selber dich vorüberfliehn!
> Danke, dass die Gunst der Musen
> Unvergängliches verheißt:
> Den Gehalt in deinem Busen
> Und die Form in deinem Geist.

---

145 Vgl. dazu auch Günther.

Bleibt zum Schluss noch kurz auf die Frage einzugehen, wie Stefan George zu den ihn umgebenden geschichtlich-politischen Ereignissen persönlich stand. Bezüglich des ersten Weltkrieges habe ich anderswo bereits das Nötige gesagt. Insofern er, wie gesagt, ein Dichter mit seherischem Blick in die Zukunft war, ist die Frage durchaus berechtigt und bedeutsam, wie er die Zukunft Deutschlands sah, besonders auch konkret die Zukunft, wie sie sich unter dem neuen Regime des Nationalsozialismus, dessen Anfänge er noch erlebte, anbahnte. George hat es konsequent vermieden, sich in irgendeiner Weise für Tagespolitik vereinnahmen zu lassen. Er tat dies seit er sich Hofmannsthals frühen Aufruf zum Kriegspatriotismus sowie jeder Beteiligung an der Kriegsbegeisterung des ersten Weltkriegs entschieden verweigerte.[146] Er lehnte das deutsche Kaiserreich genauso ab wie die Weimarer Demokratie und den heraufziehenden Nationalsozialismus, da er die unkorrigierbare Schieflage der politischen Entwicklung Deutschlands seit der Bismarckschen Reichsgründung erkannte, und er erkannte sie, weil er wusste, dass Deutschland als konkret politische Größe zum Scheitern verurteilt war. Wenn sich der Kreis später 'Staat' nannte (im übrigen eine keineswegs unumstrittene Terminologie von Wolters), dann konnte das im Sinne Georges nur bedeuten, dass auch das wahre politische Deutschland nur in einem Kreis von gemeinsam dem geistigen Deutschland Geweihten als dem geheimen Deutschland bestehen konnte. Sein Neues Reich ist pointiertes ein geistiges universelles Reich, das jeder konkreten Tagespolitik inkommensurabel gegenübersteht. Wie hätte George sich denn auch konkret die von ihm in dem Staufer Friedrich ii verkörperte Erfüllung des deutschen Menschen in seinen lateinischen Wurzeln in der Politik vorstellen sollen? Im Anschluss der Schweiz und Italiens an das deutsche Reich?[147] Das wäre ein noch besserer Witz als der seiner Kritiker, George wolle die Deutschen zu einem Volk von Bamberger Reitern machen. Alles, was George von konkreter deutscher Tagespolitik erwarten konnte, war der Stolz, 'im missglück fest' zu sein – das Gegenteil von militaristischem Protzertum und chauvinistischer Expension.

Wenn George sich hie und da gegenüber Personen des Kreises wie etwa Edith Landmann zur Tagespolitik äußerte,[148] so sind Bemerkungen wie etwa, man habe Frankreich bereits 1890 in seiner Schwäche angreifen sollen – was seinen

---

146　Günther (2015).

147　Liest man George statt verfehlter Interpretationen seiner Jünger und benutzt zudem etwas gesunden Menschenverstand, so kommt genau das Gegenteil heraus von dem, was Robertson 2005 behauptet.

148　Landmann 1963.

STEFAN GEORGE ALS POLITISCHER DICHTER                                    97

früheren Äußerung zu deutscher Kriegspolitik diametral widerspricht[149] – aus
der Empörung des Moments über die Demütigung von Versailles durchaus
verständlich, aber für seine Grundhaltung bedeutungslos, ebenso wie seine
Empörung über Schwarze in den französischen Truppen, die ihn selbst in seiner
Dichtung vor der Gefahr der Blutschmach warnen lassen sollte.[150] Als Mensch
war George auch ein Kind seiner Zeit, der auch anlässlich des Boxeraufstandes
von 'gelben Affen' sprach.[151] Derartige zeitbedingte Entgleisungen müssen
weder verschwiegen noch sollen sie verharmlost werden: der Mensch George
war weder ein Gott noch unfehlbar. Sie betreffen freilich sein Werk und dessen
Gehalt in keiner Weise. Und Äußerungen in denen George von einer mögli-
chen Kandidatur zum Reichskanzler gesprochen haben soll,[152] sind allenfalls
'tongue in cheek' zu verstehen. Dass George selbstverständlich eine nationale
Erneuerung wünschte, dass er der Aufbruchstimmung der Anfänge der Zeit
unmittelbar nach der Machtergreifung ebenso etwas abgewinnen konnte wie
dem 'ungewohnten Eingefühl' zu Beginn des ersten Weltkriegs, ist etwas anderes. Er hatte damals keinen seiner Jünger gewarnt, nicht in diesen Krieg zu
ziehen, den er freilich explizit als nicht seinen Krieg bezeichnete und schon
im Vorfeld scharf verurteilte – im Gegenteil. Warum sollte er nun irgendeinen
explizit warnen, sich der nationalsozialistischen Bewegung anzuschließen,
auch wenn sie nicht die seine war?[153] Die einzige Größe, die George repräsen-
tierte, war er selbst.

---

149   S. Günther (im Druck).

150   "Die ihr die fuchtel schwingt auf leichenschwaden ·/ Wollt uns bewahren vor zu leichtem
      schlusse/ Und vor der ärgsten · vor der Blut-schmach!‹ Stämme/ Die sie begehn sind wahl-
      los auszurotten/ Wenn nicht ihr bestes gut zum banne geht"; heißt es in 'Der Krieg'.

151   Salin 1954: 260. Entsprechend steht es um die Zeugnisse, die für George persönlich oder
      Personen seines Kreises immer wieder angeführt werden, etwa in Lane 2011 oder .

152   Norton 2002: 543.

153   Wie oben gesagt, die jungen Leute des Kreises nahm George ohnehin nicht als geistige
      Partner, sondern als Erziehungsbedürftige wahr, und von ihnen zu erwarten, dass sie viel
      von ihm verstanden, wäre naiv. George hat weder mit dem Nationalsozialismus etwas
      zu tun noch, wie man ihn gerne stilisiert, war er ein Vater des militärischen Widerstands
      gegen Hitler, der immer wieder zum Alibi dafür gemacht wird, dass es in der deutschen
      Wehrmacht aufrechte (sogar zutiefst christliche!) Männer mit Gewissen gab, von denen
      einige einst als junge Leute im Banne Georges gestanden haben. Das Hitlerattentat
      Stauffenbergs und der ganze damit verbundene Zirkus war der dilettantische Versuch
      von hoffnungslos naiven politischen Kindern, die sich allenfalls fünf Minuten nach zwölf
      so ungefähr bewusst wurden, auf welch ungeheure Beihilfe zum Verbrechertum sie sich
      jahrelang eingelassen hatten, die dann ein dilettantisches Attentat planten, das nur schief
      gehen konnte, weil man zu einem direkten Attentat zu feige war, die ein lächerliches
      nationalistisches politisches Konzept von einem pseudoaristokratischen Deutschland

Wenn George in der Stimmung nach der Machtergreifung mehr als lau sagte, hier klänge ihm doch zumindest einmal von außen etwas von dem entgegen, was er schon immer gesagt habe,[154] so ist das schlichtweg unvereinbar mit der Deutung des enthusiastisch angekündigten Mann des Gedichtes 'Der Dichter in der Zeit der Wirren' auf Hitler; und wie hätte es auch je eine politische Partei sein können, die das im Sinne Georges *wahre* Sinnbild auf das völkische Banner heftet'. Wenn nicht in seinen bewusst uneindeutigen Äußerungen im Gespräch, so hat George in seiner Dichtung, liest man sie genau, unmissverständlich klargemacht, was er meinte. Unter seine mündlichen Aussagen ist allerdings das oft zitierte Wort zum Nationalsozialismus, "man solle nicht alles an der kleinen Judenfrage messen", höchst aufschlussreich, nur bedeutet es das Gegenteil von dem, was man auch im Kreis selbst hineingelesen hat. Man muss es im Zusammenhang mit der Äußerung sehen, er sehe für Deutschlands Zukunft so grauenhafte Dinge, wie niemand sie sich vorstelle und er sie weder aussprechen wolle noch könne. Weit davon entfernt, den lächerlichen Antisemitismus der Nazis entschuldigen zu wollen, meinte George mit dieser Bemerkung, dass mit dieser Bewegung weit Grauenhafteres auf Deutschland zukommen sollte als das, was sich im Judenhass der Nazis ankündigte (man lese dazu nur wieder vergleichend, was er in 'Der Krieg' über die vom Dichter geschaute Zukunft Deutschlands sagte). Und in der Tat hat der Nationalsozialismus nicht nur Massenmord an Juden, sondern auch

---

hatten, das nicht die geringste Chance auf Verwirklichung hatte, selbst abgesehen davon, dass es kaum auf alliierte Gegenliebe gestoßen wäre (was immer man von den Alliierten hält: Kinder waren sie nicht und mit Kindern hätten sie gewiss nicht verhandelt). Wenn es einen Mann des militärischen Widerstandes gab, der jedenfalls die Realitäten erkannte – und zwar sehr früh –, dann war das Canaris, aber deshalb war er allenfalls der größere Verbrecher (längst vor der Machtergreifung). Die deutsche Wehrmacht, die sich Hitler nach der Blomberg-/Fritzschaffäre noch zur Verfügung stellte, war eine Verbrecherbande – ohne Ausnahme. Das einzige, was man manchen zugute halten kann, ist, dass sie es früher oder später erkannten. Ein Persilschein ist das Affenthather des militärischen Widerstandes nicht. Dass manche in der deutschen Wehrmacht durchaus ein Gewissen hatten, zeigt nicht zuletzt das Schuldbekenntnis Keitels im Nürnberger Prozess, das mir jedenfalls Respekt abnötigt, wenn man es mit dem schäbigen Verhalten von Leuten wie Dönitz und Mannsfeld (oder auch Speer) vergleicht, die mehr oder weniger davongekommen sind, während man Keitel sein Recht, als Offizier durch das Erschießungskommando zu sterben, verweigerte und seine Leiche mit dem Strang um den Hals in der Wochenschau zeigte. Ein eindrücklicheres Beispiel für die widerwärtige Siegerjustiz der Alliierten gibt es nicht. Aber leider erging und ergeht man sich in solchen Situationen – und zwar tun das alle Beteiligten – in hohlen Phrasen und der Schaffung von Mythen.

154  Landmann 1963: 209.

STEFAN GEORGE ALS POLITISCHER DICHTER

unzähligen anderen verübt, vor allem war er aber wie George es in 'Der Krieg'
ausgedrückt hat, nicht nur ein 'Mord an Hunderttausenden', er war ein 'Mord
am Leben selbst'. George sah voraus, dass dieses Regime nur in der endgültigen
Zerstörung des Deutschtums als konkret politischer Entität enden konnte, wie
es ja auch tatsächlich kam. Deutschland gibt es seit dem zweiten Weltkrieg
nicht mehr; das sollte uns gerade heute nach der schäbigen und würdelosen
Wiedervereinigung klar sein[155], und ebenso wenig gab es seit Ende des zweiten
Weltkriegs noch etwas, was das Recht hätte, sich Europa zu nennen.

George sprach vom Krämern der Politiker des Kaiserreiches und der Weimar
Republik, dem eitlen Dünkel des Pochens auf hohle Überlegenheitsansprüche,
dem seichten Sumpf erlogener Brüderei, von Sachwaltern und Händlern. Ich
weiß nicht, welche Worte er für die Politiker Europas und Deutschlands heute
finden würde, wo man konsequenterweise in prosaischer Sprache bestenfalls
von Messerstechern und Taschendieben reden könnte, die sich für ein gutes
Taschengeld zu Handlangern des noch grauenhafteren Massenmords an
Hunderttausenden, des Mords am Menschen selbst durch die letzte Entartung
des Menschlichen im Amerikanismus gemacht haben. Doch obwohl George
all dies vorausgesehen hat, endet sein 'Sang nicht im Fluch', denn er weiß:

> Dass die erkoren sind zu höchstem ziel
> Zuerst durch tiefste öden ziehn dass einst
> Des erdteils herz die welt erlösen soll . .

Das geistige Deutschland, von dem George spricht, bedarf keines konkret
geschichtlichen Staatsgebildes, nein, sein Wesen liegt gerade im Ertragen

---

155    Da man sich heute so gerne für diese großartige Veranstaltung immer wieder auf die
Schultern klopft, kann ich es mir nicht verkneifen, einmal darauf zu verweisen, dass ich
den Fall der Mauer in England miterlebt habe. Ich kann nur sagen, als ich im englischen
Fernsehen die Mehrzahl der deutschen Politiker der zweitgrößten deutschen Partei und
den damaligen Berliner regierenden Bügermeister im englischen Fernsehen sah, wie sie
sich gegen die Wiedervereinigung aussprachen, fühlte ich mich an Kaiser Wilhelms II
Worte erinnert, als er im Exil von der Judenverfolgung der Nazis erfuhr und sagte: "Zum
ersten Mal schäme ich mich, ein Deutscher zu sein." Diese Würdelosigkeit und abgrund-
tiefe Dummheit, so als könne man unseren Landsleuten, die noch teurer für den verlorenen Krieg bezahlt hatten, die Tür ins Gesicht schlagen, ist für die Schieflage (wieder
einmal) der heutigen Bundesrepublik wesentlich verantwortlich. Ein Volk, das nicht
einmal soviel Würde besitzt, in solcheiner Situation durch eine Regierung der nationalen Einheit, die Probleme anzugehen, den Osten dagegen auf schäbige Weise kolonisiert
und seinen Menschen die Würde nimmt, verdient es nicht ein Volk zu sein. Von anderen
Erlebnissen und Personen möchte ich hier besser schweigen.

des Scheiterns im Äußeren, im Verzicht. Der Verzicht macht es frei, frei von jeder geographischen Bindung, das geistige Deutschland lebt überall dort, wo die Dichtung Goethes, Hölderlins, Georges gelebt wird, überall dort 'ist deutscher Geist', wie es der einzige Jünger, der groß genug war, ihn zu verstehen, Karl Wolfskehl ausgedrückt und im Exil in Neuseeland gelebt hat, in Neuseeland, soweit weg wie nur möglich von dem Deutschland, das, indem es ihm sein Deutschtum abgesprochen hat, sein eigenes Deutschtum verloren hat. Wolfskehl hat vorausgelebt, was wir heute erleben: während Deutschland sich selbst zerfleischt, Kant und Goethe allenfalls noch als Emblem primitiv rassistischen Überlegenheitswahns einer Mischung von verkorksten Bildungsspießern und kaum maskierten halbgebildeten Proleten im Munde geführt werden, wo Deutschland seinen größten modernen Denker als Nazi und Antisemiten zum Kehricht bestimmt, ist deutsche Kultur, die deutschen Klassiker, deutsche Musik, deutsche Philosophie in Ostasien lebendiger als bei uns, ist in Japan, Korea und inzwischen auch China Heidegger einer der meistgelesenen und rezipierten Denker, während Europa und Deutschland kaum noch zu belangloser Philosophiehistorie fähig ist.

George lehrt uns, das zu sehen und darin zu sehen, dass deutscher Geist auf Deutschland, auf Europa verzichten kann. Das geistige Deutschland ist ein Reich, das *vivit et non vivit*, das nicht untergeht, solange das Menschliche nicht untergeht. Geistiges Deutschtum ist der höchste Ausdruck *einer* – nicht der! – Grundkonstante menschlichen Wesens: es ist Heimischwerden im Fremden, es bedeutet den stolzen Verzicht auf hartnäckiges Zueigenhabenwollen, und dies ist der Verzicht, der gibt und nicht nimmt: er schenkt das Heimischwerden in einer langen Herkunft.

### Literatur

Aurnhammer, A. (2012), *Stefan George und sein Kreis: ein Handbuch* (Berlin – New York).

Günther, H.-C. (2006), 'Heidegger und Sophokles', in: H.-C. Günther/ A. Rengakos (edd.), *Heidegger und die Antike, Zetemata* 126 (München).

Günther, H.-C. (2015), 'Augustus nach 2000 Jahren', in: H.-C. Günther (ed.) *Augustus und Rom nach 200 Jahren* (Nordhausen).

Günther, H.-C. (im Druck), 'Stefan George und der erste Weltkrieg', erscheint in: A. Larcati (ed.), *Tra due fronti/ Zwischen den Fronten* (Nordhausen).

Günther, H.-C. (in Vorbereitung), 'Bossuet's Place in the Intellectual History of Europe', erscheint in: G. Ferreyrolles/ B. Guion/ H.-C. Günther (edd.), *Bossuet en contexte* (Leiden – Boston).

## STEFAN GEORGE ALS POLITISCHER DICHTER

Günther, H.-C./ Kerkhecker, A. (2008), *Der Dichter Konstantinos Kavafis: Einführung, Übersetzung und erläuternde Anmerkungen von Hans-Christian Günther, Nachwort Arnd Kerkhecker* (Nordhausen).

Heiseler, B. (1958), *Lebenswege der Dichter* (Gütersloh).

Heiseler, B. (1936), *Stefan George* (Lübeck).

Helting, H. (1999), *Heideggers Auslegung von Hölderlins Dichtung des Heiligen: ein Beitrag zur Grunsdlagenforschung der Daseinsanalyse* (Berlin).

von Hermann, F.-W. (1999), *Die zarte, aber helle Differenz: Heidegger und Stefan George* (Frankfurt)

Karlauf, Th. (2007), *Stefan George; die Entdeckung des Charismas* (München).

Kerkhecker, A. (ed.) (2007), *Litterae Augustae: Augusteische Dichtungen und Texte des Princeps in deutscher Übertragung von Josef Liegle* (Basel).

Kerkhecker (2009), 'Josef Liegle (1893–1945)', in: I. De Gennaro, I./ H.-C. Günther, *Artists and Intellectuals and the Requests of Power*, IATP 1 (Leiden – Boston) 17–24.

Landmann, E. (1963), *Gespräche mit Stefan George* (Düsseldorf).

Lane, M.S. (ed.) (2011), *A Poet's reich: politics and culture in the George circle* (Rochester).

Leo, F. (1967), *Geschichte der römischen Literatur: 1. Die archaische Literatur* (Nachdruck, Darmstadt).

Norton, R.E. (2002), *Secret Germany: Stefan George and his Circle* (Ithaka – London).

Richardson, R. (2005), 'George, Nietzsche and Nazism', in: J. Riekman (ed.), *A Companion to the Works of Stefan George* (Canden House) 189–206.

Salin, E. (1954), *Um Stefan George: Erinnerung und Zeugnis* (2. ed. München).

Schefold, B. (2013), 'Karl Wolfskehl: Der Fernblick des 'Exul' auf Deutschland und Israel', in: G. Margagliotta/ A. Roboglio (edd.), Art, Intellect and Politics: A Diachronic Perspective (Leiden – Boston) 435–470.

Schmitt, C. (1991), *Glossarium. Aufzeichnungen der Jahre 1947–1951*, herausgegeben von Eberhard Freiherr von Medem (Berlin).

Schröder, R.A. (1972), 'Horaz als politischer Dichter' in: H. Oppermann (ed.), *Wege zu Horaz* (Darmstadt) 37ff.

CHAPTER 7

# Patriotism and Pacifism: The Year 1914 for Futurist Vladimir Mayakovskiĭ

*Luigi Magarotto*

1. On October 26th, 1914, the famous Russian philosopher Nikolaĭ Berdyaev wrote an article for the Petersburg newspaper entitled "The Messenger of the Stock Exchange" ("Birzhevye Vedomosti"):

> The futurist war of the Germans has already given results. A part of the futurist program of Marinetti was achieved by German soldiers. They destroy old culture, raze ancient towns, churches, rob works of art. In order to justify this barbarism, German newspapers write that there is no reason to be sad because of the destruction of the ancient monuments, being Germany called to build new and more beautiful monuments. This is an absolutely futurist attitude that it was difficult to expect from Germany.[156]

According to Berdyaev:

> Futurism had to originate in Italy, in the land of the ancient and great Latin culture. Futurism is the feverish attempt to shake off the exhausting power of passed greatness, to burn the past in order to begin to live freely in a different way, creating a new life and a new beauty, which you may not compare with neither the early nor with the late Renaissance. In the futurist movement there is the insolence of the poor children of great fathers. [...] Futurism as ideology had to blossom in Italy, however, in Italy the futurist ideology has reached no authentic result. These results can be rather observed in the futurist war of the German soldiers.[157]

---

156  Berdyaev 2004: 19.

157  *Ibidem*: 92–93.

# PATRIOTISM AND PACIFISM

Russian futurists were also against the past. They promised to "throw Pushkin, Dostoevskiĭ, Tolstoĭ overboard from the Ship of Modernity" and for them "The Academy and Pushkin [were] less intelligible than hieroglyphics".[158] Berdyaev did not put the Russian futurists on trial because, in his opinion, there was no exhaustive power of passed greatness in Russia. Therefore, Russian futurists were simply modest followers, foolish imitators of the Italian futurists.

In 1915, Maksim Gor'kiĭ expressed a similar opinion; indeed, he even denied the existence of Russian futurism:

> In Russia there is no futurism, the authentic one, as the primitive Italian futurism represented by Marinetti. [...] You understand, in Italy oppress museums, beautiful architecture, the ancient sources of the culture and outdated ideas. They must get out of these bulky protections, jump out of this shell and Marinetti with the strength of his talent and the colour of his word infects youth and leads to an undoubted thaw. You cannot stop him. On the contrary, here in Russia, we have no fear of antiquity, it does not oppress us.[159]

Nevertheless, if the basis of both Italian and Russian futurism was a deep aversion towards the culture of the past, the attitudes of the two movements toward the war was very different. In his manifesto from 1909, Marinetti glorified war as the only "hygiene of the world", and in 1911, during the invasion of Libya, he published his serialized futurist reportage entitled *Battle of Tripoli* (*La battaglia di Tripoli*), where he celebrated the war as a form of adventure and theatre.

In 1914, when the First World War broke out, the Italian futurists showed an unbridled interventionism by using crude, vulgar and ferocious arguments. With the intention of pushing the Italian government towards war, on October 10th, 1913, the Italian futurists wrote a *Political Futurist Program* (*Programma politico futurista*) that was openly anti-pacifist. It glorified the conception of war and, once again, considered war to be the only hygiene of the world.

At the beginning of 1914, Giacomo Balla published a work entitled *Futurist Manifesto of the Man's Suit* (*Manifesto futurista del vestito da uomo*) in Italian. Almost immediately after, he translated the work into French and on May 20th, he gave it to the press under the title of *Le vêtement masculin futuriste*. Balla, however, was an ardent interventionist and a few months later, he prepared a

---

158    Burlyuk, Kruchënykh, Mayakovskiĭ, Khlebnikov 2000: 41.
159    Gor'kiĭ 2006: 252–253.

third manuscript, which he published on September 11th under the very eloquent title of *The Anti-Neutral Suit – Futurist Manifesto* (*Il vestito antineutrale – Manifesto futurista*). At the beginning of 1915, Carlo Carrà created a new style of painting that he dubbed "guerrapittura" (war-painting), according to which he produced various 'warlike' designs.

On May 24th, 1915, Italy went to war and when the government ordered the mobilization of troops, many futurists were called to arms: Umberto Boccioni, Luigi Russolo, Antonio Sant'Elia, Achille Funi, Carlo Erba, Ugo Piatti, Mario Sironi and of course Filippo Tommaso Marinetti. Apparently, they fought courageously and some of them were wounded, while Boccioni, Erba and Sant'Elia fell on the battlefield.

Participation in the war gave a strong boost to Marinetti's creativity. In any case, all his work is closely related to the war. However, for the Italian futurists and for Marinetti in particular, war, aggression, violence and struggle were not only the hygiene of the world and the tools to educate the world as a community of people, but "the truth of the world: the ultimate truth of nature and history".[160]

2. Mayakovskiĭ's point of view and that of other Russian futurists on the subjects of war and peace were completely different from that of the Italian futurists. In November 1914, Mayakovskiĭ began to deal with the matters of war, literature and art. He published some articles in the Moscow liberal newspaper "Virgin Land" ("Nov'"). In the article entitled "Russia. Art. We" ("Rossiya. Iskusstvo. My") from November 19th, 1914, the poet intended to show the "prophetic strength of the artist Velimir Khlebnikov" and to draw the consequences that "the formation of cubo-futurist poets, counting among its ranks such a warrior, had the right to require the primacy in the realm of poetry".[161] First and foremost, Mayakovskiĭ was interested in the defence of Russian art and Russian style. In particular:

> of that literature, which, having among its ranks Khlebnikov and Kruchënykh, did not arise from the imitation of books published in the 'educated' nations, but from the bright river bed of the native, primeval word of the Russian nameless poetry.[162]

For the twenty-one year-old Mayakovskiĭ:

---

160    Sanguineti 1975: 43.

161    Mayakovskiĭ 1955, I: 319.

162    *Ibidem.*

PATRIOTISM AND PACIFISM

It was time to learn that "to be Europe" did not mean slavishly imitating the West, did not mean being commanded by Verzhbologo,[163] but to tend to *one's own* forces in the same way that is done *there*.[164]

In the early months of the war, the Russian *intelligentsia* exhibited a decisively patriotic orientation, which was shared by the futurists. According to Berdyaev, they were not moved by the aggressive, interventionist spirit, characteristic of the Italian futurists, but by a more noble feeling "of love for the homeland, by the instinctive impulse to defend it from the enemy, by a holy wrath against the oppressors".[165]

Benedikt Livshits immediately participated in the military operations and was wounded. Vasilisk (Vasiliĭ) Gnedov was also called up during the outbreak of the war. Vadim Shershenevich volunteered to be sent to the front. Konstantin Bol'shakov left university and enrolled at the Academy of Cavalry Nikolaĭ and from 1915 was assigned to a unit at the front. Il'ya Zdanevich was drafted into the army, but for unknown reasons[166] was discharged in 1915 and began working as a correspondent for the daily newspaper of Petrograd, "The Word" ("Rech'"), which was an organ of the Constitutional Democratic (*kadet*) Party. Zdanevich primarily sent correspondences from the southern regions of Georgia.

In the early days of the war, Vladimir Mayakovskiĭ and Velimir Khlebnikov decided to volunteer to be sent to the front, but their requests were denied because they did not exhibit – in the words of Mayakovskiĭ himself – good political behaviour. Let us see what Mayakovskiĭ wrote in his autobiography *I, Myself (Ja sam)* about his desire to defend his homeland:

> The war. I took it with emotion. At the beginning only from the decorative, thunderous side. I draw posters to order and, of course, about the war. Therefore, the poem *War has been declared (Voĭna ob"yavlena)*.
>
> August: the first battle. Immediately the horror appears. War is disgusting. Behind the lines, it is even more disgusting. To speak of war, one

---

163    An important train station at the border of the Russian and the German empires.

164    Mayakovskiĭ 1955, 1: 319.

165    Berdyaev 2004: 6.

166    The critic Andreĭ Krusanov [Krusanov 2010, 1, 2: 481] claims he was unsuitable for the sight, while his wife Hélène Douard-Iliazd asserted that he was reformed for his short stature [actually was high m. 1,55].

should see it. I went to volunteer. They did not take me. Lack of good political behaviour.[167]

In the summer 1915, Russia suffered continuous defeats on the front, forcing it to retreat hundreds of miles. Continuously needing new recruits to replace the dead and wounded soldiers, the Russian army decided to call all men to arms, even if they did not have a spotless police record. Therefore, in October 1915 Mayakovskiĭ was enlisted, but the desire to defend his country –, as we can understand from his own words – had now completely vanished and he tried to do his military service far from the front, managing to find a place as a draftsman. In his autobiography, he writes as follows:

> They enlisted me. Now I do not want to go to the front. I pretend to be a designer. At night, I learn from some engineer to make drawings of cars. As regards publications, it is even worse. Soldiers cannot publish. Only Osip Brik is satisfied. He buys all my poems at fifty kopecks every verse. He published the poems *The Backbone Flute* (*Fleĭta-pozvonochnik*) and *A Cloud in Trousers* (*Oblako v shtanakh*). In printing, *The Cloud* became a cirrus. The censor blew inside. About six pages of dots.
> Since then I hated points. And commas too.[168]

In that same month, he reassured his mother and sisters, Lyudmila and Ol'ga, on his new position of enlisted subject:

> I was called up and sent to the motor school of Petrograd where I found a position with the technical design, as a skilled and experienced designer.
> Worry for me is not really the case. After work, in the school I can take care of the things I was doing before.[169]

Khlebnikov was called to arms in April 1916. Among the others enlisted were young painters such as Mikhail Larionov, Pëtr Konchalovskiĭ, Georgiĭ Yakulov, Vladimir Burlyuk, Nikolaĭ Burlyuk, Kazimir Malevich, Vasiliĭ Chekrygin, Pavel Filonov, Mikhail Le-Dantyu, etc.

There is no doubt that Mayakovskiĭ, along with his futurist companions, felt revulsion towards war. This is clear from his writings in his autobiography and his poems at the time.

---

167    Mayakovskiĭ 1955, I: 22–23.
168    *Ibidem*: 24.
169    Mayakovskiĭ 1961, XIII: 22–23.

## PATRIOTISM AND PACIFISM

According to their manifestos, Russian futurists pursued a clear program of dismantling the culture of the past in their literary and artistic endeavours:

> As you can see –, Mayakovskiĭ wrote in December 1915, summarizing the program of the futurists – no building, no comfortable corner, only destruction and anarchy.[170]

However, according to Mayakovskiĭ, the war itself contributed to their program of annihilation because "in history, violence is a step towards perfection, a step towards the ideal state".[171] The destruction of the old world shows that life does not stop; that "life goes on, creating a new beauty," a new art: futurist art. Because of the war, art is dead (that is, academic art: "The painters can get rid of the lying canvases making bandages for wounded soldiers"),[172] so it is necessary to shout "hurrah for art" – Mayakovskiĭ incites – because futurists have already prepared the way for a new art, post-war art, or the art of the future.

The cubo-futurist Mayakovskiĭ was disgusted by the war, but he was excited by its power and its destructiveness of the classical heritage, much like the futurist Marinetti, but for different reasons.

Mayakovskiĭ thought that the war stopped the development of the old art, thus simplifying the task of the futurists, while the leader of Italian futurism loved war as such, as a fundamental expression of being.

In the article *A drop of tar* (*Kaplya dëgtya*) of 1915, Mayakovskiĭ wrote:

> We consider the first part of our program of destruction to be settled. Therefore, do not be surprised if you see today in our hands, instead of the rattle of the clown, the project of the architect, and if the voice of futurism, yesterday still sweet of dreaming sentimentalism, today will melt into the bronze of the sermon.[173]

From these words, it seems that up until the years of the war, the futurists had behaved as 'jokesters' and 'fools'. After the war, the futurists proposed to become creators or inventors (following Khlebnikov's famous opposition between inventors [*izobretateli*] and acquirers or consumers [*priobretateli*]). However not all futurists shared Mayakovskiĭ's opinion. During the world war, the Russian cubo-futurists were divided into roughly two different camps. One,

---

170    Mayakovskiĭ 1955, I: 350.

171    *Ibidem*: 304.

172    *Ibidem*: 302.

173    *Ibidem*: 351.

led by Mayakovskiĭ, defended the logical and rational aspects of futurism, and found its realization in the October Revolution of 1917, just because that event would lead to the "third bloodless, but terrible Revolution, the Revolution of the Spirit".[174] The second, led by Kruchënykh, defended the alogical and transmental (*zaumnyĭ*) aspects of futurism. Picking up the "rattle of the clown" abandoned by Mayakovskiĭ and his companions, they furiously agitated it for several years.

Mayakovskiĭ addressed academic painters, advising them as follows:

> You, Repin, Korovin, Vasnetsov fill us with the last joy: sacrifice your paintbrushes making toothpicks for spineless vegetarians.[175]

In his opinion, academic painters were out of step with the times. They had formerly been important people, perhaps even great people. The poet, expressing a lavish, but hypocritical deference, promised to bury them "with honour in the front row".[176] He also addresses the writers of the old literature:

> Now there can be no place for those who do not understand us! [...] Now life has adopted us. There is nothing to be afraid of. Now, we will show daily that under the yellow blouses of the clowns were hidden vigorous bodies, essential to you as warriors.[177]

Defending the basic principles of cubo-futurism in literature, he argues:

> We must also show that the cruelty and the improbability of our language are not the result of grammatical mistakes of teenagers, but the conscious betrayal of innovators.[178]

In his article entitled *The Futurians* (*Budetlyane*), Mayakovskiĭ discusses the birth of Russian futurism and extolls the collectivist concept of 'us', stressing that the war generated this notion. Quoting a stretcher-bearer, who had just returned from the front, Mayakovskiĭ writes:

---

174    Burlyuk, Kamenskiĭ, Mayakovskiĭ 1918: 1.
175    Mayakovskiĭ 1955, I: 308.
176    *Ibidem*: 309.
177    *Ibidem*: 311–312.
178    *Ibidem*: 323.

PATRIOTISM AND PACIFISM

When the regiment goes on the attack in the mighty collective 'hurray', nobody can discern the voice of Ivan from that of the other soldiers, so in the mass of flying deaths, nobody can discern mine from others' death. Death swoops down on the whole mass of soldiers, but, powerless, it grabs only an insignificant part of them. Our collective body remains intact: in the war, all soldiers breathe as one person and therefore, they are immortal.[179]

We observe that the notion of the collective 'us' defended by Mayakovskiĭ during the years of socialism is the result of his experience in the futurist movement as well as his reflections on patriotism and war.

3. During the war, Mayakovskiĭ did not just write articles in the "Virgin Land" newspaper. At the very beginning of the conflict, between August and October 1914, he also created numerous anti-German captions in verse for popular prints and postcards. This sentiment in defence of Russia and against the German aggressor was revealed in both the postcards and posters drawn by him during those months. He worked in a team that included avant-garde artists such as David Burlyuk, Kazimir Malevich, Mikhail Larionov, Aristarkh Lentulov, Vasiliĭ Chekrygin and others. The war became a very important matter for Mayakovskiĭ and it became the primary source of his poetic activity. He wrote poems such as *The War Has Been Declared*, which was published in August 1914, and *Mama and the Evening that Was Murdered by the Germans* (*Mama i ubityĭ nemtsami vecher*), which was published in November 1914, dominated by a clear pacifism and, therefore, in direct conflict with the preeminent spirit of his captions in verse and of his posters.

Viktor Shklovskiĭ recalls:

In October 1914 in the magazine "Apollo" ("Apollon"), Georgiĭ Ivanov published the article *Ordeal by Fire* (*Ispytanie ognëm*). Here is what he writes: "Although it is strange, those who responded more weakly to the war are the futurists, although in the years of peace they had made it famous by all means. In a Moscow magazine, there appeared the scrubby and unpleasant verses of V. Mayakovskiĭ, V. Shershenevich and others".[180]

The poet Ivanov was right. When conflict broke out, many futurists, beginning with Mayakovskiĭ, began to write verses that were not patriotic, but pacifist.

---

179  *Ibidem*: 332.
180  Shklovskiĭ 1940: 74.

In 1915–1916, Mayakovskiĭ wrote a laconic and anti-militarist poem entitled *War and the Universe* (*Voĭna i mir*), which depicts the horrors of war:

> Everywhere the same:
> stone,
> swamp
> and hovel
> are soaked in human blood world-wide.
> Everywhere
> footsteps
> splashing
> kneading the smoking mass of the world.
> In Rostov,
> a worker
> on a holiday
> wanted some water for his samovar,
> but recoiled:
> in all the water pipes
> the same red slime oozed out.[181]

There is no drop of blood in this mass of carnage, of which Mayakovskiĭ declares not to bear the responsibility. The critic Vyacheslav Polonskiĭ found that the poet "shocked by the spectacle of the war, he stated the matter of the expiation of that horror".[182]

On this subject, Lilya Brik writes: "Like Dostoevskiĭ, Mayakovskiĭ was also dominated by the following obsessive thought: 'I alone am responsible for all'. We see it in his first tragedy *Vladimir Mayakovskiĭ*, when people bring tears to the poet. Then we observe it in the poem *War and the Universe*:

> I repent:
> I alone
> bear the guilt
> for the growing crackle of lives being broken;[183]

and again in the poem *About This* (*Pro éto*):

---

181    Mayakovskiĭ 1955, I: 225, trans. by Barooshian 1974: 51.

182    Polonskiĭ 1988: 222.

183    Mayakovskiĭ 1955, I: 230–231, trans. by Barooshian 1974: 52.

PATRIOTISM AND PACIFISM

On the bridge of the years,
   derided,
     scorned,
a redeemer of earthly love I'll be, alone,
I must stand,
    stand up for everyone born,
for everyone I'll moan,
       for everyone atone".[184]

In the early poems, such as *The Cloud in Trousers, The Backbone Flute, Man* (*Chelovek*) and in the tragedy *Vladimir Mayakovskiĭ*, the poet comes into conflict with God. Conversely, in the poem entitled *War and the Universe*, the author becomes a Christ-like figure, purifying humanity from evil and promising, in the conclusion, the final resurrection of the dead (according to Ezekiel,[185] Isaiah,[186] Daniel[187] and Jesus[188]). Human remains rise from the soil and take on human flesh:

---

184    Brik 1966: 207. Mayakovskiĭ 1957, IV: 172, trans. by Marshall 1965: 212. On this subject see Katsis 2000: 61.

185    The hand of the Lord was upon me, and carried me out in the spirit of the Lord, and set me down in the midst of the valley which *was* full of bones, and caused me to pass by them round about: and, behold, *there were* very many in the open valley; and, lo, *they were* very dry. And he said unto me, Son of man, can these bones live? And I answered, O Lord God, thou knowest. [...] So I prophesied as I was commanded: and as I prophesied, there was a noise, and behold a shaking, and the bones came together, bone to his bone. And when I beheld, lo, the sinews and the flesh came up upon them, and the skin covered them above: but *there was* no breath in them. Then said he unto me, Prophesy unto the wind, prophesy, son of man, and say to the wind, Thus saith the Lord God; Come from the four winds, O breath, and breathe upon these slain, that they may live. So I prophesied as he commanded me, and the breath came into them, and they lived, and stood up upon their feet, an exceeding great army (Ez 37, 1:10).

186    Thy dead *men* shall live, *together with* my dead body shall they arise. Awake and sing, ye that dwell in dust: for thy dew *is as* the dew of herbs, and the earth shall cast out the dead (Is 26, 19).

187    And many of them that sleep in the dust of the earth shall awake, some to everlasting life, and some to shame *and* everlasting contempt (Dn 12, 2).

188    Jesus answered and said unto them, Ye do err, not knowing the scriptures, nor the power of God. For in the resurrection they neither marry, nor are given in marriage, but are as the angels of God in heaven. But as touching the resurrection of the dead, have ye not read that which was spoken unto you by God, saying, I am the God of Abraham, and the God of Isaac, and the God of Jacob? God is not the God of the dead, but of the living

Whispering.
The whole earth
has unclenched its black lips.
Louder.
It is seething
with the hurricane's roar.
"Swear,
you won't mow anyone else down!"
This is the bones, now clothed in meat,
rising from the grave barrows.

Has it ever happened
that cut off legs
went looking for their owners,
that torn off heads were called by their names?
Now
onto a hacked corpse's skull
a scalp has leapt,
legs have come running,
and they are alive under the hacked corpse.[189]

---

(Mt 22, 29:32). And Jesus answering said unto them, Do ye not therefore err, because ye know not the scriptures, neither the power of God? For when they shall rise from the dead, they neither marry, nor are given in marriage; but are as the angels which are in heaven. And as touching the dead, that they rise: have ye not read in the book of Moses, how in the bush God spake unto him, saying, I [am] the God of Abraham, and the God of Isaac, and the God of Jacob? He is not the God of the dead, but the God of the living: ye therefore do greatly err (Mk 12, 24:27). And Jesus answering said unto them, The children of this world marry, and are given in marriage: But they which shall be accounted worthy to obtain that world, and the resurrection from the dead, neither marry, nor are given in marriage: Neither can they die any more: for they are equal unto the angels; and are the children of God, being the children of the resurrection. Now that the dead are raised, even Moses shewed at the bush, when he calleth the Lord the God of Abraham, and the God of Isaac, and the God of Jacob. For he is not a God of the dead, but of the living: for all live unto him (Lk 20, 34:39). Verily, verily, I say unto you, The hour is coming, and now is, when the dead shall hear the voice of the Son of God: and they that hear shall live. For as the Father hath life in himself; so hath he given to the Son to have life in himself; And hath given him authority to execute judgment also, because he is the Son of man. Marvel not at this: for the hour is coming, in the which all that are in the graves shall hear his voice, And shall come forth; they that have done good, unto the resurrection of life; and they that have done evil, unto the resurrection of damnation (Jn 5, 25:29).

189    Mayakovskiĭ 1955, 1: 236. Thanks to Donald Rayfield for the translation.

PATRIOTISM AND PACIFISM

In his review of the poem, poet and critic Dmitriĭ Semënovskiĭ notes that:

> unfortunate impression produce bizarre rhymes *glaz zare* – *Lazarej* [in
> the dawn of the eyes – Lazarus], *skòsite* – *kosti* [you shall mow – bones],
> *zalezhi* – *glaza lizhi* [layers – eyes licks], indeed they are monstrous.[190]

Boris Ĕĭkhenbaum asserts, rather, that precisely those "bizarre rhymes" show
the young poet's extraordinary creative abilities:

> Such the rhythm and such is also the rhyme. It appears in Mayakovskiĭ
> only there, where it is necessary, where it must be heard. Moreover, its
> nature is new. It resides on the stressed syllable because only this last
> syllable flies until the ear of the last listener, being always Mayakovskiĭ
> in front of the crowd and never in his study. He puts into rhyme *grjaz'*
> *vy* – *razve* [mud you – perhaps], *naprasno vam* – *prazdnovat'* [in vain
> to you – celebrate]. He cannot? No, he does not want because does not
> need the old compact rhyme. From his lips, loudly invoking the crowd,
> the accented vowels start flying with extraordinary strength and in them
> there is the whole dynamics of the poet, while the other sounds in any
> case lose their way, choke, jump off: it would be a strange pedantry 'boil'
> them until the end.[191]

During the writing of *War and the Universe*, Mayakovskiĭ was close to Maksim
Gor'kiĭ's political-ideological positions. In fact, the writer invited the poet to
become a permanent contributor to his review "The Chronicle" ("Letopis'"),
the first issue of which was published in December 1915.

At that time, Gor'kiĭ's political attitude towards the war was "defeatist".[192] He
asserted that Russia should put an immediate end to the war at all costs. One
can assume that Gor'kiĭ's anti-militaristic convictions, his views on the revolution and on democratic socialism exercised some influence upon the young
Mayakovskiĭ, who in the epilogue of his poem describes the reconciliation
of enemies[193] and the development of a utopian, idyllic post-war world that
would be dominated by peace and love:

---

190   S-kiĭ [Semënovskiĭ, D.N.] 2006: 408–409.
191   Ĕĭkhenbaum 2006: 385.
192   Brown 1973: 146.
193   Kantor 2008: 306–319.

Earth,
where do we find such love?
Just imagine –
there
under the tree
Christ was seen
playing checkers with Cain.[194]

Unfortunately, the fate of the world in the twentieth century took a very different direction from that as predicted by Mayakovskiĭ. In Russia, the Bolshevik revolution ushered in a terrible form of socialism, while in Italy, the government and the state came to be ruled by fascism. Nazism rose to power in Germany and then, a new world war broke out... It seems that Mayakovskiĭ was too optimistic in the epilogue of his poem.

## Bibliography

Barooshian, V.D. (1974), *Russian Cubo-Futurism: 1910–1930. A Study in Avant-Gardism* (The Hague & Paris).

Berdyaev, N.A. (2004), *Futurizm na voĭne. Publitsistika vremën Pervoĭ miravoĭ voĭny* (Moskva).

Brik, L.Yu. (1966) *Predlozheniya issledovatelyam*, "Voprosy literatury", 9 (Moskva).

Brown, E.J. (1973), *Mayakovky. A Poet in the Revolution* (Princeton).

Burlyuk, D., Kamenskiĭ, V., Mayakovskiĭ, V. (1918), *Deklaratsiya letucheĭ federatsii futuristov*, "Gazeta futuristov", mart (Moskva).

Burlyuk, D., Kruchënykh, A., Mayakovskiĭ, V., Khlebnikov, V. (2000), *Poshchëchina obshchestvennomu vkusu*, in: Terëkhina, V.N., Zimenkov, A.P. (edd.), *Russkiĭ futurizm* (Moskva).

Éĭkhenbaum, B. (2006), *Trubnyĭ glas*, in: *V.V. Mayakovskiĭ: Pro et Contra* (Sankt-Peterburg).

Gor'kiĭ, M. (2006), *O futurizme*, in: *V.V. Mayakovskiĭ: Pro et Contra* (Sankt-Peterburg).

Kantor, K. (2008), *Trinadtsatyĭ Apostol* (Moskva).

Katsis, L.F. (2000) *Vladimir Mayakovskiĭ. Poét v intellektual'nom kontekste épokhi* (Moskva).

Krusanov, A. (2010), *Russkiĭ avangard 1907–1932. Istoricheskiĭ obzor*, I, t.1–2 (Moskva).

Mayakovskiĭ, V.V. (1955–1961), *Polnoe Sobranie Sochineniĭ*, I–XIII (Moskva).

*Mayakovsky*, translated and edited by Marshall, H. (1965) (London).

---

194 Mayakovskiĭ 1955, I: 241, trans. by Barooshian 1974: 52.

PATRIOTISM AND PACIFISM     115

Polonskiĭ, Vyach. (1988), *O literature* (Moskva).

Sanguineti, E. (1975), *Ideologia e linguaggio* (Milano).

S-kiĭ [Semënovskiĭ, D.N.] (2006), *V. Mayakovskiĭ. Voĭna i mir*, in: *V.V. Mayakovskiĭ: Pro et Contra* (Sankt-Peterburg).

Shklovskiĭ, V. (1940), *O Mayakovskom* (Moskva).

*Beyond Europe*

∵

CHAPTER 8

# Dichtung, Propaganda und Polemik im Konflikt zwischen Schah Isma'īl und Sultan Selīm

*Max Scherberger*

In unserem Beitrag möchten wir einen Eindruck von den iranisch-türkischen Beziehungen unter Schah Isma'īl I. und Sultan Selīm I. zu Beginn des 16. Jahrhunderts vermitteln. Diese Phase der iranisch-türkischen Beziehungen war für die politische und religiöse Entwicklung in Iran und im Osmanischen Reich von herausragender Bedeutung. Sie bietet gleichzeitig eine reiche Auswahl an politisch und religiös motivierter Dichtung, Propaganda und Polemik in türkischer, persischer und arabischer Sprache, von denen hier einige ausgewählte Beispiele vorgestellt werden sollen. Beginnen werden wir mit dem Aufstieg Isma'īls zum Herrscher Irans, der in vieler Hinsicht außergewöhnlich ist und der die historische Entwicklung in Iran und seinen Nachbarstaaten entscheidend und nachhaltig beeinflusste.[195]

Isma'īl (1487–1524) stammte vom Derwisch-Orden der Safawiden in Ardabil in Nordwestiran ab. Die Safawiden waren ein ursprünglich sunnitischer Derwisch-Orden, der sich in Iran und in den umliegenden Gebieten, gerade auch im Osmanischen Reich, großer Beliebtheit erfreute. Im 15. Jahrhundert nahmen die Safawiden jedoch eine Entwicklung, die sie zusehends in einen religiösen und politischen Konflikt mit den muslimischen Herrschern der Region brachte. Zum Einen fielen die Safawiden von der Sunna ab und traten zu einer extremen und militanten Form der Zwölferschia über. Zum anderen wandten sie sich von der Mystik ab und begannen, nach politischer Macht zu streben. Sie warben Anhänger an, indem sie dazu aufriefen, einen „heiligen

---

[195] Die in der vorliegenden Darstellung umrissenen historischen Abläufe und Sachverhalte sind ausführlich in einer Vielzahl älterer und neuerer Abhandlungen nachlesbar. Außer den Beiträgen, auf die in den folgenden Anmerkungen verwiesen wird, seien hier noch genannt: a) zu den iranisch-osmanischen Beziehungen unter Isma'īl und Selīm: Allouche 1983: 30–130; Bacqué-Grammont 1993: 7–17; Özgüdenli 2006; b) zur Biographie Isma'īls: Gündüz 2010; Savory 1998; c) zur Biographie Selīms: Emecen 2009; İnalcık 2007; d) des Weiteren: Roemer 1989: 219–273, 389–408; Savory 1995: 765–768. Auf Wikipedia gibt es zwischenzeitlich ebenfalls zahlreiche themenrelevante Artikel, von denen wir die wichtigsten am Ende unseres Beitrages zusammengestellt haben.

Krieg" zur Verbreitung der Schia zu führen. Besonderen Erfolg hatte ihre Propaganda bei den turkmenischen Nomaden in Aserbaidschan, Anatolien und Irak, die sich ihnen in großer Zahl anschlossen. Auf diese Weise bauten sie eine Armee auf und dehnten ihre Herrschaft allmählich aus. Die safawidischen Krieger trugen rote Mützen mit zwölf Zwickeln, die die zwölf schiitischen Imame symbolisierten. Daher bezeichnete man sie auf Türkisch als *Kızılbaş* („Rotkopf" bzw. „Rotkappe").

Die Schia der frühen Safawiden war nach sunnitischen, aber auch nach herkömmlichen schiitischen Maßstäben extrem heterodox. 'Alī, die übrigen Imame und das Oberhaupt der safawidischen Bewegung wurden mit Gott gleichgesetzt. Sie galten als menschliche Hüllen, in denen sich das Göttliche manifestierte. Demnach waren sie alle miteinander und mit Gott wesenseins. Dies wird besonders bei Ismaʿīl augenfällig, der seine Anhänger dazu aufrief, sich wie beim rituellen Gebet vor ihm niederzuwerfen. Er verfasste Gedichte in aserbaidschanisch-türkischer Sprache, mit denen er seine turkmenischen Gefolgsleute mobilisierte. Sie sind ein wichtiges Zeugnis der aserbaidschanisch-türkischen Literatur. Sie zeugen von Ismaʿīls Vorstellung, dass 'Alī (ca. 600–661)[196] mit Gott wesensgleich ist, dass er selbst mit 'Alī, mit Muḥammad (570/573–632), mit anderen Propheten und Heiligen (Moses, Salomo, Jesus, Ḫiḍr[197] etc.) sowie mit Gott wesensgleich ist, und dass er gekommen ist, um das Licht des ewigen Lebens in die Welt zu bringen. Dadurch schlüpft er gleichzeitig in die messianische Rolle des verborgenen Imams, des Mahdīs,[198] der nach zwölferschiitischer Auffassung am Ende der Zeit auf der Erde wiederkehren wird, um die Menschheit zu retten. Außerdem setzt sich Ismaʿīl mit den vorislamischen Königen und Helden des persischen „Königsbuches"[199] (Farīdūn, Ḫusraw, Ǧamšīd, Żaḥḥāk, Rustam, Alexander der Große) gleich, die für sein Selbstverständnis von ähnlicher Bedeutung wie

---

196  'Alī b. Abī Ṭālib, Vetter und Schwiegersohn des Propheten Muḥammad, erster Imam der Schia.

197  Arab. „der Grüne", Gestalt, die mit dem nicht namentlich genannten geistigen Führer von Moses im Koran (Sure 18, 65–82) identifiziert und die in der gesamten islamischen Welt als Heiliger bzw. als Prophet verehrt wird (z. T. auch mit dem heiligen Georg identifiziert), Krasnowolska 2009.

198  Muḥammad b. Ḥasan al-Mahdī („der Rechtgeleitete"), der zwölfte (verborgene) Imam, nach zwölferschiitischer Überlieferung 869 geboren und 874 in die Verborgenheit entrückt.

199  Pers. *Šāhnāma*, epische, versifizierte Monumentaldarstellung der vorislamischen Geschichte Irans, vollendet von Firdawsī (940/941–1020) Anfang des 11. Jahrhunderts, Nationalepos der persisch-sprachigen Welt.

DICHTUNG, PROPAGANDA UND POLEMIK 121

die islamischen Heiligen waren. Hierzu die folgenden Beispiele aus Ismaʿīls Diwan:[200]

> Mein Name ist Schah Ismaʿīl, ich bin Gottes Geheimnis,
> ich bin der Anführer all dieser Glaubenskrieger,
> meine Mutter ist Fāṭima[201], mein Vater ist ʿAlī,
> auch bin ich der geistliche Führer der zwölf Imame,
> …
> ich bin der lebende Ḫiḍr und Jesus, Sohn der Maria,
> ich bin der Alexander unter meinen Zeitgenossen,
> …
>
> Ich bin Ḫaṭāʾī[202], mein Reitpferd ist rotbraun, meine Worte sind süßer als Zucker,
> ich habe die Essenz von ʿAlī, ‚der gebilligt ist‘,[203] ich bin die Religion des Schahs (ʿAlī),
> …
>
> Die, die ʿAlī nicht als Wahrheit (bzw. Gott) anerkennen, sind absolut ungläubig,
> sie haben keine Religion und keinen Glauben und sind keine Muslime,
> …
>
> Ich bin Farīdūn, Ḫusraw, Ǧamšīd und Żaḥḥāk,
> ich bin Zāls Sohn (Rustam) und Alexander,
> das Geheimnis von ‚Ich bin die absolute Wahrheit‘[204] ist in meinem Herz versteckt,
> ich bin die absolute Wahrheit, und was ich sage, ist Wahrheit,
> ich gehöre zur Religion des ‚Gottesfreundes‘ (ʿAlī), auf dem Weg des Schahs (ʿAlī)
> bin ich ein Führer für den, der sagt: ‚Ich bin Muslim‘,
> mein Zeichen ist die ‚Krone des Glücks‘ (rote Kappe der Safawiden),
> ich bin der Ring an Salomons Finger,

---

200  Zu Transkription und stilistischen Merkmalen unserer Texte vgl. Anhang.

201  Fāṭima (606–632), Tochter des Propheten Muḥammad und Frau ʿAlīs.

202  Arab. „Sünder“, Dichtername Ismaʿīls.

203  Arab. *Murtaḍā*, Beiname ʿAlīs, übersetzt nach Schimmel 1995b: 89.

204  Arab. *anā ʾl-Ḥaqq*, ekstatischer Ausruf, der ursprünglich von dem Sufi al-Ḥallāǧ (857–922) stammt, übersetzt nach Schimmel 1995a: 103.

Muḥammad ist aus Licht, ʿAlī aus Geheimnis,
ich bin eine Perle im Meer der absoluten Wahrheit,

…

Ich bin Gottes Auge (bzw. Gott selbst),
nun komm, verirrter Blinder, und schaue die Wahrheit (Gott),
ich bin das erste absolute Agens, von dem sie sagen,[205]
Sonne und Mond stehen in meiner Macht,
meine Existenz ist Gottes Haus, sei dir dessen gewiss,
du musst dich abends und morgens vor mir niederwerfen,

…

Sein Name ist Ismaʿīl, er ist wesenseins mit dem ‚Gebieter der Gläubigen‘,[206]
bei seinem Anblick wären die Abtrünnigen bereit, zu Stein zu werden,

…

Der perfekte Führer ist gekommen, allen Geschöpfen ist Glaube gebracht
worden,
alle Glaubenskrieger haben sich darüber gefreut, dass das ‚Siegel der
Propheten‘[207] gekommen ist,
ein Mensch ist zur Manifestation der Wahrheit geworden, wirf dich (vor
ihm) nieder, füge dich nicht dem Teufel,
Er (Gott) ist in Adams Kleid geschlüpft, Gott ist gekommen, Gott ist
gekommen,

…

o mein schöner Schah (ʿAlī), mein Mond, die Erfüllung meiner Wünsche,
Geliebter meines Herzens,
o Du, in dessen Schönheit sich Gott offenbart, der Auserwählte der
Heiligen ist gekommen,
erliege nicht den Pfeilen der Heuchelei des Asasel genannten Teufels,
nimm seine Hand, zeige ihm den Weg, der rechtgeleitete Imam ist
gekommen,
Pharao hat sich die Welt mit Zauberei unterworfen,
doch der Stab von Moses ist gekommen wie ein Drache, um ihn zu
verschlucken,
die heldenhaften Glaubenskrieger sind vorgetreten, auf ihrem Kopf ist
die ‚Krone des Glücks‘ (rote Kappe der Safawiden),

---

205  Erste Vershälfte übersetzt nach Halm 1988: 105.
206  Arab. *Amīru ʾl-muʾminīn*, Beiname ʿAlīs, übersetzt nach Schimmel 1995b: 87.
207  Arab. *Ḫātamu ʾl-anbiyāʾ*, Beiname des Propheten Muḥammad.

DICHTUNG, PROPAGANDA UND POLEMIK                                    123

die Epoche des Mahdīs hat begonnen, das Licht des ewigen Lebens in der
Welt ist angebrochen...[208]

Bemerkenswert ist ferner, dass Ismaʿīl im Jahre 1499, als er an die Spitze der
safawidischen Bewegung trat, erst zwölf Jahre alt war. In den folgenden Jahren
dehnte er seine Herrschaft über ganz Iran und noch darüber hinaus aus. 1500
stürzte er den Schah von Širwān. 1501 besiegte er die Aq Qoyunlu und besetzte
die damalige persische Hauptstadt Tabriz. Er nahm den alten persischen
Königstitel eines Schahs an und erhob die Zwölferschia zur Staatsreligion. Von
1503 bis 1508 eroberte er Hamadan, Isfahan, Schiraz, Yazd, Kerman, Diyarbakır
und Bagdad. 1510 besiegte er die Usbeken in der Schlacht von Marw und
dehnte seine Herrschaft bis nach Maschhad, Herat und Balch aus. Dadurch
erreichte das Safawiden-Reich seine größte Ausdehnung und erstreckte sich
von Irak und Ostanatolien bis nach Afghanistan. Das alte persische Imperium,
das durch die arabisch-muslimische Eroberung Irans Mitte des 7. Jahrhunderts
untergegangen war, war damit neugegründet. Durch seine vielen Siege erschien
Ismaʿīl vielen Zeitgenossen bald als unbesiegbar, und dadurch schien sich sein
Anspruch, eine übermenschliche, göttliche Natur zu besitzen, zu bestätigen.

Iran war zum damaligen Zeitpunkt noch ein weitgehend sunnitisches
Land, und der neue Glaube, die Zwölferschia, wurde von Ismaʿīl und seinen
Anhängern auf kompromisslose Weise verbreitet. Der islamische Gebetsruf
wurde um die Formeln „Ich bekenne, dass ʿAlī der Freund Gottes ist" (arab.
*ašhadu anna ʿAlīyan walīyu 'llāh*) und „Auf zum besten Tun" (arab. *ḥayya ʿalā
ḫayri 'l-ʿamal*) erweitert. Die Freitagspredigt wurde künftig im Namen des
Schahs und der zwölf Imame gehalten. Es wurde der Brauch eingeführt, die
drei ersten Kalifen Abū Bakr (ca. 573–634), ʿUmar (592–644), ʿUṯmān (574–656),
Muḥammads Frau ʿĀʾiša (613/614–678) sowie die übrigen Prophetengefährten,
die das Kalifat ʿAlīs nicht unterstützt hatten, zu verfluchen. Die Sunna wurde
unterdrückt und verfolgt. Muslime, die die zwölferschiitischen Neuerungen
zurückwiesen, mussten damit rechnen, exekutiert zu werden. Vor Moscheen
und Mausoleen der anderen Konfession scheint die Inquisition der Safawiden
ebenso wenig halt gemacht zu haben. So soll Ismaʿīl etwa in Bagdad die Gräber
Abū Ḥanīfas (699–767), des Gründers der hanafitischen Rechtsschule, und
ʿAbd al-Qādir al-Gīlānīs (1077/8–1166), eines der bedeutendsten Mystiker des

---

208  Gandjeï 1959, Nr. 16, 1–2, 4, Nr. 20, 7, Nr. 197, 3, Nr. 198, 2–6, Nr. 207, 1–3, Nr. 214, 4, Nr. 252,
     4–5, 9–12; Minorsky 1942 (Faksimile des aserbaidschanisch-türkischen Textes S. 1030–1041,
     englische Übersetzung S. 1042–1053): Nr. 15, 1–2, 4, Nr. 18, 7, Nr. 194, 3, Nr. 195, 2–6, Nr. 204,
     1–3, Nr. 211, 4, Nr. 249, 4–5, 9–12. Zu Ismaʿīls Poesie vgl. ferner Anıl 2010; Gandjeï 1978;
     Karamustafa 1998.

sunnitischen Islam, zerstört haben.[209] Immer wieder verließen Sunniten die von der Expansion der Safawiden betroffenen Gebiete und nahmen Asyl bei den Osmanen oder Usbeken, den sunnitischen Nachbarn Irans. Ein berühmtes Beispiel hierfür ist der Gelehrte Faḍlallāh b. Rūzbihān Ḫunǧī (1456–1521) aus Isfahan, der am Hof des usbekischen Khans Muḥammad Šaybānī (1451–1510) in Buchara aufgenommen wurde. Ḫunǧī rief den usbekischen Khan dazu auf, einen Feldzug gegen Ismaʿīl zu führen und die islamische Welt von ihm zu befreien. 1510 kam es tatsächlich zur Schlacht zwischen Ismaʿīl und den Usbeken, doch nicht Ismaʿīl wurde dabei besiegt und getötet, sondern Muḥammad Šaybānī. Danach blieb für Ḫunǧī nur noch die Perspektive, dass der osmanische Sultan die Safawiden besiegen würde.

Die Osmanen hatten ebenfalls eine feindliche Haltung gegenüber den Safawiden, weil ein großer Teil der Turkmenen, die von safawidischer Seite mobilisiert wurden, in Anatolien auf osmanischem Reichsgebiet beheimatet war. Die Osmanen versuchten seit langem, die Verbreitung der Schia in Anatolien aufzuhalten und die *Ḳızılbaş*-Turkmenen an der Ausreise nach Persien zu hindern. Außerdem kam es in den anatolischen Provinzen immer wieder zu religiös gefärbten Aufständen, die sich zu einer Staatsgefahr entwickelten. Damit waren die Safawiden für die Osmanen nicht nur eine äußere, sondern auch eine innere Bedrohung. Dies führte zu einem Wandel in der offiziellen osmanischen Ideologie. Die Osmanen waren von Anbeginn an sunnitische Muslime gewesen. Bisher hatten sie ihre religiöse Einstellung aber nicht mit Nachdruck vertreten und sich schiitischen oder anderen heterodoxen Bewegungen gegenüber relativ tolerant verhalten. Angesichts der schiitischen Herausforderung der Safawiden gingen sie jedoch dazu über, sich stärker ihrer sunnitischen Identität bewusst zu werden und sich zunehmend als Verteidiger „islamischer Rechtgläubigkeit" zu definieren.[210] So kam es nun auch im Osmanischen Reich zu Übergriffen auf die andere Konfession. Rebellische *Ḳızılbaş* wurden inhaftiert, zur Zwangsarbeit herangezogen, verbannt oder hingerichtet. Die öffentliche Verfluchung der drei ersten Kalifen war unter Todesstrafe verboten. Gemäßigte Schiiten, die keine staatsfeindlichen Tendenzen zeigten, blieben hingegen weitgehend unbehelligt.[211]

Sultan Selīm I. (1470–1520) war der erste osmanische Herrscher, der nicht nur die extreme Schia in seinem Reich bekämpfte, sondern der sich zu einem Feldzug gegen Ismaʿīl selbst entschloss. Der religiös-rechtlichen Schwierigkeit, dass er als Muslim nicht gewaltsam gegen andere Muslime vorgehen durfte,

---

209 Niewöhner-Eberhard 1975: 109–110, 116.
210 Eberhard 1970: 33.
211 Sohrweide 1965: 162–163.

DICHTUNG, PROPAGANDA UND POLEMIK                                    125

begegnete er mit religiöser Propaganda. Ṣarıgörez Nūreddīn Ḥamza (st. 1522),
der damalige Kadi von Istanbul, erließ eine Fatwa in osmanisch-türkischer
Sprache, die Ismaʿīl und seine Anhänger nicht nur zu Ungläubigen, sondern
zu aktiven Feinden des Islam erklärte.[212] Dabei wurde zum Einen Bezug auf
Verstöße gegen die Scharia wie etwa die Vergöttlichung Ismaʿīls genommen.
Zum Anderen spielte man auf Ismaʿīls Verfolgung der Sunniten an, die wie
eine Aggression gegen alles Islamische und gegen alle Muslime dargestellt
wurde. So erschien es geradezu als „heilige Pflicht" des Sultans, Krieg gegen
Ismaʿīl und seine Bewegung zu führen. Hierzu der folgende Auszug aus der
genannten Fatwa:

> … Muslime! Seid euch bewusst, dass diese Gruppe der *Ḳızılbaş*, deren
> Anführer Ismaʿīl, der ‚Sohn Ardabils' ist, die Scharia und die Sunna unseres
> Propheten (Gott segne ihn und schenke ihm Heil), die Religion des Islam,
> das Wissen der Religion und den unbestreitbaren Koran verachten, dass
> sie sagen, dass die Dinge, die Allah verboten hat, erlaubt sind, dass sie den
> mächtigen Koran, die Koranexemplare sowie die Gesetzesbücher belei-
> digen und im Feuer verbrennen, dass sie die Gelehrten und die Frommen
> hintergehen und töten, dass sie die Moscheen zerstören, dass sie ihren
> verfluchten Anführer zum Gegenstand der Anbetung machen und sich
> vor ihm niederwerfen, dass sie seine Majestät Abū Bakr (Gott möge mit
> ihm zufrieden sein) und seine Majestät ʿUmar (Gott möge mit ihm zufrie-
> den sein) beschimpfen und deren rechtmäßiges Kalifat bestreiten, dass
> sie die Frau unseres Propheten, unsere Mutter ʿĀʾiša (Gott möge mit ihr
> zufrieden sein) verleumden und beschimpfen, und dass sie das Gesetz
> unseres Propheten (Gott segne ihn und schenke ihm Heil) und die isla-
> mische Religion abschaffen wollen. Da sie die erwähnten und noch wei-
> tere ähnliche gesetzeswidrige Dinge sagen und tun, haben wir aus diesem
> bekannten und offenbaren Grund in gegenseitiger Übereinstimmung
> zwischen meiner Wenigkeit und den anderen Gelehrten der islamischen
> Religion gemäß der Scharia und in der Tradition unserer Bücher eine
> Fatwa mit dem Urteil erlassen, dass die erwähnten Personen Ungläubige
> und Ketzer sind. Alle, die mit ihnen sympathisieren und die mit ihrer
> falschen Religion einverstanden sind und sie unterstützen, sind eben-
> falls Ungläubige und Ketzer. Sie zu töten und ihre Gemeinschaften auf-
> zulösen ist eine unbedingte Pflicht und Obliegenheit für alle Muslime.

---

212   Einige weitere polemische Schriften gegen die Safawiden, die von dieser Zeit an im
      Osmanischen Reich entstanden, sind hingegen in arabischer Sprache verfasst. Zu diesen
      Texten vgl. ausführlich Eberhard 1970.

> Die Muslime, (die im Kampf gegen sie) umkommen, sind Selige und
> Märtyrer und kommen ins oberste Paradies. Diejenigen aber, die von
> ihnen umkommen, sind niedrig und verachtenswert und für den Grund
> der Hölle bestimmt...[213]

1514 zog Selīm mit seinem Heer nach Osten, um die safawidische Hauptstadt Tabriz zu erobern. Unterwegs ließ er zahlreiche *Kızılbaş* hinrichten. An Ismaʿīl schickte er mehrere Briefe, darunter eine Kriegserklärung in persischer Sprache. Darin bezeichnete sich Selīm als „Hort des Kalifats" und als „Sultan der Glaubenskämpfer". Dadurch kam sein Anspruch zum Ausdruck, der höchste Führer und Schutzherr der islamischen Ökumene zu sein. Außerdem bezeichnete er sich als „Demütiger der Pharaonen", womit er bereits auf sein Vorhaben anspielte, Ägypten zu erobern, das damals von den Mamluken beherrscht wurde. Ferner gebrauchte er Motive aus dem *Šāhnāma* und aus der vorislamisch-persischen Geschichte. So identifizierte er sich mit den großen persischen Königen Farīdūn und Kayḫusraw, mit Darius dem Großen (549–486 v. Chr.) und mit Alexander dem Großen (356–323 v. Chr.). Ismaʿīl setzte er mit dem Tyrannen Żaḥḥāk, mit dem König der Barbaren Afrāsyāb und mit dem letzten König der Achämeniden Darius III. (ca. 380–330 v. Chr.) gleich. Damit deutete er an, dass er wie die Helden der persischen Mythologie einen Kampf im Namen des Guten gegen das Böse führte, und dass er Ismaʿīl besiegen würde, so wie einst Farīdūn Żaḥḥāk, Kayḫusraw Afrāsyāb und Alexander Darius III. besiegt hatte. Hierzu das folgende Zitat aus Selīms Kriegserklärung:

> ... Diese vorzügliche Anrede erging von unserer Seite, von uns, die wir der
> Hort des Kalifats, der Schlächter der Ungläubigen und Götzenanbeter,
> der Zerstörer der Feinde des Glaubens, der Demütiger der Pharaonen,
> der, der die Kronen der Khane mit Staub überzieht, der Sultan der
> Glaubenskämpfer, der Farīdūn-prächtige, der Alexander-königliche,
> der Kayḫusraw-gerechte, der Darius-edle Sultan Selīm Schah, Sohn
> Sultan Bāyezīds, Sohn Sultan Meḥmed Khans sind, an dich, der du der
> Befehlshaber der Barbaren, der mächtige Feldherr, der große Anführer,
> der Żaḥḥāk der heutigen Zeit, der letzte Darius, der Afrāsyāb der heutigen Zeit, der berühmte Emir Ismaʿīl bist.[214]

Abgesehen davon erfolgte wieder die religiöse Rechtfertigung für den Feldzug, indem die Vergehen Ismaʿīls ähnlich wie zuvor in der Fatwa noch einmal Punkt

---

213   Tansel 1969: 35, Anm. 61.

214   Browne 1959: 13–14 (persischer Text mit englischer Übersetzung); Ferīdūn 1858: 379.

DICHTUNG, PROPAGANDA UND POLEMIK

für Punkt aufgezählt wurden. Selīm stellte zudem Frieden in Aussicht, wenn Ismaʿīl „zum Islam zurückkehren", seine Taten bereuen sowie die den Osmanen zustehenden „Burgen und Länder" aufgeben würde.[215] Die eben genannte Quelle ist nicht das einzige Zeugnis, das von Selīms Affinität zur persischen Kultur kündet. Er verfasste einen ganzen Diwan mit Gedichten auf Persisch. Auf Türkisch scheint er hingegen nur selten gedichtet zu haben. Bei Ismaʿīl war es genau umgekehrt. Seine Poesie ist größtenteils auf Türkisch und in deutlich geringerem Maße auf Persisch. Dies zeigt ein weiteres Mal, dass die osmanisch-safawidische Auseinandersetzung kein Konflikt zwischen Türken und Persern war, sondern dass sich vielmehr auf beiden Seiten sowohl persische als auch türkische Elemente finden.

Auf der Hochebene von Tschaldiran in Aserbaidschan kam es zur Schlacht, in der das mit Artillerie ausgerüstete osmanische Heer Ismaʿīl und seinen Kriegern, die über keine Feuerwaffen verfügten, eine schwere Niederlage zufügte.[216] Ismaʿīl musste fliehen und den Osmanen seine Hauptstadt Tabriz überlassen. Selīm ließ zahlreiche „Siegesbriefe" ( *fetiḥnāme* ) anfertigen, mit denen sein Sieg ausgewählten Persönlichkeiten wie etwa seinem Sohn und späteren Nachfolger Süleymān, dem Khan der Krim, den Anführern der Kurden, den Notabeln von Tabriz etc. verkündet wurde.[217] Diese Siegesbriefe enthalten noch einmal dieselbe Polemik wie die Fatwa und die Korrespondenz vor der Schlacht. Sie liefern keinen Bericht vom tatsächlichen Hergang der Kämpfe und erwähnen nicht, dass die Osmanen militärisch besser gerüstet waren als die Safawiden. Dadurch sollte der Eindruck entstehen, dass Selīm nicht aufgrund seiner technischen, sondern aufgrund seiner ethischen Überlegenheit über Ismaʿīl triumphiert hatte. Die folgenden Zeilen stammen aus dem „Siegesbrief", den Selīm an seinen Sohn Süleymān gerichtet hatte, einem Text in osmanisch-türkischer Sprache:

> Mein vortrefflicher Sohn, sehr vornehmes, glückliches, rechtgeleitetes Licht des Augapfels des Sultanats, Ländereroberer des Lichts des Gartens des Kalifats, mit allerlei göttlichen Gnaden Überhäufter, Stütze des Reiches, der Welt und der Religion, mein Sohn Süleymān Schah...: Weil sich der Aufrührer, der Ketzer und Häretiker, den man ‚Sohn Ardabils' nennt, Zwietracht und Aufruhr zum Untergewande (sowie)

---

215 Ferīdūn 1858: 380–381. Zu dieser Kriegserklärung vgl. ferner Hammer-Purgstall 1963: 404–405.
216 Zur Schlacht von Tschaldiran vgl. McCaffrey 1990.
217 Ferīdūn 1858: 386–396.

Unglaube und Häresie zum Überwurfe (d.h. zur Gewohnheit) machte,[218] sich mit der Heimsuchung der Diener Gottes brüstete und sich mit der Verwüstung der Länder schmückte, setzte ich ihm im Vertrauen auf Gott (möge Er gelobt und gepriesen sein) und auf die segensreichen Wunder des Herrn des Universums (Muḥammad) (Heil und Segen sei mit ihm) mit einem flinken, feindjagenden Reiterheer in die östlichen Länder nach; nur, um den Unglücklichen beizustehen und um den Unterdrückten zu helfen, um die Zeremonien des Glaubens wieder-zubeleben und um die Satzungen des göttlichen Gesetzes unversehrt zu halten. In den Tagen, in denen man das Meer überquerte, wurde (ihm) ein großherrliches Schreiben geschickt, das aus dem (folgenden) wertvollen Inhalt (besteht): In Anbetracht dessen, dass es einstimmig bezeugt wurde, dass du (Ismaʿīl) den Islam entehrtest, und dass sämtli-che Scheiche und Religionsgelehrten dich für ungläubig erklärten sowie eine Fatwa zu deiner Tötung erließen, wurde es zu meinem erhabenen großherrlichen Streben und zu meiner erlauchten Herrscherpflicht, den unreinen Fleck deiner Existenz mit den Klauen des Messers und mit der glänzenden Klinge vom Blatt der Zeit zu löschen...[219]

Des Weiteren erhielt Selīm zwei Lobgedichte, die der zuvor erwähnte sun-nitische Gelehrte und Dichter Ḥunǧī aus Isfahan zu seinen Ehren verfasst zu haben scheint.[220] Der eine Text ist in persischer, der andere in tschagha-taisch-türkischer Sprache. In dem persischen Text pries der Verfasser den siegreichen Selīm als Restaurator von Muḥammads Gesetz, als Erneuerer der islamischen Religion, als Garanten der Herrschaft der Scharia, als Kalif Gottes und Muḥammads, dem die ganze Welt zu Dank verpflichtet sei. Er forderte Selīm auf, den Kampf gegen Ismaʿīl fortzusetzen und diesen vollends zu ver-nichten. Außerdem setzte er Selīm mit dem „Zweigehörnten" (arab. *Ḏū 'l-qar-nayn*) gleich, einer Gestalt, die im Koran (Sure 18, 83–98) erwähnt und in der islamischen Überlieferung v. a. mit Alexander dem Großen identifiziert wird.[221] Ḥunǧī berichtet, dass der „Zweigehörnte" Kaiser in Rom gewesen sei und Persien erobert habe. Dadurch habe er die Reiche Roms und Persiens unter

---

218 Metapher übers. nach Zenker 1994: 545a.

219 Ferīdūn 1858: 386. Zu diesem und weiteren „Siegesbriefen" zur Schlacht von Tschaldiran vgl. ferner Lewis 1962: 193–195.

220 Glassen 1979: 178. Das genaue Entstehungsdatum dieser Gedichte ist nicht bekannt. Hammer-Purgstall zufolge scheint Selīm sie noch in Tabriz erhalten zu haben, Hammer-Purgstall 1963: 419. Alışık schreibt hingegen in Bezug auf den tschaghataisch-türkischen Text, dass er irgendwann zwischen 1514 und 1520 entstand, Alışık 2005: 78.

221 Hanaway 1998: 609.

DICHTUNG, PROPAGANDA UND POLEMIK

seiner Herrschaft vereint und sei zum Herrscher über West und Ost aufgestiegen. Auf die gleiche Weise solle nun der osmanische Sultan, der Nachfolger des römischen Kaisers, Persien erobern und mit seinem Reich vereinen. Hierzu der folgende Auszug aus dem persischen Gedicht:

O Bote mit glücklichem Aussehen,
bringe mein Gebet zum siegreichen König,
sage: o König der ganzen Welt,
an deinem Edelmut kann heute kein Zweifel sein,
du hast die Grundlagen für die Religion in der Welt gelegt,
du hast das heilige Gesetz des auserwählten Propheten restauriert,
du hast mit deiner Anstrengung die Religion erneuert,
die Welt bricht zusammen unter der Last ihrer Dankbarkeit,
wenn die Herrschaft der Scharia standhaft ist,
dann ist dies alles wegen des Glücks Sultan Selīms,
aus Ehrfurcht vor dir erzittern Persien und die Türkei,
denn du hast ihm die Krone der Rotkappen vom Kopf geworfen,
du hast ihm die Krone vom Kopf geworfen, o du Siegreicher,
und nun schlage ihm in deinem Mut den Kopf ab,
die Rotkappe ist wie eine Giftschlange,
du musst ihren Kopf zerstören, anders geht es nicht,
du bist jetzt aufgrund deiner edlen Eigenschaften
Gottes und Muḥammads Kalif,
willst du zulassen, dass die ungläubige und gottlose Bestie
die Gefährten Muḥammads beschimpft?
Wenn du ihn nicht zerbrichst mit Mannesgewalt,
wenn du zurückkommst, ohne ihn enthauptet zu haben,
wenn er begnadigt wird und in Sicherheit ist,
dann ergreife ich dich am Tag des Jüngsten Gerichts,
ich habe in den Prophetenüberlieferungen gelesen,
dass der ,Zweigehörnte' Kaiser in Rom war,
er nannte sich ,Besitzer zweier Hörner',
weil er das Reich Persien dem Reich Rom hinzufügte,[222]
seine zwei Hörner wurden zur Herrschaft in der Welt,
seine Verordnungen gingen nach Ost und West,
komm und zerbrich mithilfe des Glaubens das Götzenbild,
füge dem Thron Roms das Perserreich hinzu!...[223]

222 Zur Übersetzung von Vers 13 und 14 vgl. Glassen 1979: 178.
223 Browne 1959: 78–80 (persischer Text mit englischer Übersetzung); Ferīdūn 1858: 416–417.

Selīm wollte in Aserbaidschan überwintern und anschließend erneut gegen Ismaʿīl ziehen. Dann brach jedoch eine Hungersnot aus, und die Osmanen mussten sich nach Anatolien zurückziehen. Dieses Muster sollte sich auch bei künftigen Persienfeldzügen wiederholen. Aufgrund der großen Entfernungen konnten die Osmanen den Nachschub an Lebensmitteln nicht dauerhaft gewährleisten. Die Safawiden trugen ihren Teil dazu bei, indem sie die Kulturlandschaft der Umgebung zerstörten, so dass dort nichts Essbares mehr auffindbar war. Ismaʿīls Sohn und Nachfolger Ṭahmāsb I. (1514–1576) trat den Osmanen nicht mehr mit dem Heer entgegen, sondern ließ sie in seine Hauptstadt einrücken und solange auf seinem Territorium verharren, bis Hunger und Kälte sie zum Rückzug zwangen. Dies war die Ursache dafür, dass die Osmanen trotz ihrer lange Zeit gegebenen militärischen Überlegenheit das Safawiden-Reich nie erobern konnten. So gingen Selīms nordwestiranische Eroberungen zwar wieder verloren, doch hatte sich das Osmanische Reich durch seinen Feldzug bis zum Van-See im äußersten Osten Anatoliens ausgedehnt.

Ismaʿīl stürzte durch die Niederlage in eine Identitätskrise und erlitt bei seinen Anhängern einen Prestigeverlust. So konnte er nicht länger in Anspruch nehmen, unbesiegbar zu sein und eine übermenschliche Natur zu besitzen. Dennoch konnte er seine Herrschaft über Iran bis zu seinem Tod 1524 aufrechterhalten. Unter Ismaʿīls Sohn Ṭahmāsb kam es aber zu Aufständen der *Ḳızılbaş*, weil diese die Göttlichkeit des Schahs zunehmend infrage stellten. Doch auch aufseiten des Schahs vollzog sich ein Wandel. Bereits unter Ṭahmāsb wurde damit begonnen, die Schia der frühen Safawiden zu reformieren und extreme Elemente wie etwa die Vergöttlichung ʿAlīs und des Schahs abzuschaffen. Dies hatte zur Folge, dass Ismaʿīls Diwan ebenfalls teilweise überarbeitet und in seinem Wortlaut entsprechend geändert wurde.[224] Es wurde eine Form der Zwölferschia entwickelt, die mit der Scharia in Einklang stand.

Selīm scheint zwar die Absicht gehabt zu haben, nach 1514 erneut gegen Ismaʿīl vorzurücken. Tatsächlich unternahm er jedoch bis zu seinem Tod 1520 keinen weiteren Feldzug mehr nach Iran. Stattdessen führte er sein Heer nach Syrien und Ägypten und stürzte das Sultanat der Mamluken. Der Syrien- und Ägyptenfeldzug war rechtlich noch problematischer, weil die Mamluken keine Schiiten, sondern Sunniten waren. Doch auch hier wurden religiöse Rechtfertigungen gefunden. So hatten die Mamluken etwa ein Bündnis mit den Safawiden geschlossen. Daraufhin wurde auf osmanischer Seite u. a. der zuvor in der Fatwa angeklungene Beschluss wirksam, dass jeder, der die „Gottlosen" unterstütze, selbst „gottlos" sei und damit ohne religiös-rechtliche Einwände

---

224    Halm 1988: 109.

DICHTUNG, PROPAGANDA UND POLEMIK 131

bekämpft werden könne.[225] Der bis dahin in Kairo residierende Nachfolger der Kalifen von Bagdad übertrug Selīm nun auch offiziell den Titel eines Kalifen. Durch die Eroberung Syriens und Ägyptens fiel zudem der Hijaz mit den heiligen Städten Mekka und Medina unter osmanische Hoheit. Seitdem bezeichneten sich Selīm und seine Nachfolger als „Diener der beiden heiligen Stätten" (arab. *ḫādimu 'l-ḥaramayn aš-šarīfayn*) und übten die Schutzherrschaft über die religiösen Zentren der islamischen Welt aus.

Der Aufstieg Ismaʿīls und sein Konflikt mit den Osmanen waren für die Genese der neuzeitlichen Staaten Iran und Türkei von entscheidender Bedeutung. Iran wurde eine Monarchie und blieb dies bis zum Sturz des Schahs durch die Islamische Revolution 1979. Die Zwölferschia wurde eingeführt und entwickelte sich zur endgültigen Staatsreligion Irans. Im Osmanischen Reich und in der Türkei setzte sich hingegen bis heute der sunnitische Islam als herrschende Konfession durch. Durch die Eroberungen Ismaʿīls und Selīms waren ferner wichtige Grundlagen für den territorialen Bestand Irans und der Türkei gelegt worden. Iran wurde in seinen historischen Grenzen neugegründet, und die Osmanen gewannen Ostanatolien hinzu. Nicht zuletzt war die osmanisch-safawidische Auseinandersetzung auch für die europäische Geschichte von Bedeutung. So hätten die Osmanen, die bis vor Wien zogen, ihre Herrschaft noch weiter über Europa ausdehnen können, wenn sie im Osten ihres Reiches nicht in die Kämpfe mit den Safawiden verwickelt worden wären.

Mit dieser Einordnung der osmanisch-safawidischen Beziehungen in einen größeren historischen Kontext kommen wir zum Ende unseres Beitrages. Wir hoffen, dass wir unsern Lesern damit einen Eindruck von dieser wichtigen Phase der persisch-türkischen Geschichte sowie von der politischen und religiösen Propaganda, Dichtung und Polemik dieser Epoche vermitteln konnten.

Anhang: Transkription der aserbaidschanisch-türkischen, osmanisch-türkischen und persischen Texte

Alle unsere Texte sind im Original in arabischer Schrift geschrieben und werden im Folgenden in Transkription präsentiert.[226] Unsere Transkription des Aserbaidschanisch-Türkischen orientiert sich an der heutigen aserbaidschanisch-türkischen Lateinschrift und verwendet darüber hinaus bestimmte Zeichen der Transkription der Deutschen Morgenländischen Gesellschaft (DMG), um den Besonderheiten der arabischen Schrift gerecht zu werden.

---

225 Hammer-Purgstall 1963: 537.
226 Quellennachweise s. oben in unserer deutschen Übersetzung der Texte.

132          SCHERBERGER

Ähnlich verhält es sich mit unserer Transkription des Osmanisch-Türkischen, die auf der heutigen türkeitürkischen Lateinschrift beruht und ebenfalls entsprechende Transkriptionszeichen der DMG gebraucht. Unsere Transkription des Persischen erfolgt gänzlich nach den Regeln der DMG.

## 1     Schah Isma'īl (Ḫaṭā'ī), Diwan (Aserbaidschanisch-Türkisch)

Bei den folgenden Beispielen handelt es sich nicht um ein zusammenhängendes Gedicht, sondern um Auszüge aus sieben verschiedenen Gedichten, die in Isma'īls Diwan enthalten sind. Alle sieben Gedichte lassen sich aufgrund der Anzahl ihrer Strophen, aufgrund ihres Metrums sowie aufgrund ihres Reimschemas der Gattung des Ghasels zuordnen. Das Ghasel ist eine in den islamischen Literaturen (Arabisch, Persisch, Türkisch, Urdu etc.) weitverbreitete Gedichtform und seit dem 18./19. Jahrhundert (Goethe, Rückert, Platen) auch in der deutschen Lyrik anzutreffen. Ghaselen bestehen in der Regel aus drei bis fünfzehn Strophen (Doppelversen) und sind in quantitierendem Metrum (arabisch ʿArūḍ, persisch/türkisch ʿArūż) verfasst. Die beiden Verse der ersten Strophe enden auf einen Paarreim. Dieser Reim setzt sich in den weiteren Strophen als unterbrochener Kreuzreim fort, d.h. er kehrt immer nur am Ende des zweiten Verses jeder weiteren Strophe wieder. Der erste Vers der weiteren Strophen bleibt gewöhnlich ungereimt.

Der Inhalt des Ghasels weist in vielen Fällen sowohl erotische als auch religiöse Aspekte auf, und häufig lässt sich nur schwer beantworten, ob der entsprechende Vers von weltlicher Erotik oder von mystischer Gottesliebe handelt. Ein erotisch-religiöser Charakter tritt uns auch in den vorliegenden Dichtungen entgegen, die den Glauben an die Zwölferschia propagieren, die göttliche Schönheit 'Alīs und Isma'īls preisen und die Verehrung, Liebe und Sehnsucht gegenüber diesen hier als Manifestationen des Göttlichen bezeichneten Persönlichkeiten zum Ausdruck bringen.

Die angesprochenen stilistischen Merkmale sind in unseren Beispielen nur teilweise erkennbar, weil wir hier nicht die vollständigen Ghaselen, sondern nur einzelne Strophen daraus zitieren. So wird das angesprochene Reimschema etwa nur in den Beispielen richtig deutlich, die mit der ersten Strophe des jeweiligen Gedichtes beginnen und die mehr als eine Strophe umfassen (Beispiele 1, 5). In unseren weiteren mehrstrophigen Beispielen (4, 7) ist es ebenfalls noch weitgehend nachvollziehbar. Das quantitierende Versmaß taucht in unseren Gedichten in den Varianten *Hazaǧ* und *Ramal* auf:[227]

---

227    Zu den genauen Silbenlängen vgl. Gandjeï 1959: Nr. 16, Nr. 20 (Metrum wie bei Nr. 19), Nr. 197, Nr. 198, Nr. 207, Nr. 214, Nr. 252.

## DICHTUNG, PROPAGANDA UND POLEMIK

Beispiel 1 (insgesamt neun Doppelverse, *Hazaǧ*):

*adum Şāh İsmaʿīl Ḥaqquñ sırrıyam,*
*bu cümlə ġāzīlərüñ sərvəriyəm,*
*anam dur Fāṭimə atam ʿƏlī dur,*
*on iki imāmuñ mən dax pīriyəm,*
*...*
*Xıżr-ı zində ilə ʿİsā Məryəm,*
*zamānə əhlinüñ İsgəndəriyəm,*
*...*

Beispiel 2 (insgesamt sieben Doppelverse, *Hazaǧ*):

*Xəṭāʾī-am al atluyam sözü şəkərdən datluyam,*
*Murtəżā ʿƏlī ẕātluyam ġāzīlər dīn-i şāh mənəm,*
*...*

Beispiel 3 (insgesamt fünf Doppelverse, *Ramal*):

*ʿƏlīni Ḥaqq bilməyənlər kāfir-i müṭləq olur,*
*dīni yox imānı yox ol nā-müsəlmān dur bugün,*
*...*

Beispiel 4 (insgesamt sieben Doppelverse, *Hazaǧ*):

*Fərīdūn Xusrəv ü Cəmşīd ü Żəḥḥāk,*
*ki ibn-i Zāl həm İsgəndərəm mən,*
*ənā ʾl-Ḥaqq sırrı uş göñlümde gizlü,*
*ki Ḥaqq-ı müṭləqəm ḥaqq söylərəm mən,*
*mövlā məẕhəbəm şāhuñ yolında,*
*müsəlmānam deyənə rəhbərəm mən,*
*nişānum dur mənüm tāc-ı səʿādət,*
*Süleymān əlinə əngüştərəm mən,*
*Məḥəmməd nūrdan dur ʿƏlī sırrdan,*
*ḥəqīqət bəḥr içində gövhərəm mən,*
*...*

Beispiel 5 (insgesamt sieben Doppelverse, *Hazaǧ*):

*ʿƏynu ʾllāham ʿƏynu ʾllāham ʿƏynu ʾllāh,*
*gəl imdi Ḥaqqı gör ey kör-i gümrāh,*

*mənəm ol Fā'il-i müṭləq ki derlər,*
*mənüm ḥökmümdə dür xūrşīd ilə māh,*
*vücūdum Beytü 'llāh dur yəqīn bil,*
*sücūdum səñə dur şām ü səḥər-gāh,*
*…*

Beispiel 6 (insgesamt vier Doppelverse, *Ramal*):

*ismi İsma'īl dur ū-rā həm ẕāt-ı əmīrü 'l-mö'minīn,*
*yüzini görgəç xəvāric rāżī dur daş olmaġa,*
*…*

Beispiel 7 (insgesamt 15 Doppelverse, *Hazaǧ*):

*erişdi mürşid-i kāmil xamu xalqa īmān oldı,*
*sevindi ġāzīlər cümlə ki xətm-i ənbiyā gəldi,*
*Ḥaqqa məẕhər durur ādam sücūd et uyma şeyṭāna,*
*ki Ādəm donına girmiş Xudā gəldi Xudā gəldi,*
*…*
*gözəl şāhum qamər māhum murād-gāhum göñül-xwāhum,*
*cəmāli məẕhər-i Allāhum gözin-i övliyā gəldi,*
*'Əẕāzīl adlu şeyṭānuñ tīr-i təqlīdinə uyma,*
*əlin dut Ḥaqq yolın görsət imām-ı rəh-nümā gəldi,*
*cihānı siḥr ilən Fir'ovn özinə tābi' etmişdi,*
*olları yutmaġa Mūsā 'əşāsı əždahā gəldi,*
*bahādır ġāzīlər qopdı başında tāc-ı dövlət var,*
*olur mehdī-i zamān dövri cihān nūr-i bəqā gəldi…*

## 2 Nūreddīn Ḥamza Şarıgörez, Fatwa gegen Isma'īl und die *Kızılbaş* (Osmanisch-Türkisch)

Bei dem folgenden Abschnitt handelt es sich um einen Prosatext mit religiös-rechtlichem Anspruch, der keine poetischen Aspekte aufweist:

*…müslümānlar bilüñ ve āgāh oluñ şol ṭā'ife-i Kızılbaş ki re'īsleri Erdebīl-oġlı İsma'īl-dir peyġamberimiziñ 'aleyhi 'ṣ-ṣalātü ve 's-selām şerī'atını ve sünnetini ve dīn-i İslām ve 'ilm-i dīni ve Kur'ān-ı mübīni istiḥfāf etdikleri ve daḥi Allāhu te'ālā ḥarām kılduġı günāhlara ḥelāldir dedikleri ve istiḥfāfları ve Kur'ān-ı 'aẓīm ve muṣḥafları ve kütüb-i şerī'atı taḥkīr edüb oda yakdıkları ve daḥi 'ulemāya ve ṣuleḥāya ihāne edüb kırub mescidleri yıkdıkları ve daḥi*

# DICHTUNG, PROPAGANDA UND POLEMIK

135

*re'īsleri la'īni ma'būd yerine ḳoyub secde etdikleri ve daḫi ḥażreti-i Ebū Bekr'e*
*raḍiya 'llāhu te'ālā 'anhu ve ḥażret-i 'Ömer'e raḍiya 'llāhu te'ālā 'anhu söğüb*
*ḫilāfetlerine inkār etdikleri ve daḫi peyğamberimiziñ ḫātūnı 'Ā'iṣe anamıza*
*raḍiya 'llāhu te'ālā 'anhā iftirā edüb söğdükleri ve daḫi peyğamberimiziñ*
*'aleyhi ṣ-ṣalātü ve 's-selām ṣer'ini ve dīn-i İslāmı götürmek ḳaṣdın etdikleri*
*bu ẕikr olunan ve daḫi bunlaruñ emẟāli ṣer'a muḫālif ḳavilleri ve fi'illeri bu*
*faḳīr ḳatında ve bāḳī 'ulemā'-ı dīn-i İslām ḳatlarında tevātürle ma'lūm ve*
*ẓāhir oldığı sebebden biz daḫi ṣerī'atıñ ḥükmi ve kitāblarımızıñ naḳli ile*
*fetvā verdük ki ol ẕikr olunan ṭā'ife kāfirlerdir ve mülḥidlerdir ve daḫi her*
*kimse ki anlara meyl edüb ol bāṭıl dīnlerine rāżı ve mu'āvin olalar anlar*
*daḫi kāfirlerdir ve mülḥidlerdir bunları ḳırub cemā'atların ḍaǧıtmaḳ cem'-i*
*müslümānlara vācib ve farżdır müslümānlardan ölenler sa'īd ve ṣehīd cen-*
*net-i a'lādadır ve anlardan ölenler ḫor ve ḥaḳīr cehennemiñ dibindedir...*

3  **Sultan Selīm, Kriegserklärung an Schah Isma'īl (Persisch)**

Der Text, aus dem der folgende Abschnitt stammt, stellt kein Gedicht im
eigentlichen Sinn dar. Er ist weder in Versen angeordnet noch folgt er einem
bestimmten Metrum. Allerdings weist er insofern einen poetischen Aspekt
auf, dass er die für das herrschaftliche türkische und persische Schrifttum typi-
schen Aufzählungen enthält, die aus zahlreichen sich reimenden Einzelteilen
bestehen (*ḫiṭāb-i mustaṭāb, ǧināb-i ḫilāfat-ma'āb, qātilu 'l-kafara wa 'l-muṣrikīn,*
*qāmi'-i a'dā'i 'd-dīn, murǧim-i unūfi 'l-farā'īn* etc.):

> ... *īn ḫiṭāb-i mustaṭāb az ǧināb-i ḫilāfat-ma'āb-i mā ki qātilu 'l-kafara wa*
> *'l-muṣrikīn qāmi'-i a'dā'i 'd-dīn murǧim-i unūfi 'l-farā'īn mu'affiru tīǧāni*
> *'l-ḥawāqīn sulṭānu 'l-ǧuzāt wa 'l-muǧāhidīn Farīdūn-far Sikandar-dar*
> *Kayḫusraw-i 'adl u dād Dārā-yi 'ālī-niẓād Sulṭān Salīm-ṣāh bin Sulṭān*
> *Bāyazīd bin Sulṭān Muḥammad Ḫān-īm ba-sū-yi tū ki farmān-dih-i 'Aǧam*
> *sipahsālār-i a'ẓam sardār-i mu'aẓẓam Żaḥḥāk-i rūzigār Dārāb-i gīr u dār*
> *Afrāsyāb-i 'ahd Amīr Isma'īl-i nāmdārī samt-i ṣudūr yāft...*

4  **Sultan Selīm, „Siegesbrief" (*fetiḥnāme*) an Süleymān**
   **(Osmanisch-Türkisch)**

Der Text, aus dem der folgende Abschnitt stammt, ist wieder kein Gedicht
im eigentlichen Sinn, weist aber wie die Kriegserklärung zuvor zahlreiche
Aufzählungen sich reimender Einzelteile auf (*Ferzend-i ercümend, fitne ü fesād*
*ṣi'ār, küfr ü ilḥādı dīṧār, ta'ẕīb-i 'ibādı iftiḫār* etc.):

136  

*Ferzend-i ercümend emced erşed es'ad nūr-u ḥadaḳa-ı salṭanat ve kişver-
küşa-yı nūr-u ḥadīḳa-ı ḫilāfet ve fermān-revā-yu 'l-maḫfūf bi-şünūfi
laṭāyıfı 'avāṭıfı 'llāh 'aḍuḍu 'd-devle ve 'd-dünyā ve 'd-dīn oġlım Süleymān
Şāh ... Erdebīl oġlı denen müfsid ve zındīḳ ve mülḥid fitne ve fesād şi'ār ve
küfr ü ilḥādı diṣār ve ta'ẕīb-i 'ibādı iftiḫār ve taḥrīb-i bilādı pīrāye-i rüzgār
edindiği sebebden mahzan i'ānet-i melhūfīn ve iġāṣet-i mazlūmīn ve iḥyā'-ı
merāsim-i dīn ve ibḳā'-ı nevāmīs-i şer'-i mübīn etmek içün ḥaḳḳ-ı sübḥān ve
te'ālāya tevekkül ve seyyid-i kā'ināt 'aleyhi 'ṣ-ṣalātü ve 's-selāmıñ mu'cizāt-i
bā berekātına tevessül edüb leşker-i tāzī-süvār-ı ḥaşm-şikār ile anıñ ḳaṣdına
bilād-ı şarḳa teveccüh etmişidim deñizden 'ubūr olındıġı eyyāmda ḥükm-ü
şerīf gönderilüb maẓmūn-u 'izzet-maḳrūnında hetk-i perde-i İslām etdiğiñ
ḥadd-ı tevātüre yetişüb meşāyiḫ ve 'ulemā bi-esrihim küfrine ḥükm eyleyüb
ḳatline fetvā verdikleri cihetden noḳṭa-ı vücūd-u nāpākıñı aẓfār-ı ḥancer ve
tīġ-i ābdārla ṣafḥa-ı rüzgārdan ḥakk eylemek himmet-i 'alīye-i şāhāne ve
ẕimmet-i senīye-i pādişāhānemize vācib ve lāzım olmışdır ...*

5     **Faḍlallāh b. Rūzbihān Ḫunǧī (wahrscheinlicher Verfasser),
Lob- und Bittgedicht an Sultan Selīm (Persisch)**

Das folgende Beispiel ist Teil eines Gedichtes, das sich aufgrund der Anzahl
seiner Strophen, aufgrund seines Versmaßes sowie aufgrund seines Inhalts als
Qaside erweist. Die Qaside ist neben dem Ghasel (s. o. 1) eine weitere klassische
Gedichtform der islamischen Literatur. Qasiden bestehen häufig aus fünfzehn
bis dreißig oder noch mehr Strophen (Doppelversen) und sind wie Ghaselen
in quantitierendem Metrum verfasst. Nicht selten liegt ihnen dasselbe
Reimschema wie den Ghaselen zugrunde, d.h. der Reim der ersten Strophe
taucht im letzten Vers jeder weiteren Strophe auf. In dieser Hinsicht nimmt das
vorliegende Gedicht eine Sonderstellung ein, weil es nicht dem durchgängigen
Reimschema folgt, sondern aus Paarreimen besteht, d.h. sich in jeder Strophe
jeweils der erste und zweite Vers reimen. Bei Qasiden handelt es sich in der
Regel um Gedichte, die zum Lob Gottes oder bestimmter Persönlichkeiten
(der Prophet, Heilige, Herrscher, politische oder religiöse Würdenträger) bzw.
zur Schmähung von Feinden verfasst werden und in denen der Dichter Bitten
und Wünsche an seine Adressaten richtet. Daher auch die Bezeichnung dieser
Gedichtform als Qaside, was man mit „Zweckgedicht" (von arabisch *qaṣada*
„abzielen auf, bezwecken") übersetzen kann. Das vorliegende Gedicht weist
alle diese Aspekte auf: Der Dichter lobt und preist den siegreichen Selīm, er
verunglimpft Isma'īl und seine Anhänger, und er möchte mit seinen Versen
den osmanischen Sultan zu einem Feldzug gegen die Verunglimpften zur

## DICHTUNG, PROPAGANDA UND POLEMIK

„Befreiung der islamischen Gemeinde" bewegen. Bei den folgenden Versen handelt es sich um die Strophen 2 bis 17 dieses Gedichtes, das insgesamt aus sechsundzwanzig Strophen besteht:

*alā ay qāṣid-i farḫunda-manẓar,*
*nīyāzam bar sū-yi Šāh-i muẓaffar,*
*ba-gū ey pādšāh-i ǧumla ʿālam,*
*tuʾī imrūz dar mardī musallam,*
*asās-i dīn tu dar dunyā nihādī,*
*tu šarʿ-i Muṣṭafā bar ǧā nihādī,*
*muǧaddad gašt dīn az himmat-i tu,*
*ǧahān dar zīr-i bār-i minnat-i tu,*
*agar mulk-i šarīʿat mustaqīm ast,*
*hama az dawlat-i Sulṭān Salīm ast,*
*zi bīmat dar tazalzul Fārs u Turk,*
*čū afgandī zi sar tāǧ-i qizil-burk,*
*fagandī tāǧ-iš az sar ay muẓaffar,*
*figan aknūn bi-mardī az tan-iš sar,*
*qizil-burk ast hamčūn mār-i afʿī,*
*sar-iš-rā tā nakūbī nīst nafʿī,*
*tuʾī imrūz zi awṣāf-i šarīfa,*
*ḫudā-rā wa Muḥammad-rā ḫalīfa,*
*rawā dārī ki gabr u mulḥid-i dad,*
*dihad dušnām-i aṣḥāb-i Muḥammad,*
*tu ū-rā našikanī az zūr-i mardī,*
*sar-iš-rā nā-burīda bāz gardī,*
*agar gīrad amānī dar salāmat,*
*ba-gīram dāman-at-rā dar qīyāmat,*
*čanīn dīdam zi aḫbār-i payambar,*
*ki ẕū ʾl-qarnayn bud dar Rūm qayṣar,*
*ba-ẕū ʾl-qarnayn az ān ḫud-rā ʿilm kard,*
*ki mulk-i Fārs-rā bā Rūm żamm kard,*
*du qarn-i ū šahī andar ǧahān šud,*
*ba-šarq u ġarb ḥukm-i ū rawān šud,*
*bīyā az naṣr-i dīn kasr-i żanam kun,*
*ba-taḫt-i Rūm mulk-i Fārs żamm kun …*

Verzeichnis relevanter Wikipedia-Artikel (vgl. Anm. 195)

In dem folgenden Verzeichnis werden nur die jeweiligen Artikel in deutscher und englischer Sprache angeführt. Es sei aber darauf hingewiesen, dass einige der hier erwähnten Artikel ferner auf Türkei-Türkisch, Aserbaidschanisch-Türkisch, Persisch etc. (vgl. Sprachenmenü auf der jeweiligen Seite) vorliegen und z. T. Informationen beinhalten, die sich in den entsprechenden deutschen und englischen Artikeln nicht finden.

http://de.wikipedia.org/wiki/Alevitenverfolgungen_im_Osmanischen_Reich
http://en.wikipedia.org/wiki/Ottoman_persecution_of_Alevis
http://en.wikipedia.org/wiki/Islam_in_Iran
http://de.wikipedia.org/wiki/Ismail_I._(Schah)
http://en.wikipedia.org/wiki/Ismail_I
http://de.wikipedia.org/wiki/Kizilbasch
http://en.wikipedia.org/wiki/Qizilbash
http://en.wikipedia.org/wiki/Safavid_conversion_of_Iran_to_Shia_Islam
http://de.wikipedia.org/wiki/Safawiden
http://en.wikipedia.org/wiki/Safavid_dynasty
http://de.wikipedia.org/wiki/Schlacht_bei_Tschaldiran
http://en.wikipedia.org/wiki/Battle_of_Chaldiran
http://de.wikipedia.org/wiki/Selim_I
http://en.wikipedia.org/wiki/Selim_I

## Bibliographie

Alışık, Gülşen Seyhan (2005), 'Fażlullāh B. Rūzbihān-i Huncī'nin yaşamı ve Yavuz Sultan Selim Han'a yazdığı Türkçe manzum yakarışı' [„Das Leben Fadlallāh b. Rūzbihān-i Ḫungīs und die türkische Bittschrift in Gedichtform, die er Yavuz Sultan Selīm Khan geschrieben hat"] in: Modern Türklük Araştırmaları Dergisi 2/4, 70–87. Publikation im Internet: http://mtad.humanity.ankara.edu.tr/II-4_Aralik2005/54_MTAD_2-4_GSeyhanA.pdf.

Allouche, Adel (1983), *The Origins and Development of the Ottoman-Ṣafavid Conflict (906–962/1500–1555)*, Islamkundliche Untersuchungen 91 (Berlin).

Anıl, Adile Yılmaz (2010), 'Şah İsmâil. Edebiyat' [„Schah Ismā'īl. Literatur"] in: TDVİA 38, 256. Publikation im Internet: http://www.islamansiklopedisi.info/.

Bacqué-Grammont, Jean-Louis (1993), 'Les Ottomans et les Safavides dans la première moitié du XVIe siècle' in: *La Shī'a nell'Impero Ottomano, Accademia Nazionale dei Lincei Fondazione Leone Caetani* 25 (Rom) 7–24.

Browne, Edward G. (1959), *A Literary History of Persia 4. Modern Times (1500–1924)* (Cambridge).

DICHTUNG, PROPAGANDA UND POLEMIK

Eberhard, Elke (1970), *Osmanische Polemik gegen die Safawiden im 16. Jahrhundert nach arabischen Handschriften, Islamkundliche Untersuchungen* 3 (Freiburg i. Br.).

Emecen, Feridun (2009), 'Selim ı' in: TDVİA 36, 407–414. Publikation im Internet: http://www.islamansiklopedisi.info/.

Ferīdūn Beg, Aḥmed (1858), *Maǧmūʿa-yi Munšaʾāt as-Salāṭīn* 1 [„Sammlung der Briefe der Sultane 1"] (Istanbul).

Gandjeï, Tourkhan (1959), *Il canzoniere di Šāh Ismāʿīl Ḫaṭāʿī* (Napoli).

——— Ders. (1978), 'Ismāʿīl I. 2. His Poetry' in EI 2/4, 187–188.

Glassen, Erika (1979), ‚Krisenbewusstsein und Heilserwartung in der islamischen Welt zu Beginn der Neuzeit' in: Ulrich Haarmann/Peter Bachmann (edd.): *Die islamische Welt zwischen Mittelalter und Neuzeit. Festschrift für Hans Robert Roemer zum 65. Geburtstag, Beiruter Texte und Studien* 22 (Beirut – Wiesbaden) 167–179. Publikation im Internet: https://www.freidok.uni-freiburg.de/fedora/objects/freidok:4346/data streams/FILE1/content.

Gündüz, Tufan (2010), 'Şah İsmâil' [„Schah Ismāʿīl"] in: TDVİA 38, 253–255. Publikation im Internet: http://www.islamansiklopedisi.info/.

Halm, Heinz (1988), *Die Schia* (Darmstadt).

Hammer-Purgstall, Joseph von (1963), *Geschichte des Osmanischen Reiches 2. Von der Eroberung Konstantinopels bis zum Tod Selims I. 1453–1520* (Graz) (1. Aufl. Pest 1828).

Hanaway, William L. (1998), 'Eskandar-nāma' in: EncIr 8, 609–612 Publikation im Internet: http://www.iranicaonline.org/articles/eskandar-nama.

İnalcık, Halil (2007), 'Selīm I' in: EI 2/9, 127–131.

Karamustafa, Ahmet T. (1998), 'Esmāʿīl I Ṣafawī. 2. His Poetry' in: EncIr 8, 635–636. Publikation im Internet: http://www.iranicaonline.org/articles/esmail-i-safawi.

Krasnowolska, Anna (2009), 'Ḵeżr' in: EncIr, online edition. Publikation im Internet: http://www.iranicaonline.org/articles/kezr-prophet.

Lewis, Geofrey Lee (1962), 'The Utility of Ottoman Fetḥnāmes' in: Bernard Lewis/P.M. Holt (edd.), *Historians of the Middle East* (London – New York – Toronto) 192–196.

McCaffrey, Michael J. (1990), 'Čālderān' in: EncIr 4, 656–658. Publikation im Internet: http://www.iranicaonline.org/articles/calderan-battle.

Minorsky, Vladimir (1942), 'The Poetry of Shāh Ismāʿīl I' in: *BSOAS* 10/4, 1006–1053.

Niewöhner-Eberhard, Elke (1975), ‚Machtpolitische Aspekte des osmanisch-safawidischen Kampfes um Bagdad im 16/17. Jahrhundert' in: *Turcica* 6, 103–127.

Özgüdenli, Osman G. (2006), 'Ottoman-Persian Relations 1. Under Sultan Selim I and Shah Esmāʿil I' in: EncIr, online edition. Publikation im Internet: http://www.iranica online.org/articles/ottoman-persian-relations-i-under-sultan-selim-i-and-shah-esmail-i.

Roemer, Hans Robert (1989), *Persien auf dem Weg in die Neuzeit. Iranische Geschichte von 1350–1750, Beiruter Texte und Studien* 40 (Beirut).

Savory, Roger Mervyn (1995), 'Ṣafawids. 1. Dynastic, political and military history' in: EI 2/8, 765–771.

—— Ders. (1998), 'Esmāʻīl I Ṣafawī. 1. Biography' in: EncIr 8, 628–635. Publikation im Internet: http://www.iranicaonline.org/articles/esmail-i-safawi.

Schimmel, Annemarie (1995a), *Mystische Dimensionen des Islam. Die Geschichte des Sufismus* (Frankfurt a. M. – Leipzig) (1. Aufl. München 1985).

—— Dies. (1995b), *Von Ali bis Zahra. Namen und Namengebung in der islamischen Welt* (München) (1. Aufl. München 1993).

Sohrweide, Hanna (1965), ‚Der Sieg der Ṣafaviden in Persien und seine Rückwirkung auf die Schiiten Anatoliens im 16. Jahrhundert' in: *Der Islam* 41, 95–223.

Tansel, Selâhattin (1969), *Yavuz Sultan Selim* [„Sultan Selīm der Grausame (bzw. der Strenge)"] (Ankara).

Zenker, Julius Theodor (1994), *Türkisch-Arabisch-Persisches Handwörterbuch I–II* (Hildesheim – Zürich – New York) (1. Aufl. Leipzig 1866).

CHAPTER 9

# Maos Gedichte – Versuch einer soziagogischen Analyse[228]

*Harro von Senger*

## 1      Was verstehe ich unter soziagogischer Analyse?

Die Bezeichnung „Soziagogie" weist einen Bezug zu „ago" im Sinne von „führen", „lenken", und zu „societas" im Sinne von „Gesellschaft" auf. Es ergibt sich der Sinn „Gesellschafsführungskunde", „Gesellschaftslenkungskunde." „Soziagogisch" bedeutet „gesellschaftsführungskundlich", „gesellschaftslenkungskundlich".

Die Analyse, welche untersucht, welche Rolle Literatur und Kunst bei der Verbreitung von ästhetischem Genuss spielt, möchte ich als literarische Analyse bezeichnen. Die Analyse, welche untersucht, welche Rolle Literatur und Kunst bei der Verankerung und Veränderung bestimmter sozialer Normen und Verhaltensweisen und somit bei der Lenkung und Steuerung der Gesellschaft spielt, nenne ich „soziagogische Analyse". Es geht um die „Wirkung auf das Publikum"[229], insbesondere um die inspirierende, ermunternde, anfeuernde, verhaltensgestaltende Ausstrahlung auf das Publikum. Mir scheint, von der gesellschaftslenkenden Funktion von Literatur und Kunst zu sprechen, sei genauer als wenn man bloss sagt, Literatur und Kunst dienten „der Politik"[230] und der Politik dienende Poesie sei „politische Poesie"[231]. Dies umso mehr, als es bei der Soziagogie um Gesellschaftslenkung nicht nur durch Literatur und Kunst, sondern auch durch andere Medien wie z.B. durch das Recht und die Religion geht.[232]

---

228    Für die Umschrift chinesischer Schriftzeichen benutze ich das System Pinyin. Sofern in zitierten Texten eine andere Umschrift verwendet wird, übernehme ich diese.

229    Klaus Birnstiel: Der Literaturgelehrte M.H. Abrams ist tot, in: *Süddeutsche Zeitung*, 24.4.2015: 12.

230    Gu Zhengkun: Einleitung. Die Dichtung Mao Zedongs, in: Mao Zedong 2013: 33.

231    Handbuch der politischen Poesie, in: *Neue Zürcher Zeitung*, 2.2.2015: 43; http://www.sued deutsche.de/kultur/nachruf-der-literaturgelehrte-m-h-abrams-ist-tot-1.2449024.

232    Siehe Harro von Senger: Literatur und Kunst – nicht nur Gegenstand der Ästhetik, sondern auch der Soziagogie (Lehre von der Gesellschaftslenkung), in: Giusy M.A. Margagliotta; Andrea A. Robiglio 2013: 23–68.

© KONINKLIJKE BRILL NV, LEIDEN, 2016 | DOI 10.1163/9789004323537_010

Im vorliegenden Aufsatz versuche ich, eine soziagogische Analyse von Maos Gedichten vorzunehmen. Mao war nicht nur ein Guerillakämpfer und Politiker sowie Verfasser von marxistischen Schriften, sondern auch ein Poet. Als Verfasser marxistischer Schriften hat Mao einen wesentlichen Beitrag zur Entstehung der sogenannten Mao-Zedong-Ideen geleistet. Diese werden offiziell nicht als die individuelle Schöpfung Mao Zedongs betrachtet, sondern gelten als „eine Kristallisation der kollektiven Weisheit der Kommunistischen Partei Chinas".[233] Als Poet hat Mao Zedong zahlreiche Gedichte hinterlassen.[234] Über deren Verhältnis zu den Mao-Zedong-Ideen gehen die Meinungen auseinander. Teils wird behauptet, sie seien ein wichtiger Teil der Mao-Zedong-Ideen[235], teils wird gesagt, sie seien eine künstlerische Kristallisation[236] beziehungsweise Manifestation der Mao-Zedong-Ideen.[237] Würde diese Einschätzung stimmen, so würde dies zugunsten der Sichtweise sprechen, welche weniger die ästhetische denn die gesellschaftslenkende Funktion dieser Gedichte hervorheben würde. Auf grossen Schautafeln kann man in der Volksrepublik China immer wieder Reproduktionen von Gedichten Maos in dessen kalligraphischer Handschrift in Amtsstuben, Hotelhallen usw. betrachten. Mehrere dieser Gedichte wurden vertont.[238] Dadurch sollte wohl ihre Wirkung auf die chinesische Gesellschaft verstärkt werden.

---

233    Resolution über einige Fragen in unserer Parteigeschichte seit Gründung der Volksrepublik China (27.6.1981), Punkt 29 Ziff.4, in: Beijing Rundschau, Beijing, Nr. 28, 7.7.1981: 29.

234    Siehe „die bislang vollständigste Sammlung seiner Gedichte in freier deutscher Nachdichtung", Mao Zedong 2013: 11.

235    毛新宇 Mao Xiyu: 毛泽东诗词属于中国革命事业、毛泽东思想的重要组成部分 Mao Zedong shici shuyu Zhongguo geming shiye, Mao Zedong Sixiang de zhongyao zucheng bufen (Die Gedichte Mao Zedongs gehören zur Sache der chinesischen Revolution [und] sind ein wichtiger Bestandteil der Mao-Zedong-Ideen), am 19.10.2014 verbreitet auf der Webseite 乌有之乡 Utopia, http://www.wyzxwk.com/Article/lishi/2014/10/330638.html.

236    Li Shichang 季世昌: 试论毛泽东诗词与中国革命和建设的关系 Shi lun Mao Zedong shici yu Zongguo geming he jianshe de guanxi (Versuchsweise Erörterung des Verhältnisses zwischen den Gedichten Mao Zedongs und der Revolution und dem Aufbau in China), am 1.2.2013 verbreitet auf der Webseite 中共中央文献研究室 Zhong Gong Zhongyang Wenxian Yanjiushi (CCCPC Party Literature Research Office), http://www.wxyjs.org.cn/zgzgmzdscyjh_614/mslt/201207/t20120720_54903.htm.

237    毛泽东诗词有关思想 Mao Zedong shici youguan sixiang (Gedanken über die Gedichte Mao Zedongs), am 13.12.2014 verbreitet auf der Webseite 作业帮 zuoyebang (Arbeitshilfe) http://zuoye.baidu.com/question/0ac4e77c053e5c6316ec685b3788acac.html.

238    So gibt es eine CD mit dem Titel 毛泽东诗词歌曲 Mao Zedong Shici Geju (Lieder zu Gedichten Mao Zedongs) mit Vertonungen der Gedichte *Changsha, Jinggangshan, Gegen*

MAOS GEDICHTE – VERSUCH EINER SOZIAGOGISCHEN ANALYSE 143

Für den Versuch einer soziagogischen Analyse von Maos Gedichten möchte ich zwei Gedichte auswählen, die in der Volksrepublik China zu Neujahr 1976 veröffentlicht und über den Campus-Lautsprecher der Beijing-Universität beinahe unaufhörlich tagelang deklamiert wurden. Es waren die letzten Gedichte Maos, die zu seinen Lebzeiten veröffentlicht wurden.[239] Da ich damals an der Beijing-Universität studierte, habe ich die Intensität, mit denen diese beiden Mao-Gedichte verbreitet wurden, selbst erlebt. Natürlich wurden die Gedichte auch reichlich kommentiert, und zwar keineswegs in erster Linie unter ästhetischem Gesichtspunkt.

Beide Gedichte wurden sogleich in mehrere Sprachen übersetzt. Die deutsche Übersetzung der Gedichte verbreitete, und zwar offenbar gemäss einer chronologisch begründeten Reihenfolge, erst jenes vom Mai und dann jenes vom Herbst 1965, die *Peking Rundschau* in ihrer Ausgabe Nr. 1 vom 6. Januar 1976 zusammen mit der deutschen Wiedergabe eines in mehreren chinesischen Periodika erschienenen Leitartikels, der – durchaus soziagogisch – an ein zur Willenskraft und Strebsamkeit aufrufendes Zitat aus einem der beiden Mao-Gedichte anknüpfte. Bei der *Peking Rundschau* handelte es sich um eine quasioffizielle Wochenzeitschrift, die in Beijing in deutscher, englischer, französischer, spanischer und japanischer Sprache erschien.

In der Ausgabe Nr. 2 vom 13. Januar 1976 doppelte die *Peking Rundschau* nach. Erneut pries sie unter einem nicht so sehr ästhetischen, als vielmehr soziagogischen Aspekt die Gedichte an, indem sie deren Funktion, zum Kampf anzuspornen, hervorhob.

Am Beispiel von Kommentaren zu den beiden Gedichten möchte ich im Folgenden deren Instrumentalisierung zum Zwecke der Gesellschaftsführung veranschaulichen. Dabei stütze ich mich auf in deutscher Sprache in der *Peking Rundschau* erschienene Beiträge.

---

*die erste grosse Einkreisung, Der Gelbe-Kranich-Turm, Dabaidi, Der Loushanpass* und *Kunlun*, 毛泽东诗词歌曲, ohne genaue Datumsangabe im Jahr 2015 verbreitet auf der Webseite 豆瓣音乐 Douban Yinyue (Musik aus der [Pekinger] Douban[-Gasse]), http://music.douban.com/subject/2788947/; 豆瓣网 Douban Wang (Das Douban-Webportal) http://baike.baidu.com/link?url=J7KoPmCU-_cq9SqI9nF9D2q5QHPWyoFVLe4b6T daUdSXg8xoo3OVrQskYh_hvJV_uftIR2vLTIsXvOZQSqasWa#2.

239 纪念毛主席诞辰120周年——毛泽东诗词的重大革命意义 Jinian Mao zhuxi danchen 120 zhou nian – Mao Zedong shici de zhongda geming yiyi (Im Gedenken an den 120. Geburtstag des Vorsitzenden Mao – Die gewaltige revolutionäre Bedeutung von Mao Zedongs Gedichten), am 23.12.2013 verbreitet auf der Webseite 华声论坛 Hua Sheng Luntan (Diskussionsforum für Stimmen aus China) http://bbs.voc.com.cn/topic-5710316-1-1.html.

FIGURE 9.1  *Titelseite der* Peking Rundschau, *Nr. 1, 6. Januar 1976.*

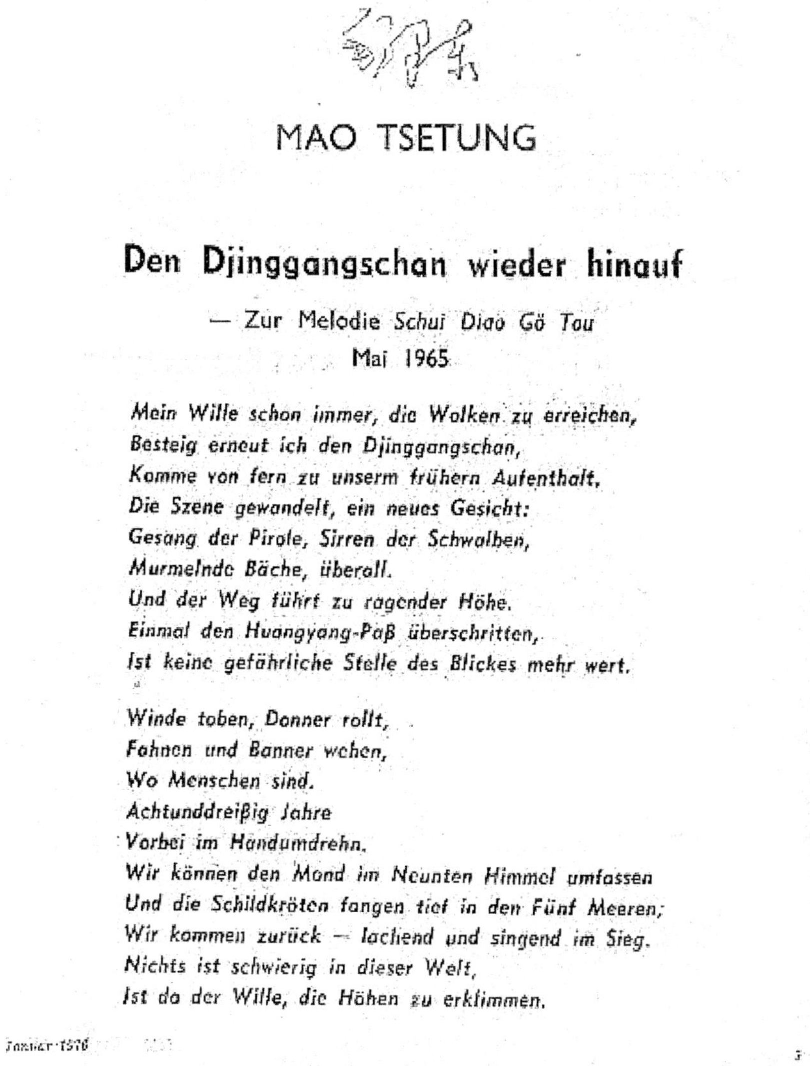

# MAO TSETUNG

# Den Djinggangschan wieder hinauf

— Zur Melodie *Schui Diao Gö Tou*
Mai 1965

Mein Wille schon immer, die Wolken zu erreichen,
Besteig erneut ich den Djinggangschan,
Komme von fern zu unserm frühern Aufenthalt.
Die Szene gewandelt, ein neues Gesicht:
Gesang der Pirole, Sirren der Schwalben,
Murmelnde Bäche, überall.
Und der Weg führt zu ragender Höhe.
Einmal den Huangyang-Paß überschritten,
Ist keine gefährliche Stelle des Blickes mehr wert.

Winde toben, Donner rollt,
Fahnen und Banner wehen,
Wo Menschen sind.
Achtunddreißig Jahre
Vorbei im Handumdrehn.
Wir können den Mond im Neunten Himmel umfassen
Und die Schildkröten fangen tief in den Fünf Meeren;
Wir kommen zurück — lachend und singend im Sieg.
Nichts ist schwierig in dieser Welt,
Ist da der Wille, die Höhen zu erklimmen.

Januar 1976

FIGURE 9.2 *Das erste zu Neujahr 1976 veröffentlichte Mao-Gedicht, in*: Peking Rundschau,
Nr. 1, 6. Januar 1976: 5.

# Gespräch zweier Vögel

— Zur Melodie Niān Nu Djiao
Herbst 1965

Der Riesenvogel schlägt die Schwingen,
Stößt neunzigtausend Li empor,
Aufrührt einen Wirbelsturm.
Den blauen Himmel tragend, sieht er
Die Menschenwelt mit ihren Städten.
Geschützfeuer steigt zum Firmament,
Granaten graben ihre Spur.
Im Busch der Spatz zu Tod erschrocken:
„Die Hölle ist los,
Nur weg von hier!"

„Darf man fragen, wohin?"
Darauf der Spatz:
„Zum Berg der Götter, ins Jadeschloß!
Weißt du nichts vom Vertrag der Drei,
Geschlossen unter hellem Herbstmond vor zwei Jahren?
Auch zu essen gibt es dort,
Kartoffeln, schon fertig,
Und Rindfleisch dazu."*
„Hör' auf mit diesem Furz!
Sieh', die Welt wird umgewälzt!"

*(Originaltexte veröffentlicht in der Januarausgabe 1976 der Zeitschrift „Schikan" <Poesie>)*

*\* Anspielung auf Gulasch – Anmerkung der Hsinhua <Xinhua> – Redaktion*

FIGURE 9.3  *Das zweite zu Neujahr 1976 veröffentlichte Mao-Gedicht, in*: Peking Rundschau,
Nr. 1, 6. Januar 1976: 6.

# PEKING RUNDSCHAU 2

13. Januar 1976

**Glänzende Gedichte, die uns zum Kampf anspornen**

12 Millionen Mittelschulabsolventen lassen sich auf dem Land nieder

Wachsende Gefahr eines neuen Weltkrieges

FIGURE 9.4 *Titelblatt der* Peking Rundschau, *Nr. 2, 13. Januar 1976.*

Zunächst wende ich mich dem Aufsatz „Nichts ist schwierig in dieser Welt, Ist da der Wille, die Höhen zu erklimmen – Leitartikel von ‚Renmin Ribao', ‚Hongqi' und ‚Jiefangjun Bao' zum Neujahr 1976"[240] zu. „Nichts ist schwierig in dieser Welt, Ist da der Wille, die Höhen zu erklimmen" sind die Schlusszeilen des Gedichts „Den Jinggangshan[241] wieder hinauf." Bei der *Renmin Ribao* (*Volkszeitung*) handelt es sich um das Sprachrohr des Zentralkomitees der

---

240  In: *Peking Rundschau*, Nr. 1, 6. Januar 1976: 8–11.
241  Der Jinggangshan, das Jinggangshan-Gebirge, ist ein steiler Gebirgsstock mit vielen Tälern. Einige Kreise im Westen der Provinz Jiangxi und in der Provinz Hunan haben an ihm Anteil. Mao errichtete hier im Oktober 1927 Chinas erstes ländliches revolutionäres Stützpunktgebiet; Zitat aus einer Fussnote zu dem Artikel „Glänzende Gedichte, die uns zum Kampf anspornen – Notizen beim Studium der zwei Gedichte des Vorsitzenden Mao", in: *Peking Rundschau*, Nr. 2, 13. Januar 1976: 7.

Kommunistischen Partei Chinas. Dasselbe gilt von *Hongqi* (*Rote Fahne*), nur dass es sich hierbei um eine Zeitschrift und nicht um eine Tageszeitung handelte. Die *Jiefangjun Bao* (*Volksbefreiungsarmeezeitung*) und die *Renmin Ribao* (*Volkszeitung*) gibt es auch heute (2015) noch, aber die Zeitschrift *Hongqi* (*Rote Fahne*) wurde umbenannt in *Qiushi* (*Wahrheitssuche*). Zitate aus den Gedichten Maos wurden in der *Peking Rundschau* in fetter Schrift wiedergeben. Diese Vorgehensweise übernehme ich in diesem Aufsatz.

Einleitend heisst es:

> Das Jahr 1976 ist angebrochen. Heute werden zwei Gedichte veröffentlicht, die unser grosser Führer, der Vorsitzende Mao, im Jahr 1965 verfasste. [...] Diese beiden glänzenden Werke beschreiben in poetischen Bildern, welche revolutionären Realismus und revolutionäre Romantik aufs innigste verbinden, die ausgezeichnete Lage im In- und Ausland. Von ihr heisst es:
> Die Welt wird umgewälzt
> und
> Die Szene gewandelt, ein neues Gesicht.
> Sie besingen den Heldenmut der revolutionären Völker. Sie
> können den Mond im Neunten Himmel umfassen und die Schildkröten
> fangen tief in den Fünf Meeren.
> [...] Die Veröffentlichung dieser zwei Gedichte des Vorsitzenden Mao ist ein Ereignis von grosser politischer und aktueller Bedeutung und ein gewaltiger Ansporn für das ganze Volk. Wenn wir beim Eintritt in das neue Jahr die Gedichte des Vorsitzenden Mao rezitieren, unsere Blicke über das weite Territorium des Vaterlandes schweifen lassen und die revolutionären Stürme auf der Welt ins Auge fassen, erfüll[en] uns grosse Begeisterung und ein Gefühl des Stolzes, sind wir noch zuversichtlicher, neue Siege zu erringen.
> Gesang der Pirole, Sirren der Schwalben überall.
> [Das besagt, dass] unser Volk noch enthusiastischer ist, [dass] unser Land immer besser gedeiht.

Nun zählt der Leitartikel zahlreiche Erfolge auf, um dann fortzufahren:

> All diese Tatsachen haben das Geschwätz von der „guten alten Zeit" überzeugend widerlegt. [...] Im neuen Jahr müssen die ganze Partei, die ganze Armee und die Volksmassen aller Nationalitäten des Landes [...] unter Führung des Zentralkomitees der Partei mit dem Vorsitzenden Mao an

der Spitze [...] die ganze Reihe wichtiger Weisungen des Vorsitzenden Mao weiter in die Tat umsetzen [und] die sozialistische Revolution [...] vorantreiben.

Dann folgen seitenlange Aufforderungen, was alles zu tun sei. Der Leitartikel endet mit den letzten Zeilen des Gedichts „Den Jinggangshan wieder hinauf" und einem Schlusskommentar, in welchem – sehr soziagogisch – das Wort „anleiten" zur Beschreibung der erwünschten Funktion des Gedichts benutzt wird:

> Nichts ist schwierig in dieser Welt, ist da der Wille, die Höhen zu erklimmen.
> Dieser glänzende Vers des Vorsitzenden Mao eröffnet uns die lichte und herrliche Zukunft und zeigt gleichzeitig den windungsreichen Verlauf des Kampfes auf unserem Weg vorwärts. Er wird uns anleiten, auf dem breiten Weg der Weiterführung der Revolution durch Stürme und Gewitter hindurch mutig vorwärtszuschreiten.. [...] Wir werden, das ist gewiss, alle Schwierigkeiten und Hindernisse überwinden und im neuen Jahr noch grössere Siege erringen können.

Ein weiterer von der *Peking Rundschau* veröffentlichter Kommentar war überschrieben mit „Die Gedichte des Vorsitzenden Mao – Ansporn für das Volk des ganzen Landes."[242] Darin hiess es:

> Zahlreiche Arbeiter, Bauern und Soldaten gelobten, die vom Vorsitzenden Mao und vom Zentralkomitee der Partei für das neue Jahr gestellten Kampfaufgaben zu erfüllen [...] und mit jener heroischen Entschlossenheit nach noch grösseren Siegen zu streben, wie sie im Gedicht formuliert wird:
> Wir können den Mond im Neunten Himmel umfassen. Und die Schildkröten fangen tief in den Fünf Meeren.
> Die Menschen in ganz China riefen sich die ausgezeichnete internationale und inländische Lage ins Gedächtnis, ausgedrückt in den Zeilen:
> Die Welt wird umgewälzt
> und
> Die Szene gewandelt, ein neues Gesicht.

---

242  In: *Peking Rundschau*, Nr. 2, 13. Januar 1976: 5 f.

150 VON SENGER

[...] Einhellig wurde darauf hingewiesen, dass die Praxis in der sozialistischen Revolution seit über zwei Jahrzehnten die unumstössliche
Wahrheit bestätigt hat:
Nichts ist schwierig in dieser Welt / Ist da der Wille, die Höhen zu
erklimmen.

Ein dritter von der *Peking Rundschau* verbreiteter Beitrag trug den Titel
„Glänzende Gedichte, die uns zum Kampf anspornen – Notizen beim Studium
der zwei Gedichte des Vorsitzenden Mao."[243]
Es heisst hier, die Gedichte seien für das chinesische Volk ein

machtvoller Ansporn, [...] die Revolution beharrlich weiterzuführen,
[...] unser Land zu einem starken und modernen sozialistischen Staat
aufzubauen und hart für die grosse Sache, den Kommunismus, zu
kämpfen.
Ob das Volk besungen oder der Feind verspottet wird, das Thema [der
Gedichte] ist stets das gleiche: Strategisch gesehen ist der Feind und sind
die Schwierigkeiten nicht zu fürchten. [...] Die revolutionären Massen
[...] werden alle Hindernisse aus dem Weg räumen. Die alte Welt
wird umgewälzt
von ihnen [...].
Das Gedicht ‚Den Jinggangshan wieder hinauf' [...] schildert das
schöne neue Antlitz des Jinggangshan, der Wiege der chinesischen
Revolution, rühmt die sozialistische Revolution und den sozialistischen
Aufbau in diesem alten revolutionären Stützpunktgebiet. Die Finsternis
des alten China[s] ist besiegt, an seine Stelle ist blühendes, kraftvolles
Leben getreten.
Gesang der Pirole, Sirren der Schwalben. Murmelnde Bäche, überall.
Und der Weg führt zu ragender Höhe.

Nach längeren Ausführungen werden die folgenden Gedichtzeilen zitiert:

Wir können den Mond im Neunten Himmel umfassen / Und die
Schildkröten fangen tief in den Fünf Meeren.

Und es heisst dann:

In den nächsten zwei Jahrzehnten werden wir [...] China zu einem modernen und starken sozialistischen Staat aufbauen [...].

---

243    In: *Peking Rundschau*, Nr. 2, 13. Januar 1976: 7–11.

MAOS GEDICHTE – VERSUCH EINER SOZIAGOGISCHEN ANALYSE          151

> Nichts ist schwierig in dieser Welt / Ist da der Wille, die Höhen zu erklimmen.
>
> Dieser grandiose Schlussvers [...] gibt uns grosse Impulse. Die chinesische Revolution hat bereits grosse Siege errungen, aber der vor uns liegende Weg ist noch länger, noch schwierigere und gewaltigere Aufgaben harren unser [...]
>
> Das Gedicht ‚Gespräch zweier Vögel' [...] wurde im Herbst 1965 geschrieben. Der Vorsitzende Mao formte [die] alte Fabel [vom Dialog zwischen dem Riesenvogel Peng und dem Spatzen] um und nutzte sie für das wichtige Thema des Kampfes gegen den Revisionismus. Der Riesenvogel versinnbildlicht den Marxisten, während der Spatz im Busch für die sowjetisch-revisionistische Renegatenclique steht [...].
>
> Nichts ist schwierig in dieser Welt / Ist da der Wille, die Höhen zu erklimmen.
>
> [Diese] zwei Zeilen [...] spornen uns an, weiterzuschreiten und eine Höhe nach der anderen zu erklimmen [...]

Wie man aus den Kommentaren zu den beiden Gedichten ersehen kann, sollten sie das Volk anspornen und ermutigen. Die Gedichte dienten also nicht einfach nur zur Vermittlung ästhetischen Genusses, sondern sie sollten anfeuernd wirken. Die Gedichte sollten zahlreiche politische Anforderungen an das Volk untermauern.

Dass die Gedichte auf das Volk einwirken, wurde von den Kommentatoren erhofft. Dass sie tatsächlich anspornend gewirkt haben, lässt sich wohl schwerlich nachweisen. Gleichwohl hoffe ich, mittels der obigen Darlegungen in etwa aufgezeigt zu haben, wie zu Beginn des Jahres 1976 in der Volksrepublik China der Versuch unternommen wurde, Gesellschaftsführung mit Hilfe von Poesie in die Tat umzusetzen.

Professor Gu Zhengkun, unter anderem Direktor des Instituts für Weltliteratur der Beijing-Universität, schreibt:

> [...] während der Kulturrevolution reagierte ganz China auf [Maos] Lieder mit frenetischem Enthusiasmus, so dass er vielleicht mehr zitiert wurde, als jeder andere Dichter eines anderen Landes zu einer anderen Zeit. Der enorme Einfluss der Dichtung Maos auf die zeitgenössische chinesische Kultur, insbesondere die Literatur, fühlt man überall aufs Deutlichste [...].[244]

---

244   Gu Zhengkun: Einleitung, in: Mao Zedong 2013: 21.

Nach meinen Erfahrungen vor Ort im letzten Jahr der „Kulturrevolution" waren die Reaktionen der Menschen auf irgendwelche offiziellen Vorgänge, darunter die Verbreitung von Mao-Gedichten, nicht natürlich und spontan. Man konnte gar nicht anders als für Mao Zedong Begeisterung an den Tag zu legen. Bemerkenswert an der zitierten Äusserung Gu Zhengkuns finde ich den Umstand, dass er zwar den Einfluss der Dichtung Maos auf Kultur und Literatur, aber nicht auf das politische Verhalten des chinesischen Volkes erwähnt. Widerspiegelt diese Absenz einer Bemerkung über die das chinesische Volk zu hehren Taten aufrüttelnde Funktion der Mao-Gedichte die rein ästhetische Betrachtungsweise Gu Zhengkuns, die mit einem blinden Fleck für die soziagogische Funktion von Kultur und Kunst behaftet ist? Oder ist die gesellschaftslenkende Wirkung, die, um bei diesem Beispiel zu bleiben, laut den Kommentaren der *Renmin Ribao* von den beiden kurz vor dem Tode Maos publizierten Gedichten hätte ausgehen sollen, aus der Sicht Gu Zhengkuns ins Leere verpufft, weshalb er darauf nicht eingeht?

Im Jahre 1976 ging es jedenfalls drunter und drüber. Am 8. Januar 1976 starb Ministerpräsident Zhou Enlai, am 7. April 1976 wurde der stellvertretende Ministerpräsident Deng Xiaoping seiner Ämter enthoben, am 9. September 1976 verschied Mao Zedong, und im Oktober 1976 wurde die sogenannte Viererbande verhaftet. Deshalb standen die beiden Gedichte nur ganz kurz im Fokus. Allerdings erschien noch im Februar 1976 ein Kommentar zu einem der beiden Mao-Gedichte, und zwar unter dem Titel „Der Bankrott des ‚Gulaschkommunismus' - Zum Studium des Gedichts des Vorsitzenden Mao ‚Gespräch zweier Vögel' – zur Melodie ‚Niàn Nu Djiao'".[245] In diesem Kommentar wird unter anderem ausgeführt:

> Zum grossen Vergnügen aller Revolutionäre geisselt der Vorsitzende Mao mit beissendem Spott die Moskauer Kreaturen, die sich den Gulaschkommunismus ausgedacht haben, verhöhnt sie als vor den revolutionären Stürmen erzitternden Spatzen.[246]

Zu Beginn des 21. Jahrhunderts sind die Gedichte Mao Zedongs keineswegs vergessen. Der Staatspräsident der Volksrepublik China und Generalsekretär der Kommunistischen Partei Xi Jinping zitiert ab und zu aus Mao-Gedichten, durchaus auch zur Motivierung und Anfeuerung. Allerdings werden Zitate aus Maos Gedichten nicht mehr, wie in seinem letzten Lebensjahr, in fetter

---

245  In: *Peking Rundschau*, Nr.6, 10.Februar 1976: 11–13.
246  A.a.O.: 11.

# MAOS GEDICHTE – VERSUCH EINER SOZIAGOGISCHEN ANALYSE

Schrift wiedergegeben. In seiner Rede „Verwirklichung der grossen nationalen Renaissance als Traum des chinesischen Volkes" sagte Xi Jinping[247]:

> Was das chinesische Volk gestern zu überwinden hatte, das war ein
> grosser Pass, gewaltig, stark wie Eisen.[248]
> [...] Heute durchlebt das chinesische Volk einen tief greifenden Wandel, wie wenn
> blaue Meere zu grünen Maulbeerfeldern werden.[249]
> Morgen wird das chinesische Volk
> wie ein riesiges Schiff vorausfahrend starke Winde und heftige Wellen
> durchbrechen.[250]

In einer Rede zum Gedenken an Mao Zedongs 120. Geburtstag zitierte Xi Jinping am 26.12.2013 zunächst aus einem Mao-Gedicht die Zeile:

> So geschmückt sehen Berge und Pässe heute noch schöner aus[251],

um dann fortzufahren:

> Wir haben uns bereits einen hellen Weg gebahnt, wir müssen [aber] weiter voranschreiten.[252]

Darauf schrieb ein Kommentator:

---

247 Das im Folgenden leicht abgewandelt wiedergegebene Zitat stammt aus Xi Jinping: Verwirklichung der grossen nationalen Renaissance als Traum des chinesischen Volkes, in: Xi Jinping 2014: 41.

248 Zitiert aus der deutschen Übersetzung des Mao-Gedichts „Der Loushan-Pass", in: Mao Zedong 2013: 82.

249 Zitat aus dem Mao-Gedicht „Die Volksbefreiungsarmee besetzt Nanjing", etwas anders lautende deutsche Übersetzung in: Mao Zedong 2013: 99.

250 Zitat aus einem Gedicht von Li Bai (701–762).

251 Zitat aus dem Mao-Gedicht „Dabaidi", etwas anders lautende deutsche Übersetzung in: Mao Zedong 2013: 75.

252 习近平在纪念毛泽东同志诞辰120周年座谈会上的讲话 Xi Jinping zai jinian Mao Zedong tongzhi danchen 120 zhou nian zuotanhui shang de jianghua (Rede Xi Jinpings auf einem Symposium zum Gedenken an den 120. Geburtstag des Genossen Mao Zedong), am 26.12.2013 verbreitet auf der Webseite 中国共产党新闻 Zhongguo Gongchandang Xinwen (Nachrichten von der Kommunistischen Partei Chinas), http://cpc.people.com.cn/n/2013/1226/c64094-23952651-3.html.

Dieser marxistische Gesichtspunkt, dieses Ideal eines Sozialismus mit chinesischen Besonderheiten und dieser Kampfesgeist, ermuntern uns, auf dem grossen Weg des Sozialismus mit chinesischen Besonderheiten voranzuschreiten und uns unermüdlich für die Verwirklichung des chinesischen Traums, nämlich der grossartigen Wiedererstehung der chinesischen Nation, einzusetzen und mutig nach vorne zu marschieren.[253]

## Literatur

Mao Zedong (2013), *Gedichte*, mit einem Vorwort von H.C. Günther (Nordhausen).
Margagliotta, Giusy M.A./ Robiglio, Andrea A. (Hg.) (2013), *Art, Intellect and Politics. A Diachronic Perspective* (Leiden/Boston).
Xi Jinping (2014), *China regieren* (Beijing).

---

[253] Zitiert aus: Is Mao Still Dead? A ChinaFile Conversation, am 12.2.2015 verbreitet auf der Webseite *ChinaFile*, http://www.chinafile.com/conversation/mao-still-dead. Auf dieser Webseite werden „So geschmückt sehen Berge und Pässe heute noch schöner aus" und „Wir haben uns bereits einen hellen Weg gebahnt, wir müssen [aber] weiter voranschreiten" als ein zusammenhängendes Zitat in Anführungszeichen gesetzt. Das ist falsch. Der erste Satz („So geschmückt....") ist ein Zitat aus dem Mao-Gedicht „Dabaidi", der zweite Satz („Wir haben uns bereits...") stammt von Xi Jinping. Der dritte Satz („Dieser marxistische Gesichtspunkt...") wird von ChinaFile auch noch als eine Aussage Xi Jinpings hingestellt. Das stimmt erneut nicht. Beim dritten Satz handelt es sich, falls nicht eine Fälschung seitens ChinaFile vorliegt, um einen Kommentar zu Xi Jinpings Zitat aus dem Mao-Gedicht „Dabaidi" und dem darauf folgenden Satz Xi Jinpings. Leider liess sich der chinesische Originalkommentar zu Xi Jinpings Umgang mit der Mao-Gedichtzeile nicht ausfindig machen, da ChinaFile auf eine Quellenangabe verzichtet und auf eine E-Mail-Nachfrage nicht antwortete.

# Index

Abbas I, Shah of Iran   43–46, 48f., 52, 56
Anspruch   27f., 33f., 37–40
Areopagitica   57–59, 61, 68–70
Aserbaidschan   120, 127, 131
Aserbaidschanisch-Türkisch   120, 123 n. 208, 131f., 138
Augustinian missionaries   46, 48

Brache   39

Censorship   3
Chinesischer Traum   153f.
Craft   3–10

De Castelli, Cristofore   44, 48, 54
De la Valle, Pietro   48
Demiurge   3–8
Deutsches Kaiserreich   96
Deutschtum   91ff.
Dichtung   19–25

Education   8–13
Eliot, T.S.   35
Experience   67–71

Fatwa   125, 128, 130, 134
Fédier, Francois   16, 23–25
Futurism, Italian/Russian   102f., 107f.

George, Stefan   77–100
   *Der Siebente Ring*   78–80, 85
Georgekreis   77, 79–81, 96
Ghasel   132, 136
Goethe, Johann Wolfgang von   85ff.
Gryphius, Andreas   48

Heidegger, Martin   19, 25, 82
Hölderlin, Friedrich   15–25, 81ff.

Ideal state   3, 13
Ignoranz   28f., 32f.
Iran   119f., 123f., 127f., 130f.
Istanbul   125

Kampf   18f.
Ketevan, Queen of Kakheti, Saint   43–49, 56
Kulturrevolution   151f.

Licensing   57f., 61, 68–71

Majakovskij, Vladimir   102–114
Mao Zedong   141–153
Maximin   79f.
Models   6, 9–11

Nationalsozialismus   96ff.
Nizami of Ganja   50f.
Norms   10f.

Ort des Austrags   32–34, 39
Osmanisch-Türkisch   125, 127, 131, 134f.
Osmanisches Reich   119, 124, 130f.

Paradise Lost   57 n. 104, 59–62, 65f.
Persisch   119f., 123, 126–128, 131f., 135, 138
Plato *Republic*   3–13
   *Laws*   4f., 8, 11–13
Political science   9, 12
Politik   16f., 23, 25
Pound, Ezra   27–40

Qaside   136
Quli Khan, Imam (Undiladze)   45, 47

*romanitas*   91ff.
Rustaveli, Shota   47, 49f., 52f., 55f.

Saakadze, Giorgi   46, 55
Schah Ismāʿīl   119–138
Scharia   125, 128f., 130
Schia, Schiiten   120, 124, 130
Sowjetrevisionismus   151
Soziagogie   141–153
Sultan Selīm   119–138
Sunna, Sunniten   119f., 123–125, 130

# INDEX

Tabriz   123, 126–128
Teimuraz I, King of Kakheti and Kartli
   43–56
Tragedy   7, 10–12
Tree of Knowledge   63f., 66–71
Trial   58, 61, 63–70
Türkei   131f., 138

Ursprung   19, 25
Usura   37f.

Volk   16f., 19f., 24f.

Weimarer Republik   96
Wolfskehlt, Karl   100
World War I   78ff., 94ff., 103, 107, 110

Xi Jinping   152–154

Zwölferschia   119, 123, 130–132

Printed in the United States
By Bookmasters